W9-BWG-966

PROCESS ETHICS:

A
CONSTRUCTIVE SYSTEM

Kenneth Cauthen

Toronto Studies in Theology
Volume 18

The Edwin Mellen Press
New York and Toronto

Library of Congress Cataloging In Publication Data

Cauthen, Kenneth, 1930-
    Process ethics.

    Includes indexes.
    1. Christian ethics. 2. Social ethics. I. Title.
BJ1251.C28 1984   241   84-16662
ISBN 0-88946-764-1

Toronto Studies in Theology
Series ISBN 0-88946-975-X

The Edwin Mellen Press
P.O. Box 450
Lewiston, New York 14092

Printed in the United States of America

PREFACE

In a recent book James Gustafson comments, "to the best of my knowledge no one has published a systematic, inclusive theory of ethics based on process theology."[1] The present work is an effort to fill that gap. It should be noted that this is "an approach" to process ethics. Others are needed to develop the rich possibilities of this philosophical vision. I articulate a moral theory as a Christian theologian and as a process philosopher. The result is a synthesis of these two perspectives. The particularities of my angle of vision will become apparent. I offer it as one way of uniting Christian ethics and moral philosophy. The limits as well as the advantages of this approach will be evident to readers. In my defense I can only say that this way of doing it was chosen because of the advantages it offered as compared to the limits of the alternatives known to me.

It is customary and proper for authors to acknowledge those who have been especially helpful to them in bringing a book to birth. Gladly I continue this practice. This particular volume was begun during a sabbatical leave during the Fall of 1978. I am grateful to the Trustees and Administration of Colgate-Rochester/ Bexley Hall/Crozer for granting this time off for concentrated research and reflection. President Larry Greenfield and Provost Leonard Sweet have been constant in their encouragement of my writing projects, and for this support I have warm appreciation. A special word of thanks is due to John Cobb and David Griffin who made themselves and the resources of the Center for Process Studies available to me during a delightful four months in Claremont. A grant from the Association of Theological Schools made this stay in California possible. A debt of gratitude is owed to those students who patiently listened while I expounded some of the ideas contained in these pages. It is enough just to know they often understood what they

were hearing. It is pure joy to be told now and then
that a few of my thoughts might even be on the right
track. Finally, I would like to acknowledge my in-
debtedness to Jean Coombs and Debra Watkins who worked
arduously and painstakingly to produce the final typed
draft of this manuscript.

Rochester, New York   Kenneth Cauthen
March 1984

CONTENTS

INTRODUCTION

The moral life is complex. No one of the classical
types of ethical theories taken alone is adequate.
Neither deontology nor teleology includes all that is
essential to a complete accounting of duty. While
H. Richard Niebuhr argues successfully for a neglected
third approach, the responsive ethic he espouses requires the other two standard approaches for its completion. The attempt to combine all three types into a
more comprehensive theory creates its own difficulties.
Not only is moral reasoning complicated by the inclusion of three standpoints, but the possibility that divergent courses of action may be indicated threatens
the systematic neatness for which rational ethics strives.
Nevertheless, the attempt to state an inclusive theory
is the option taken here.

Since this is an essay in theological ethics, the
perennial question of revelation and reason must be examined at the beginning. How are the methods and norms
of philosophical reasoning about morality related to the
methods and norms of Christian ethics? In the first
chapter a synthesis is proposed which emerges out of a
series of alternating stances in which first philosophical and then theological interpretations are developed.
The result is a unified theory with dual grounding.

The second chapter makes the case for a combination
of deontological and teleological approaches to ethics.
In a following chapter on metaethics it becomes apparent that a third perspective is required. Deontology
and teleology are abstract unless they are incorporated
into a more comprehensive scheme which sees the moral
agent as the product of a creative process who acts
responsively in the light of an interpretation of the
total biological, social, and cosmic context in which
questions of obligation arise. We act in response to

actions upon us by other agents (including God). This
theme is pursued in a chapter on Biblical ethics which
focuses on the meaning of love and the Kingdom (Society)
of God as the central moral categories of Christian
morality. In a final section a return movement to philosophical modes of reasoning is made in the effort to
state a theory of social justice.

     Throughout a double polemic is involved, even
though the argument is more implicit than explicit. The
first is directed against theologians who are confident
that any avowed alliance with philosophy is certain to
corrupt the Gospel. My case to the contrary is developed in Chapter I. The second polemic is less visible
and requires more comment. William Frankena, a prominent moral philosopher, has complained that theologians
generally are less precise and logically rigorous as a
group than philosophers in dealing with ethics. Doubtless there is enough substance to his charge to warrant
embarrassment among Christian moralists. However, my
reading of secular philosophers is that while they are
frequently brilliant in the technical precision with
which they analyze and prescribe moral theories, the
resulting interpretations are often superficial. This
shallowness is, in part, the accompaniment of the rational humanism which dominates contemporary moral philosophy. Ethics is viewed as an autonomous discipline,
completely independent of metaphysics and religion.
Whether devoted to an interpretation of the meaning
and intent of language or to the development of a
theory of action and agents, the prevailing modes of
thought tend to move attention away from selves who ask
moral questions in the ultimate context of the cosmic
environment in and by which persons are grounded and
surrounded. My complaint is that the focus of moral

analysis in contemporary secular philosophy is too
narrow, too shallow. Disconnected from the ultimates
of religion and metaphysics, ethics lacks rootage. I
shall argue that the dilemmas and ambiguities of moral
choice require resolution in religious responses to
cosmic finalities. Apart from this, ethics is arid,
thin, incomplete. Hence, what philosophy in its dominant expressions gains in logical precision and analytical rigor, it loses in existential adequacy. I
offer a version of ethics intentionally grounded in
a metaphysical and religious framework on the assumption that anything less is philosophically inadequate,
whatever other rational virtues humanistic alternatives
may claim. The justification of a religiously-grounded
ethics as a rational option can only be in the persuasiveness of the vision as a whole. I do not expect
many converts from the ranks of philosophers. It is
important, nevertheless, that options like this be kept
open, however unpopular they may be in the philosophy
departments of leading universities.

The philosophical orientation of this essay in
ethics is indebted to the thought of Alfred North
Whitehead. However, it appears in the form of a more
generalized process philosophy and not in the full technical vocabulary of the grand metaphysician himself.
This distinguishes my effort from a major strand of process theology which might be more accurately called
Whiteheadian theology to indicate that the metaphysical
view of that thinker is taken over more or less _in toto_
as suitably translated into Christian terms. That is
not my approach, despite the obvious virtues involved in
rooting one's thought in a precise and comprehensive
world view with the penetrating power, depth, and detail of Whitehead's metaphysics. The disadvantage is

that one must first explain and then persuade the reader
of the truth of Whitehead's system. Only then can one
proceed to show its theological relevance. This obsta-
cle, one may hope, is somewhat lessened by appealing to
a more generalized vision stated for the most part in
ordinary language. Process thought should not be identified with Whitehead's thought as such, although the
influence of his seminal mind may be much in evidence.
My hope is to appeal to a larger audience who may acknowledge the values of interpreting the world in dynamic, organic, telic, and theistic terms, while not
being bound to the letter of PROCESS AND REALITY.

Some process thinkers will, therefore, be dis-
appointed at the lack of specific and detailed reference to the thought of Whitehead. They may feel that
by this omission the distinctive insights of process
ethics have been missed or obscured. Certainly one way
to develop ethical theory within this framework is to
articulate the implications of Whitehead's (or Charles
Hartshorne's) metaphysical vision for the moral life.
Instead, I have chosen to attend directly to the phenomena of the moral life, using Whiteheadian insights
when and where it seemed illuminating to do so. Others
are better equipped and more inclined to develop moral
philosophy by systematically working out the implications of Whiteheadian thought.

Process theology is sometimes criticized as being
not much more than category translation. The content is
provided by a philosophical outlook; theology provides
the language or adopts and adapts the philosophical
language. There is point to this charge. It holds in
some measure for the Whiteheadian theologies of John
Cobb and David Griffin, for example.[1] Cobb's Christian
natural theology and Griffin's theodicy are

essentially an exposition of Whitehead's ideas. The
technical language of Whitehead (and of Charles
Hartshorne) is in large measure taken over literally
into theology and used to interpret Biblical and
Christian themes.

However, the charge that process theology is nothing more than category translation is no more valid in
principle against Cobb and Griffin than against other
philosophical theologians like Paul Tillich. The
major difference is that Tillich constructs his own on-
tology, while Cobb and Griffin take over the metaphysical vision of Whitehead and use it for Christian purposes. Moreover, the fundamental question is not what
words are used but whether the words are expressive of
Christian meanings. This obviously depends on two
points: 1. How "Christian" is the philosophy that is
used? 2. How much has the Christian orientation of the
philosopher who is writing a natural theology informed
and transformed the philosophical vision? Cobb believes
that Whitehead's philosophy is the "right one" for a
Christian to use since it, unlike many recent Western
philosophies, is theistic and otherwise congenial to
basic Christian claims.

In an attempt to avoid the criticism that process
theology is frequently just "category translation" and
in search of a more "conversionist" pattern for relating revelation and reason, I have insisted on the mutual transformation of Christian ethics and moral philosophy in a continuing dialogue. It may be that in
following a method of "dialectical synthesis," I have
arrived at an ethical theory which is completely true
neither to Christian revelation nor to Whiteheadian
reason. Nevertheless, I offer this approach to ethics
because, to my mind, the options are less adequate to

describe the quest for moral truth by a person who is both a "believer in the church" and a "self in the world."

CHAPTER I
THE TASK AND METHOD OF CHRISTIAN NATURAL ETHICS
A

Christian natural ethics examines morality from the point of human reason and experience without any appeal to special revelation. It is at the same time an approach taken by a Christian informed by the witness of the Bible. The result is a philosophical ethics that can be compared, contrasted, and criticized by the criteria developed by moral philosophers. Yet the form and content of the ethical reasoning involved will show a congeniality and, at points at least, an identity with Christian ethics. [1]

The problem of faith and reason is an ancient and perennial one. It arises inevitably out of the fact that a Christian is both a self who exists in the world and a believer who lives within the church. As a SELF IN THE WORLD the question of morality and meaning is confronted as a human being who lives in a given time and place informed by the history and culture of a particular society. As a BELIEVER IN THE CHURCH the answers to the question of morality are acknowledged as having been given by divine action in the person and work of Jesus of Nazareth as interpreted by the New Testament.

H. Richard Niebuhr in his classic work CHRIST AND CULTURE has laid out some logically possible types of relating these two approaches to what is most real and most important. [2] They range from opposition on the one side to merger on the other, with the claim that faith transforms reason in the middle. Now it is no doubt true that Christians who have taken each of these positions have done so because of the way they understood the stance required by cultural wisdom and the style of life posited by faithful obedience to Christ. Some

7

ways of interpreting "Christ" are in stark contradiction
to some understandings arising in "culture." Yet what
some derive from revelation may be thought by others to
be equally the outcome of reasoning based on experience.
Christ may be one in the sense of being an identifiable
locus of truth circumscribed by the Biblical witness,
but what Christ is thought to require with respect to
truth and morality is marvelous in its variety. Likewise, culture produces forms of reasoning about life and
duty which potentially cover the gamut of logical possibilities. Hence, it is not surprising that Christians
should come to a variety of conclusions about how Christ
and culture contradict, conflict, transform, supplement,
and confirm one another. Each of them may be "right" in
the sense of providing an accurate description of the
situation from a given vantage point. The question as
to which position is ultimately and universally "right"
may not be answerable. Given the fact that all theologies are situational and partial, it is not very helpful even to ask about the "real" truth of the matter.

Each believer in the church is shaped by the history, traditions, and beliefs of a given society and has
a grasp of truth rooted in sources independent of Christian influence. Likewise, every self in the world is informed by views of reality and value derived from historically-conditioned modes of reasoning with controlling
points of reference which correspond formally to the
function that revelation plays in the church. Hence, as
Christians and as cultural beings, as believers and
reasoners, we are produced by particular histories shot
through with relativity and time-bound forms of thinking and living. It follows, then, that there is no universal and inevitable way of relating the moral reasoning of secular thinkers to that of Christian disciples.

Hence, Brunner, Barth, and Lehmann are too extreme in
insisting that there must be and always will be irrec-
oncilable conflict between them. We can only speak of
particular Christians with certain understandings of
Christ and culture who find their functioning as believers in the church and as selves in the world to
conflict, otherwise interact in various ways, or coincide. Hence, Barth, Luther, Augustine, Aquinas, and
Schleiermacher all may be right in terms of their frame
of reference. We may agree or disagree with their particular theologies, but that the formal way any one of
them views the relationship between Christ and culture
is a universal and necessary pattern is an inevitable
outcome of neither revelation nor reason.

When Paul Lehmann, for example, argues that philosophical ethics will always be insufficient, he makes
a powerful case.[3] Yet under the Barthian shadow, his
point is overdone. Admittedly, there are special features of Christian ethics that set it apart from alternatives. Chief among them, according to Lehmann, are
assumptions relating to human sinfulness and a saving
act of God which bridges the gap between the ethical
claim and the ethical act. Redemption through Christ
thereby makes possible free responsive obedience to the
divine will. Clearly any philosophical system which
contradicted or omitted these essential elements would
be, in principle, deficient. Moreover, no alternative
scheme could include the particularities of New Testament thought without actually becoming Christian ethics.
Against the prevailing ethical theories current in philosophical circles, Lehmann's charge would be largely accurate. But may one not argue on rational grounds that
human beings are egocentric and even that selfish acts
are an offense against ultimate cosmic realities? Can

one not make the case philosophically that ethics is
grounded and completed in religion with its associated
set of metaphysical claims? Cannot one even contend
that ethical action appropriately occurs in response to
a creative nisus in the universe which creates life
and evokes gratitude toward a Primordial Goodness? The
Christian natural ethics I propose here makes all these
arguments on rational grounds appealing to no principles
not based on ordinary experience potentially open to all
persons. Yet such a philosophical ethics will at least
be compatible with and actually coincide at points with
Christian ethics. Such considerations take away the
radical and necessary insufficiency which Lehmann as-
signs in principle to philosophical efforts to develop
moral theory.

A critic like Lehmann might question the Christian character of what follows, seeing it as a masked or
covert philosophical vision parading in Christian at-
tire. From the opposite corner one might object that
the rational ethics I propose is, in effect, a covert
or masked Christian theology and hence not a genuinely
autonomous philosophical perspective at all. To the
former criticism I reply that no Christian theology or
ethics, from Paul to Barth, is without principles and
content derived from the surrounding culture or from
philosophical reasoning. To the latter charge I reply
that no philosophical viewpoint arises that does not
bear the marks of some particular historical tradition.
All ethical reasoning is culturally conditioned. Why
should rational ethics consciously influenced by Biblical modes of thought be ruled out of the philosophical arena? Human reason shaped and even transformed
by Christian influence retains its rational credentials
as long as the methods and norms of philosophical

reasoning are not violated by appeal to special authority
(divine self-disclosure or revelation). Do not Kant,
Sidgwick, and Rawls give allegiance to moral values whose
origin (and I would argue ultimate foundation) can be
traced, at least in part, to the Bible?

However, if the sources and norms of moral truth
are to be found in the New Testament witness to Jesus as
the Christ, it may still be objected that reason can
never discover independently of this revelation what is
special, unique, or even distinctive of it. This is a
fundamental challenge and must be met. The answer to
it is that behind the method being proposed is a Logos
Christology. The operating assumption underlying the
entire scheme is the unity of God's being and action in
the world. The structures, dynamics, goals, and norms
revealed in the Word made flesh in Jesus of Nazareth
(John 1:14) are identical with the structures, dynamics, goals, and norms present in the whole of creation
(John 1:1-3). The pattern of the divine activity everywhere expressed in the cosmos is normatively disclosed
in the person, words, and deeds of one human being and
the complex of events in which that life was set as interpreted by the New Testament. Such is the heart of
the Christian witness.

The implication is that once having been given this
clue to reality and value in Jesus of Nazareth by revelation, it can be seen everywhere by reason and validated
by experience independently of that revelation. Were
that not the case the Creator and the Redeemer would not
appear to be the same God. The content of the moral
vision can be stated in complete abstraction from the
cluster of revelatory events to which the New Testament
gives witness. And it can be validated without special
appeal to the authority of Scripture. Were it not pos-

sible so to find the pattern and to validate its truth
in all of life, the revelation would not have the power to evoke a response of faith in the believer in the
first instance.

The persuasiveness of revelation is nothing other
than its ability to give to reason the clue it needs to
make sense of the world. The Christian believer who
has discovered the Logos of all creation in the Logos
made flesh and affirms that the Logos made flesh is the
Logos in all creation now operates with a vision contained in an ellipse with two foci. These two foci can
be designated revelation and reason or, for this particular essay, Christian ethics and philosophical ethics.
The totality is a unified whole which can be organized
in two different ways in accordance with the requirements of each perspective.

Another assumption underlying this methodology is
related to epistemology. Every world view, every comprehensive philosophy of life, has a formal counterpart to what Christians call revelation. In epistemological terms the Christian appeal to Jesus of Nazareth is the answer to a universal question: Where in
the whole of history and experience is the clue to the
meaning of life to be found? Every answer to this question provided by philosophy or religion is particular,
historical, and concrete in some of the same ways at
least that the New Testament witness to Jesus as the
Christ is. All attempts to describe reality and prescribe a way of life universally valid for all persons
uses language that is as distinctive and historically
relative as that used by Christians -- "Nirvana," "the
class struggle," "the categorical imperative," "the
social contract," and on and on. When any person is

grasped by insight into significant truth, a "revelation" is experienced and "faith" is evoked.

The reason that revelation in the Christian sense
constitutes a self-conscious focus of epistemological
attention is that the _Gestalt_ it forms has such high
visibility. This identifiability results from its
location in a particular cluster of historical events
that is interpreted in a self-conscious religious tradition which has highlighted and maintained its peculiar distinctiveness through the centuries. But there
are formal parallels in every philosophy to revelation
and reason, i.e., a reference to some particulars with
its essential clues. Hence, Christian tradition stands
out as a specifiable locus and focus of truth claims
which can be contrasted with other religious and philosophical alternatives and with other sources of knowledge about the world such as science. But, in principle, a self in the world who is convinced by the
truth of the Gospel and becomes a believer in the
church is in no different position in the formal epistemological sense from a self in the world who is convinced of the truth of a Marxist-Leninist philosophy
and becomes a member of the Communist Party. Marxists,
no less than Christians, have to relate their "faith"
to the truth produced by science, historical research,
changing social and cultural circumstances, alternative
philosophies, and so on. The same formal parallels
would hold in respect to ethics when a self in the
world becomes convinced that the Christian principle
of community-seeking love is the central ethical norm
rather than some philosophical alternative such as
egoistic hedonism -- to choose a strikingly contrasting point of view.

The epistemological premise of the Christian

natural ethics espoused in these pages assumes the
ultimate unity of revelation and reason. Truth is one,
and faith-illuminated reason is in possession of principles of truth that can, in principle, be validated in
the whole of experience. Only those who can accept this
assumption will be persuaded of the theological method
that results. Anyone who believes that reason is so im-
potent and/or so corrupted by sin that even the light
given in Christ either contradicts or radically trans-
scends its feeble or distorted reflections will see my
point of view as naively overconfident rationalism. If
revelation is thought to be a sheer gift from above that
breaks into life with coercive power and justifies itself in and through itself by the witness of the Spirit
in and to the human spirit independently of or in defiance of rational or experiential confirmation, then
Christian natural ethics can have no theological justification.

Every religious or philosophical system validates
itself in a circular manner. Judgments about the adequacy of espoused truth claims are a function of assumptions peculiar to the point of view being tested. Epistemology cannot transcend metaphysics. Claims about
what and how we know are bound up with convictions
about what is real. Systems validate themselves on the
basis of principles internal to themselves but may not
be convincing to those who stand outside the "community
of faith." Even among the faithful complete systematic
coherence is seldom achieved. Anomalies, mysteries,
and ambiguities are common when ultimate matters of fact
are under discussion. Nevertheless, we are not completely trapped by relativism. Systems do break down
because their inadequacies become apparent. People do
change their minds on the basis of evidence. New con-

victions replace old ones. The point is that theology
is no better or worse off than philosophy in this regard. To paraphrase what Whitehead said about God,
theology is not an exception to all epistemological
categories requiring special rules to save their collapse but their chief exemplification. The implication of all this is that a Christian natural theology
or ethics can justify its claims rationally but only
or mainly to those who stand within the same circle of
faith.

My chief objection to philosophical ethics is not
its inherent limits or deficiencies but to the prevailing humanism which dominates the discipline today. The
typical assumption is that ethics is an autonomous arena,
having no need for any foundation in religion or metaphysics. The prevailing point of view is humanistic.
The result is a defective rationalism. But this is an
outcome not dictated by any necessary principles of
reason but only by the reigning secularism which dominates the current intellectual landscape. I argue, not
that philosophical ethics is identical with Christian
ethics, but only that mutual contradiction is not the
only mode of coexistence possible. In relationship to
rational philosophical ethics, Christian natural ethics
stands somewhere between identity and an irreconcil-
able dichotomy.

B

Christian ethics is based on revelation (a particular historical normative tradition). Philosophical
ethics refers to the whole class of ethical views based
on reason (a present analysis based on relevant sources
and norms in principle open to everyone). What Paul
Tillich says about the relation of philosophy and
theology in general applies here as well.[4] The moral

philosopher, to adapt Tillich's language, looks at the
whole of the ethical sphere of reality to discover its
structures. The Christian ethicist must look where that
which concerns him or her ethically is manifest and must
view morality at the point where he or she has been
grasped. The moral philosopher looks at the universal
Logos wherever in the whole of reality it appears. The
Christian ethicist looks to the concrete Logos in the
Word made flesh in a particular historical event and
witness. The philosopher looks at all places to discover the right and the good. The theologian testifies
that the answers have been provided in a particular
place. Philosophers and theologians use language developed by and appropriate to these two communities of inquiry and testimony.

Philosophy has a communal aspect as well as an
individual aspect, whereas theology has an individual
aspect as well as a communal aspect. The Christian
ethics of Karl Barth and Paul Lehmann bear the marks of
their individuality as well as the marks of their participation in the church. Likewise, the utilitarianism
of individuals like John Stuart Mill and J.J..Smart
reflects their participation in a community of discourse with a history of interpretation that bears a
formal resemblance to the interpretive tradition within
the Christian household of faith. Philosophers begin
by an attempt to be open to reality wherever and however it manifests itself to critical inquiry. However,
when insight dawns, some particular truths are affirmed
which unite a given thinker with the community of those
who have been similarly grasped. Utilitarians become a
part of a school of thought with a history of interpretation in which arguments, defenses, and claims are set
forth in opposition to deontologists whose views are

regarded as inadequate. It would be instructive to map
out the ways in which Christian ethicists and moral philosophers converge and diverge in method and content, but
the major differentiation has been indicated already.

For the Christian what is of most concern is the
way in which the duality of being both a believer in the
church and a self in the world is to be understood.
What stance will a Christian natural ethics take? A
Christian is a person who lives and thinks a certain way
as a self in the world. However, it is possible to assume one orientation or the other in a self-conscious
way. In the stance of a self in the world a Christian
thinking about the ethical life does so as a moral philosopher. As a philosopher the Christian uses the methods,
the sources, norms, and language of the community of discourse common to the world of philosophy. He or she
"does" philosophical ethics. In the stance of a believer in the church a Christian thinks about the moral life
as a Christian ethicist. The sources, norms, methods,
and language are those common to the community of discourse within the church and its interpretive tradition.
These stances are taken in different and alternating
moments. What one sees as a self in the world will be
shaped by what one believes as a member of the Christian
community. What one believes as a member of the church
will be shaped by what one sees as a self in the world.

At the outset a distinction needs to be made between the historical and the logical dimensions of the
problem. Historically, existentially, and factually, I
grew up thinking of myself as a Christian and never
otherwise. This was the natural and expected outcome of
my upbringing in the rural South with Baptists, including my parents, everywhere. I also absorbed ideas and
ideals from the American culture and the whole history

of Western civilization. In actual life, faith and
reason have always been united and interacting in complex ways in my mind. However, when I stand back from
that life situation and try to think critically, objectively, and analytically, a different orientation emerges from a logical point of view. Within that framework, I propose a methodological model which begins logically with the stance of a self in the world in quest
of meaning, courage, and fulfillment. A way of living,
believing, and hoping is sought which truthfully unites
or correlates experience with reality. Experienced
reality or reality as experienced becomes the source
and provides the norm for assessing truth claims.
Truth is sought everywhere and by whatever methods are
promising and fruitful in providing a guidance system
and a coping mechanism for relating experience to reality. From this stance I am or become or remain a
Christian because the images, ideas, beliefs, motiva-
tions, meanings, and values found in that tradition are
more compelling than any others in making sense of
reality and in directing human life toward fulfillment.
It is no doubt the case that I find the Christian vision to be true because I was disposed to do so because
of my history and upbringing. But it remains the case
logically that the judgment of the adequacy and appli-
cability of Christian belief is made on the basis of its
effectiveness in interpreting reality as experienced.
Experienced by me, yes. But experienced by me as that
experience is critically interpreted by reason.

     Revelation refers, then, not to some arbitrary
appeal to an external authority established by divine
fiat. Rather revelation points to that place in the
whole of reality where the Logos of being has been manifested concretely in ways which provide the clue to

reality and value, to meaning and destiny. For Christians that place is the event of Jesus of Nazareth interpreted as the Christ (Logos) by the witness of the New Testament. Faith as the response to revelation is evoked in a transforming intuition in which one is grasped by the intrinsic truth-disclosing power of the event in which the light dawns. This moment is experienced as the most rational of all in that reality becomes transparent to reason. In its light life makes sense. Authority is granted to the heart of the Biblical witness because of its irresistibly persuasive power. Its self-authenticating truth is compelling by reason of its intrinsic intelligibility and its capacity to make reality intelligible. On its subjective side revelation appears as intuition, insight, discovery, as an experienced _Gestalt_ in which pattern and rational clarity emerge.[5] As such it is comparable in character to other instances of finding or of being grasped by truth. What distinguishes revelation in the theological use of the term is that it involves the disclosure of truth about ultimate matters of being, value, and meaning. In it the clue to God and salvation are made plain. Such an event is uniquely momentous in its import and is thus distinguished from all other truth-yielding experiences. However, revelation in its formal character corresponds to other events in which some limited aspect of reality becomes transparent to reason.

The description just given points to the essence of the phenomena of revelation in the fullness of its manifestation. However, in actual life it seldom occurs once and for all in its perfected form. Rather we usually experience a series of insightful moments in which fragments of the whole of Christian truth grasp us under particular circumstances. Moreover, dark

spots remain for most of us which never get cleared up.
But at its center revelation is that truth-event in
which all crucial life-events become intelligible.

When in the life history of a self in the world
the Christian vision becomes the norm of religious truth,
a special Gestalt of knowledge is created which can be
contrasted with the Gestalt of knowledge constituted by
the set of beliefs affirmed independently of special
revelation. The first we may call the Christian Gestalt
(Christ or revelation) and the second the secular Gestalt (culture or reason). The Christian Gestalt may be
distinguished and identified because it contains its own
special sources and norms and its own distinctive set of
affirmations which constitute Christian identity as established by the community of faith. These two stances
overlap and, in fact, potentially or latently contain
each other. However, each can become the focus of attention, a stance from which the whole of reality is viewed.
To say it differently, one can speak as a believer in
the church (the Christian Gestalt) or as a self in the
world (the secular Gestalt). Hence, a Christian natural
theology can arise when one assumes the point of view of
a self in the world. But since this self in the world
is also a believer in the church in another context or
focused Gestalt, a Christian natural theology emerges.

It may be objected that a Christian natural theology or ethics is a contradiction in terms. Natural
theology has traditionally meant that approach which
sought what could be known about God, the world, and
humanity apart from Christian revelation and doctrines.
It is inquiry based on reason and experience. Its insights are in principle available to all people everywhere. Natural theology appeals to universal principles
of reason and tests its claims by universal norms.

Christian theology, of course, is derived from a specific historic tradition and employs established norms derived from Scripture by the community of faith. How can
any theology, then, be both natural and Christian?

The clue is in the recognition that no vision of
reality can successfully claim to be the product of universal principles of reason. The philosopher may aspire
to be a "spectator of all time and existence" (Plato),
but the truth is that all ontologies and ethical systems are historically and culturally conditioned. All
reason is historical reason, somebody's reason at some
particular time and place. The recognition of relativism implies that "natural theology in its simplest
and classical sense is a pseudo-option."[6] It follows
that Christians who attempt to think about reality as
selves in the world open to whatever truths to which
reason and experience lead them will inevitably be
shaped by some historically-conditioned secular philosophy. All intended natural theology will be qualified by some adjective which relativises its alleged
or sought for universality. There is Aristotelian
natural theology, Platonic natural theology, Kantian
natural theology, Hegelian natural theology, Whiteheadian natural theology, and so on. There is no plain old
universal natural theology that wears no glasses that
affect its vision. All natural theology is adjectival. Christian natural theology is simply the open
acknowledgement that universal reason is conditioned by
particular starting points.

Christian natural theology will in fact be doubly
adjectival. It will be Christian and Kantian, Hegelian, naturalistic, pragmatic, analytic, existentialist,
Heideggerian, Whiteheadian, or whatever. This is true
because the Christian thinker who seeks only what is
true, as reason and experience can apprehend reality,

is both a historically-conditioned believer in the
church and a historically-conditioned self in the world.
Nevertheless, it is possible to make a self-conscious
attempt to be open to reality wherever and however it
appears to the inquirer, initially free insofar as
possible from specific commitments either Christian or
secular. Every person who does so will bring to that
initial moment a set of culturally-designed receiving
equipment that will pick up certain signals from reality and miss others. But that is just the human situation and the universal predicament of historical,
finite reason.

All philosophy in the West since Augustine has
been deeply influenced by Christian theology. Alfred
North Whitehead and many others have pointed out that
Biblical themes stated in medieval theology constituted
one parent of modern science.[7] Paul Tillich has noted
that all modern philosophy is existentially Biblical in
its basis.[8] Marxism, as is commonly recognized, is
rooted in Judaeo-Christian soil, especially in its philosophy of history. It has been said by some to be, in
fact, a Christian heresy. Carl Becker establishes the
thesis that "the heavenly city of the 18th century philosophers" is a secularized version of the Biblical
Kingdom (Society) of God.[9] All of this is to say that
secular philosophy in the modern Western world which
attempts to attend to the universal Logos of being actually does so with a frame of reference which is shaped
by Biblical and Christian modes of understanding, even
when Christian norms and beliefs are explicitly repud-
iated. Modern philosophical atheism, then, is Christian atheism in that it is the Christian God whose existence is denied. Philosophical ethics, then, may also
be expected to bear in varying degrees the imprint of

Biblical morality in that the duties and values espoused
by a secular philosopher in this culture will reflect
Jewish and Christian understandings. Is the deontology
of Immanuel Kant not a secular version of obligation
that Christians would ground in the will of God? Hence,
there is a sense, however limited, in which secular
ethics is or may be a form of Christian <u>natural</u> ethics
parallel to what appears in this essay as a form of
<u>Christian</u> natural ethics. However, in my case the
Christian background of my philosophical claims is much
more evident and complete than is the case with most
ethicists who inhabit university departments of philosophy these days. But the influences are there in both
cases, however dominating or shadowy the case may be from
individual to individual.

The opposite side of this coin is that those theologians who attempt to base theology solely on the revelation of God in Christ witnessed by Scripture can
never fully succeed. Those who claim that nothing goes
into their theology that did not come out of the Bible
are likely to be mistaken. The Bible itself is a human-
ly-conditioned, historically-relative document that contains beliefs about all sorts of things from astronomy
to agriculture that are common to the culture of the
period and can hardly be put forward as universal truth.
The attempt to abstract from the Biblical materials
some pure essence of the Gospel which is then put within
some contemporary framework which does not adulterate
or qualify the absolute purity of universal Christian
truth is probably doomed to failure.

Nevertheless, it is certainly possible to elaborate
a theology which resolutely intends to be attentive
solely to the Word of God given in Scripture. Karl Barth
does so brilliantly. He does not deny that all of us

have "some philosophy or other."[10] Moreover, the form
of theological speech is philosophy. But we can endeavor
to make philosophy and our human points of view into servants of the Word and never a second source of truth
alongside and in competition with Scripture.[11] We can
attend to the Word of God in Scripture as our only object, our only source and norm of Christian truth so that
what we believe as selves in the world can serve only as
a medium through which the message comes without distorting it any more than our fallible minds can avoid.

   Barth denies the necessity of a point of contact between the Word of God and our secular conceptuality and
experience. The Word of God comes from heaven and penetrates our ideological-experience world as a "wholly
other" announcement of judgment and grace. It appears
like a rock thrown through a window (Tillich). It is
there suddenly, inexplicably, and must be taken into
account though it connects with nothing that was going
on in the room when the missile appeared. This is
"theological positivism" (Bonhoeffer) which comes as a
"Take it or leave it" option. Barth's own image is that
of the manna falling from heaven in the wilderness. The
people see it but don't know what it is. They have to
ask Moses for an explanation. But it is there, and it
feeds them (Exodus 16:13-15). So it is with the Gospel. The actuality of revelation establishes its possibility. Scripture is known to be God's Word because it
is God's Word.[12] First comes the fact and the act, then
comes the recognition of the deed by revelation by the
witness of the Holy Spirit in the hearts of believers.[13]

   This is certainly a possibility for interpreting
the situation. But whether it happens that way in the
lives of most people is problematic. A more empirically
accurate description of the way faith (Christian vision)

and reason (what we believe as secular selves) interact
in the lives of most people sees them in a dialectical,
interconnected, mutually-transforming relationship.
Operationally, these two perspectives appear to be ways
of focusing self-consciously on interdependent stances
in encounter with each other in our own minds rather
than as wholly opposed methods of discerning truth,
meaning, and value.

Yet Barth's challenge is not so easily dismissed.
His assumption is that the Gospel is a specific given,
once and for all revealed to the saints. It is distinctive, unique, with its own peculiar essence that is discovered by examining the Biblical witness to the central
event on which it is based -- Jesus Christ as the Word
of God to humanity. In this light is he not right in
contending that any alliance that employs some alien perspective as a secondary or supplementary source of truth
inevitably corrupts the purity of the revealed Word of
God? Is it not better simply to witness to the given
truth and let people choose in the light of clearly defined options? It is not a sufficient refutation of
Barth merely to protest that it is nearly impossible to
read everything out of the Bible and read nothing into
it from culture. For even if this task cannot be done
perfectly, it is better to do it inadequately than to
abandon the method -- if this is the right thing to do.

At the other end of the methodological spectrum is
a philosophy like that of Henry Nelson Wieman. He
plants himself firmly in the modern world and develops
a method of religious inquiry which derives all knowledge from critical reflection on experience in ways
suggested by scientific reasoning. Wieman appeals not
to the essence or substance of Christianity but to "the
best."[14] The best is to be judged by its conduciveness

to the increase of human good. Within such a framework
Wieman can translate into this philosophical scheme
whatever is worthy of preservation in the Christian tradition. Revelation means nothing more than inherited beliefs of the Christian community, itself the product of
previous reasoning about experience. Whereas Barth
would have us accept nothing derived from cultural experience and philosophical reasoning which cannot justify itself by the criterion of the Word of God, so
Wieman would have us accept nothing allegedly derived
from divine revelation which cannot be established by
critically reflecting on what is experienced here and
now.

C

The method I propose moves beyond and between
these polar extremes to produce a synthesis of Christian
ethics based on the Bible and moral philosophy based on
reason and experience. With Barth I agree that Christian ethics must conform to the essence of the witness of
the Bible to Jesus of Nazareth. With Wieman I agree
that we in the modern world can retain only what is best
in Christianity, there being much in the Bible and
Christian history that is deplorable to the sensitive
conscience. However, I believe that what is best is
also the essence of Christianity, namely, the agape that
God manifests to us and requires of us, the gift and demand of love. Whatever does not conform to, follow from,
or is not required by the vision of God, the world, history, and humanity centered in God's agape at work in
the world to make heaven real is essential neither to
revelation nor reason.

The method of synthesis is also dialectical. One
first stands as a believer in the church examining norm-

ative Christian texts, especially the Bible but including
the history of the interpretive tradition. From this
perspective one seeks to discover what is really there,
what is the essence, the perennially-abiding Word of
God. Competing philosophies and ethical systems are
examined in the light of this norm to discover how they
support, contradict, or otherwise compare. Moreover,
they are judged for their adequacy in terms of their conformity to the vision of duty and destiny that is given
in the New Testament. In the alternate moment, one
stands squarely in the modern world as a self in quest
of the clue to meaning and purpose, the grounds of obligation, and the path to fulfillment. In this stance the
cultural wisdom of the past and present from whatever
source available is examined and tested for its coherence and adequacy to human experience, i.e., its rational cogency. The Gospel is tested by the same standards
as other truth claims. Only what is best and compelling and worthy of belief for moderns in quest of the
true, the good, and the beautiful can be accepted from
that tradition, whether or not it is identical with
the essence of Christianity or not.

One stance alternates with the other. The meaning
of being a self in the world is examined in the light
of the Gospel. The Gospel is examined by the truest
and best that a self in the world can discover. Each
stance listens to the other, learns from the other, and
judges the other in alternating moments of inquiry and
insight. In this continuing process of mutual transformation of Christian ethics by moral philosophy and
of moral philosophy by Christian ethics, an intuition
occurs and the synthesis is born. Actually, there are
likely to be many intuitions along the way, large and
small, varying considerably in the range, depth, and

inclusiveness of the data which they unite into a patterned unity. The pilgrimage of any one person will
include many changes of mind, numerous tentative stop-
ping places on the way to a mature faith and a convincing conceptuality. The quest for what is most real
and most important in human existence is lifelong.

The content of this synthesis can be developed in
two different ways. One is to articulate a system of
Christian ethics in the categories of Biblical and trad-
itional speech produced by the theologians of the
church. This is the conversation of Christians with
each other within the community of faith. The other
possibility is to articulate a system of philosophical
ethics using the categories produced by the moral traditions of Western thought from Plato to Rawls. The
latter is the option primarily followed in the pages to
follow. Whether or not the philosophical ethics produced by this effort is compatible with Christian insights will depend on whether or not what is regarded
as truest and best from the point of view of reason
and experience is congruent with the essence of Biblical ethics.

I do not share John Cobb's view that it is use-
less to search for the essence of Christianity.[15]
Granted, no formulation of the heart of the Christian
vision is likely to win everybody's approval. Every
attempt to state the abiding norm of the Gospel is
done from some point of view. It represents somebody's interpretation. Yet here, as elsewhere, a
critical realism is indicated. There is an identifiable locus and focus where the essence is to be sought,
namely, in the center and vicinity of the New Testament witness to Jesus as the Christ. All formulations
of the fundamentals of the faith must be measured by

its conformity to that body of data. But the standpoint
of the interpreter affects what one sees as being really
there. There is no escape from this predicament. No
transcending authority is available to adjudicate dis-
putes about the Christian essence. Every such alleged
source of the real truth is itself affected by the relativity from which liberation is sought. As Luther said,
Popes and Councils can err. So can Luther and all other
theologians. The fact is that no truth and no error can
be located except in someone's judgment. Yet we should
not be pessimistic about the agreement that is real and
possible. And the New Testament is abidingly there as
an objective referent to correct and judge all formulations. Hence, every interpreter needs to declare what
appears to him or her to be its essence but should re-
frain from exclusive and absolute claims for what surely
is one among many possible views. One can only speak of
what is for me or for us the heart of the matter.

     The resulting synthesis is best thought of not as a
circle with a single center but as an ellipse with two
foci. A circle suggests that there is one and the same
identical content which is expressed in two different
language systems. It is true that nothing appears in the
philosophical vision that is rejected as untrue in the
theological outlook or vice versa. Moreover, it follows that the content of the one is latent or potentially present in the other. Only at this final state
is it the case that what is involved is mainly category
translation. With respect to many parts of the total
system, the same content will appear either in different
language or in the same terms. But the philosophical
and theological components each constitute a distinctive
Gestalt, as indicated previously. A particular methodological and substantive organization comes into focus

when each stance is assumed. The Christian theological
component will contain beliefs distinctive to the community of faith which would not necessarily or likely
arise in the secular philosophical component. Beliefs
surrounding Jesus as the Christ, the church, ministry,
the sacraments, and the trinitarian pattern for thinking
about God, for example, are essential to Christian witness. These doctrines as such would not arise in the
other framework, although formal counterparts might in
some cases.

The contents of the ellipse with the two foci designated as the Christian and the secular Gestalt should
not be thought of as marking off separate compartments
in a static, spatial way so that each contains a discrete and nonoverlapping segment of the whole. Neither
are the contents arranged hierarchically in Thomistic
fashion so that "Christ" is about "culture," with the
theological component an addition on top of but including the philosophical dimensions. Rather each stance
when it is assumed brings into play a dynamic organization from within the whole in accordance with its own
distinctive methods and content. A Gestalt is created
by its own appropriate presuppositions, procedures,
categories, and norms. The believer in the church con-
fesses the faith of the community. The self in the
world proclaims whatever reason and experience dictate.
Each of these stances takes a fully concrete form when
it is self-consciously assumed. The total ellipse contains a coherent body of affirmations about reality.
Either a theological or a philosophical construct can
be formed out of that totality in accordance with its
peculiar or unique stance. An image is suggested by
the combination of a flashlight and a magnet which
attracts iron filings. The flashlight throws a focused

light around one of the foci of the ellipse. The rest
is there but remains outside the illuminated circle.
The magnet draws into the center around itself those
distinctive filings which it has been designed to
attract leaving the others untouched or pushed outside
the immediate focus.

                              D

     The methodology of this attempt to develop a Christ-
ian natural ethics can be clarified by comparing a more
liberal statement with a more orthodox formulation of
the relationship between revelation and reason. Harold
DeWolf in his A THEOLOGY OF THE LIVING CHURCH maintains
that reason is needed to determine whether revelation
has occurred.[16] Given the multiplicity of truth claims
rooted by self definition in divine disclosure, some
rational judgment must be made to determine which, if
any, are valid. In contrast to this are those Augustinian-Anselmic affirmations that revelation antecedently
provides the very principle of reason in light of which
things makes sense. Augustine said, "I believe in order
that I may know." Anselm spoke of faith seeking understanding. Here the priority is given to something from
beyond reason which establishes the very rules and norms
of rationality. Does reason judge what is revelatory?
Or does revelation determine what is reasonable? Without trying to assert what must or always be the case,
let me suggest that both of these statements define a
part of the truth, but the whole truth involves a dialectical interaction in which in alternate moments each
assumes the priority.
     The rationalism of DeWolf is correct in defining
the limits of possibility and probability within which

any alleged claims to special insight can normally be
entertained. What offends our present moral or intellectual sensibilities or stands totally outside the norms
of our present system of beliefs can hardly be regarded
as a Word from God. What purports to be revelatory must
at least be within the bounds of the possible as judged
by our reason even to be considered as a candidate for
acceptance. A person who is firmly convinced that the
world is law-abiding is not likely to be impressed with
an alleged revelation from God that depends upon the
supernatural disruption of the casual order. Yet to
press this principle to its limits practically robs
revelation of its distinctive meaning and reduces it to
nothing more than rational insight or human discovery.
It eliminates the possibility of entertaining truth
beyond the bounds of our present rationality. It con-
fines us to our little circle of possibility. The very
meaning of revelation is that it brings the new, the
different, that it shatters our present life stance and
belief system by introducing a principle of truth and
value from beyond. Revelation is the unveiling of that
which had been hidden; it pulls back the curtains dis-
closing what we had not seen and could not see until the
revelatory moment. This is the truth for which the
Augustinian-Anselmic tradition stands. We do not know
what is true until it is revealed. Believing what is
given to us from beyond ourselves establishes the very
principle and substance and norm of rationality itself.
What did not make sense before becomes clear and plain,
chaos become cosmos, light penetrates what had been
darkness and confusion. Previous criteria of truth are
shattered by a new clue that renders former reasoning
inadequate. So far Augustine is right in asking us to
believe that we may know. Anselm is correct in seeing

that faith (which appropriates revelation) is prior to
understanding.

Yet there are limits to fideism which point us back
toward rationalism. Faith requires a leap. Believing
is accepting what is more or different from what we presently know. But why leap into one belief system rather
than another? Not everything that claims revelational
authority can be believed. Not every claim to special
disclosure can be trusted. There must be some contact
between that which invites our trust and our present
rationality. Whatever transformation a new principle
of truth (revelation) may bring about, it must have
convincing marks of worthiness which establishes itself
by its intrinsic intelligibility. There is a reason
one way of believing evokes faith while another does
not. We cannot believe what we "know" to be false.
Hence, we return to the point DeWolf was making.

Faith transforms reason and provides the key which
enables it to make sense of the world. But reason
judges faith and sets the limits within which faith ordinarily does its transforming work. Revelation fulfills reason; it does not destroy it. Revelation com-
pletes reason; it does not contradict it. Revelation
persuades reason; it does not coerce it. But reason
may also transform revelation. Reason must make a
judgment about what is best in the Christian tradition
independently of what is the essence of the faith.
Obviously, if the conclusion is that what is best and
worthy of preservation is different from the essence of
historic faith, then to that extent one consciously
places oneself outside the Christian circle. Christian
reasoning proceeds within limits circumscribed by the
norms of belief as determined by the community of believers. To affirm as of the essence of the faith what

the community in its authoritative statements or representatives regard as outside that consensus is the meaning of heresy. One may, of course, claim the right to
decide for oneself what is essential to Christian belief
and defy established norms or creeds. A Christian, by
definition, is one who affirms identity between what is
believed to be most true and important about life and
what is regarded as the abiding essence of the New Testament witness to Jesus Christ. Hence, there are limits
to which reason can appropriate the insights of faith
without regarding them as incredible and irrelevant and
thus unacceptable. And there are limits to which reason
can modify or transform the claims of faith without
breaking out of the Christian circle. But within these
parameters the dialectic proceeds in a mutual criticism,
transformation, and confirmation which yields a synthesis of insights, ideas, and ideals unified into some
coherent whole by intuition and constructive reasoning.

I affirm the way of dialectical synthesis both as
an account of what actually happens when many Christians
seek truth and as a proposition about how truth is meth-
odologically and normatively to be sought. It has already been stated that it is not useful to insist how it
must be done, as if there were one and only one way that
could be called right from some universal point of view.
Logically speaking, after some initial commitment of a
self in the world to a Christian vision of reality by
which one becomes a believer in the church, there are
three steps which occur in no particular necessary
order. They may occur in all sorts of combinations and
alternations in halting and fragmentary as well in more
formal and systematic ways. Truth-seeking is a complex
matter which does not always follow any one scheme about
how it ought to be done. But it is possible upon

reflection to lay out the logical elements that are involved abstractly, whether this ordering is actually
followed in life experience.[17]

1.   One examines Biblical and other Christian texts
to discover and record what is the heart and abiding
essence of the Christian message based on the internal
testimony of the relevant witnesses. Thus, a norm is
discovered within Scripture which judges the Christian
authenticity of everything else in Scripture itself as
well as alternative visions outside Scripture.

2.   One examines the world in search of truth
about meaning and morality as a citizen of culture here
and now using whatever methods, sources, and norms are
available. The results are organized, criticized, and
creatively constructed by human reason. The test of
the product is three-fold: a. The vision is internally
coherent; that is, as free from inconsistency as possible. b. It is adequate as an account of the data
that are to be interpreted without suppressing evidence
or leaving gaps in explanation. c. It is applicable
to experience; that is, to the theory and practice of
human existence in its practical efforts to cope with
reality in individually and corporately fulfilling ways.
Underlying these principles is the epistemological dictum of Alfred North Whitehead that the sole justification for any thought whatsoever is the elucidation of
immediate experience.

3.   These two perspectives are brought together in
a series of alternate moments in which each one examines
and is examined by the other until an intuition dawns
which unites them into one patterned whole. Intuition

refers to the experience of being grasped immediately and
directly by a pattern in which the data in question fall
into place around some organizing center. Intuitions of
varying levels of complexity and inclusiveness occur.
Many such moments follow each other in steps 1 and 2 as
well as in the search for a unifying synthesis. Patterns
of thought have a Gestalt quality. What we see obviously
depends on our perspective as well as on the objective
material that is being interpreted. When the intuition
occurs that forms our peculiar Gestalt, we have no
choice but to give witness to it, critically but boldly,
as compelling truth.[18]

The methodology described in this chapter holds for
the comprehensive task of theology. This particular volume arises out of the engagement of moral philosophy and
Christian ethics. Chapters II and III set forth a
scheme of philosophical ethics using the tools, methods,
and criteria characteristic of that discipline. Chapter
IV develops a theory of Christian ethics based on the
Biblical witness to Jesus as the Christ. The remainder
of the book examines the question of justice from the
standpoint of a Christian natural ethics.

CHAPTER II

AN INCLUSIVE ETHICAL THEORY

A

The Western tradition in philosophy has produced
two major types of ethical theory. Both have continued
to be represented by thinkers of the first rank over the
centuries. Hence, there is a _prima_ _facie_ presumption
that each contains valid elements that warrant inclusion
in a comprehensive moral philosophy. Careful examination of the issues that emerge when the problem of the
right and the good is examined sustain this initial assumption. I shall argue that an adequate ethical theory
must include both teleological and deontological elements. Both of these theories have developed in a variety of forms, but at the heart of each is a basic orientation to moral issues.[1]

Teleology comes from a Greek word meaning end or
purpose. An ethics of this type asks about the proper
ends of life or the purpose that should be embodied in
moral action. It proceeds in two steps. First, it defines non-moral good. Secondly, it defines obligation
in terms of those acts or rules which will produce the
greatest good or the largest net balance of good over
evil. The end of life has been variously defined --
pleasure, happiness, self-realization, perfection,
power, the Kingdom (Society) of God, and so on. But in
every case right acts or rules are those which are most
productive of the non-moral good previously defined.
The ends of life may be one or many, but the right act
or rule is that which will result in or will probably
result in or is intended to result in the largest
achievement of good possible given the alternatives
available. Appropriate means are sought to achieve

desirable ends.

Deontology comes from a Greek word meaning that
which is binding or necessary. Deontological ethics
seeks for what is binding or necessary in human conduct.
This approach to morality denies what teleology affirms,
namely, that rightness is to be defined as actions most
productive of good. Other considerations are determinative. Rightness may inhere in the nature of an act itself. Lying may be claimed to be intrinsically wrong
or promise keeping as right in itself and thus a duty.
Rightness may inhere in the source that commands it.
A theist may hold a divine-command theory, i.e., if God
wills it, it is right by virtue of that fact. Some one
ultimate principle of morality, such as love of neighbor, may be said to determine right actions. At any
rate, some determiner of duty, some authoritative
ground of rightness, some principle or principles are
sought, some way of grounding obligation is specified
which mandates what ought to be done. However rightness
of rule or act is defined, consequences for good or ill
are not the only, the decisive, the ultimate determiner
of what is binding for conduct. Duties may be defined
by a variety of authorities -- by intuition, conscience,
custom or tradition, a social contract, rational will
(Kant), the church, God, the state, and so on. The
image is that of a citizen under authority to whoever
or whatever legitimately defines obligation. We are
bound to do what the author or ground of obligation
requires.

Both teleology and deontology come in act and
rule versions. The former asks in every situation what
is the right act for me in this particular set of circumstances here and now. The latter asks what are the
rules that everybody should always follow in order to

do one's duty or achieve the highest good.

I shall maintain that the efforts of deontologists and teleologists to encompass the strong points of
the other finally fail. Each requires the other for completion. Likewise, act and rule theories finally move
toward and merge with each other when they expand sufficiently to be adequate.

B

With this general description of the differences
between these two orientations to ethics, I shall begin
to elaborate my own version of both. The typical problems each has to face and the charges each has to defend
itself against will be dealt with in connection with
developing my own point of view. No attempt will be
made to deal with all variants that appear in each tradition, as this would be an extensive undertaking in itself. I shall try, however, to thread my own way
through the nest of issues that arise when each perspective is pursued so that my own position will become
clear. It would be tempting to claim that I will set
forth what is really at the heart of every deontological
and teleological theory or, more boldly, what is the
ultimate truth of the matter. However, a more modest
claim is simply that mine is one interpretation among
others. It appears to be self-evident, or at least
supremely rational, when surrounded by appropriate facts
and evidence, though what is self-evident to me may not
be to others.

I shall argue for a deontological theory that roots
the source of obligation in the inherent value of persons (and of all sentient beings). Duty, then, is
grounded in reality and not in arbitrary authority.
Likewise, I shall argue for a teleological theory that

is rooted in the potential of persons (and all sentient
beings) for enjoyment (self-actualization, happiness).
The deontological imperative is: Always act in ways that
appropriately honor intrinsic worth. The teleological
imperative is: Always act in ways that appropriately
maximize the range and depth (intensity) of enjoyment.
A variety of other moral principles are, of course,
necessary to bridge the gap between this high level of
abstract generality and the particulars of decision-
making in a given concrete situation, but these two basic
imperatives are at the center of the normative form of
deontological-teleologic ethics I shall elaborate.

At this point characteristic problems and peculiar weaknesses arise for both deontological and teleological theories. For deontology one important issue has
to do with resolving conflicts between duties. If one
may not use differing consequences as the crucial factor
for determining which action or rule is most right, how
does one decide? Obviously a hierarchy of duties is
required. But how is an order of precedence to be established? Four possibilities come to mind.

1. The hierarchy of duties is purely arbitrary and
depends solely on whoever or whatever determines right
acts or rules. A theist might simply say that we must
obey the will of God. Or one must obey the state and
follow the rules of precedence as they are given in the
law. I reject this option.

2. The hierarchy of duties is known intuitively.
A distinction can be made, following W.D. Ross, between
prima facie and actual duties.[3] All obligations have
some weight. In the absence of conflict or other considerations they are to be carried out. But when two

or more duties are present, we intuitively know which has
the greater weight, and that determines what actually is
to be done. I think there is an element of truth here.
We know intuitively that we should tell a lie if so
doing will save an innocent life.

    3. The order of priorities is designed to serve
the highest good. Hence, in case of conflict, consequences are to be taken into account. While this introduces a teleological element, it may nevertheless be a
legitimate deontological procedure. One might maintain
that moral imperatives are binding because of their
source, but as a matter of fact they are designed to
promote good consequences. A theist could say that the
reason we are to be kind to our neighbors is that God
commands it, but that God commands it because kindness
promotes the well-being of others. A variation of this
line of reasoning would be that obligations, including
the ordering of priorities, have an independent grounding in deontological reasoning but that teleological
considerations can be introduced to help resolve conflicts. I think this variant is the more nearly adequate, although teleological considerations should always be brought into play, since teleology too has an
independent and valid grounding.

    4. The order of moral imperatives (including its
conflict-resolving features) has a rationale which is
non-arbitrary and non-teleological. This is the view
I shall adopt. There is a rational grounding for obligations, but it is based on a different orientation
from the quest of the highest good. Deontology asks
the moral question in another way. This reasoning will
usually lead to the same conclusion regarding what one

should actually do in given situations but not necessarily always. For example, deontological reasoning may
prefer a more equal distribution of a smaller total good
on grounds of fairness or justice to a larger fund of
goods and other benefits distributed unequally (where no
claimants have grounds for differential rewards). However, it should be noted that if the inequality is quite
moderate and the larger good provides considerably more
of everything to everybody, then this option might be
justly chosen. This is especially the case if the larger good can only be had by permitting the inequality.

A complete system of deontological ethics would
require a set of principles by which one could derive a
full set of obligations from the basic premise of honoring intrinsic worth. Some guidelines for determining
which duties take precedence over others (or which acts
are more forbidden than others) are also necessary.
This will not be done in detail here, although a modest
attempt is made in a later chapter on justice. However,
the fundamental considerations need to be indicated.
Intuition serves us well in most cases to move from the
idea of honoring worth to a sense of what is required in
a specific instance. For example, we know intuitively
that if a teenager promises her mother that she will
practice her piano lesson and baby-sit with her infant
brother while her mother is out shopping, she ought to
keep the promise. Moreover, we know that while it would
be wrong for her to watch television while her mother is
out and then lie about it, it would be a much worse offense if in anger she strangled and killed her brother
because his crying interfered with watching her favorite
program. Can one state why these judgments follow? The
basic principle is that acts honor intrinsic worth to the
degree to which they preserve, enhance, and promote the

actuality and contribute to the well-being of a given
person (or any sentient organism) or a community of such
beings. As will be stated later, an organism has worth
because it is an experiencing subject. Hence, worth is
honored by whatever maintains the existence of a subject
and adds to the quality of experience. Acts honor worth
to the extent to which they support the functioning and
flourishing of a person or organism at an optimal level.

To spell out a total system and hierarchy of required and forbidden acts (or rules) would involve a full
statement of the complete set of needs, capacities, and
potentials which constitute the health and well-being of
persons. One might conveniently put these under three
headings: (1) the biological health of the individual
organism, (2) the rights, privileges, and responsibilities growing out of membership in a community (justice
and social well-being), and (3) the spiritual needs for
meaning, love, recognition, and fulfillment as a free,
self-conscious, purposive agent.

The primary guideline is that worth is honored by
acts and rules which support the actuality and undergird
the possibility of the fulfillment of potential as a
fully functioning, flourishing, healthy organism. The
emphasis is upon the present being, existence, needs,
and capacities of a person. However, deontological imperatives move toward teleological considerations when
attention shifts from present actuality toward future
states in which potential for enjoyment can be actualized. It is a deontological requirement that the good of
a subject be promoted as a way of reverencing the intrinsic worth of a being with capacities for enjoyment.
Likewise, by implication the teleological imperative to
promote the fulfillment of experiencing subjects by
actualizing their good includes the obligation to pre-

serve the existence, health, and dignity of organisms as
a presupposition and part of promoting welfare. Hence,
while deontology focuses on actuality and teleology focuses on potentiality, each by implication moves toward and
includes the other, while retaining an autonomous status
as a ground of obligation. Here is an example of the
coincidence of apposites which retain independent standing and yet fit (complete) the other.

     With such guidelines it would, in principle, be
possible to work out a set of obligations properly ordered according to importance and precedence. Such a hierarchy would reflect what is more or less essential to
the actuality, full functioning, flourishing, and welfare
of a person.[2] The system if spelled out would indicate
that raping one's sister is a more serious offence
against human worth than deliberately giving the wrong
time of day to a stranger on the street. Providing basic
political liberties and civil rights is a more fundamental demand of justice than providing free beaches for
the populace. Intuition serves well in these instances
in the absence of a fully articulated system of principles and rules to indicate the line of duty. It would
be impossible to write a set of guiding principles or a
rule book detailed enough to guide us toward correct
action with respect to all the issues we face in personal
and social life. In addition, there are complicated and
subtle factual considerations and a whole host of contextual qualifications which have to be taken into account as
well as pure moral principle. Consider the following:
divorce, abortion, tax policy, the nuclear arms race,
welfare programs for the poor, affirmative action versus
reverse discrimination, and so on and on through an endless list. A good deal of muddling through complexity
and ambiguity is inevitable along with whatever guidance

is provided by accumulated social wisdom, custom, tradition, a changing cultural consciousness embodying a more
refined human sensitivity, and reasoning on the basis of
moral principles, ideals, goals, and lures.

A variety of problems at once also confronts teleological theories. I shall touch only briefly on some of
them. If consequences are determinative of rightness or
wrongness, consequences for whom over what period of
time? The answer, in principle, is that a universal and
all-inclusive perspective must be taken. The consequences for all sentient beings for the entire future must
be taken into consideration if the end is to achieve
largest possible good. However, action must be guided
from a subjective viewpoint by the intended, foreseeable,
probable consequences. The greater consequences usually
are those which project into the immediate surroundings
and the near future. One might, of course, imagine
scenarios in which one or a few small acts at crucial
points so altered the balance of circumstances through a
whole series so that the whole of history is altered profoundly. However, ripples into the wider universe and
spans of time from one act generally become weaker and
less relevant to immediate decision. The context will
generally make clear what the pertinent factors are that
can reasonably be expected to alter the general balance
of good over evil resulting from our actions. A plan of
moral living by individuals and groups will, of course,
include short range and long range strategies. Some will
be intended to affect one individual here and now, others
to change the social context that will benefit large
numbers over an indefinite future.

A second issue is, of course, what the good is that
is to be sought and how it is to be measured. The good
is, according to the present theory, enjoyment or

happiness or self-actualization in community -- different
ways of saying essentially the same thing. Now if right
acts or rules are those which maximize enjoyment, then
one has to have a way to distinguish between more or
less. Inevitably, it seems, one must deal with the differences and interactions between quantity and quality of
goodness and the difficulties arising out of objective
standards of goodness and subjective preferences. Considerable detail is given to this set of problems in a
later chapter on justice under the headings of "The Good
Person," "The Good Life," and "The Good Society." Here
let it be said that I do believe that there is a human
essence or nature and that these structures of humanness
do give clues to what is needed to actualize the potential for enjoyment. Nevertheless, there are areas where
subjectivity reigns and individual preference is the
primary determiner of goodness. Here something is good
because it is desired. So some combination of objective
and subjective considerations must be taken into account.
Some appropriate combination of fulfilled needs and
wants leads to the self-actualization of human nature
and thus provides the clue to the good that is to be
sought. Moreover, an analysis of the different dimensions of human need including biological health, social
justice, and spiritual fulfillment, as was given in discussing deontology, gives more specific clues to the
nature of the non-moral good. Also, it provides guidelines relevant to the determination of what is the com-
paratively greater good in particular circumstances
both in quantitative and qualitative terms.

     Still a third fundamental problem is faced by teleo-
logical theories. Does it matter whose good is realized?
Or is it simply an issue of the most good regardless of
who experiences it? Once it is asserted that it matters

whose good is involved or that the good of all should be
included, even if the total good be perhaps less, a deontological principle has been introduced. The reason for
preferring a lesser good more widely distributed than a
larger good less widely distributed is that it is right
or just to do, and this is a deontological standard.
One might, of course, argue on teleological grounds that
if any potential for good should be actualized, then it
rationally (logically) follows that every such potential
should, so that no capacity for enjoyment can be left
out. Also, it could be maintained that what is at stake
is achieving the truly good and not simply the sheer quantity of good and that the truly good includes the rightful claims of all. True enough, but a dilemma still
arises when a choice must be made between seeking the
greatest good and honoring the equal claims of all equal
potential for good (justice). Pure teleology will choose
to maximize the good regardless of who experiences the
good or who is left out. I will assume here that the
distribution of good is an independent question from
that of maximizing the good and that the former rises in
the strictest sense from a deontological principle. To
incorporate the principle of justice in any way at any
point makes it a mixed theory.

Hence, utilitarianism is a classic example of the
pure form of teleological ethics. It is commonly (and
rightfully) said that the utilitarian formula is "the
greatest good of the greatest number." However, most
twentieth century utilitarians have recognized the dilemma just discussed and resolved it in favor of the single principle of the greatest good. However, they note
in most cases that the greater good is usually achieved
when the distribution is more equal due to the principle
of diminishing marginal utility. But if a choice has to

be made, the greatest total good regardless of whose
good is involved is the ultimate criterion. For this
reason I shall use utilitarianism and teleology almost
interchangeably.

C

    Teleological and deontological theories form two
distinct classes of moral reasoning. A characteristic
weakness emerges from the fundamental premises of each.
By examining this situation, further evidence can be
presented for including both perspectives into a complete accounting of morality. Utilitarianism, in particular, has been charged with a willingness to make
persons into means and even to do them injustice in
order to maximize the good. Deontological perspectives
have been indicted because they may sometimes lead to
miserable consequences that could have been avoided or
to a good less than could have been achieved. The
attack on the one is the exact counterpart of the other.
Each by guarding one essential moral principle falls
into a potential trap by virtue of that very fact. An
examination and evaluation of this situation will
further the development of the inclusive theory I wish
to defend.
    Utilitarianism has been criticized for willingness
to use any means whatsoever as long as the consequence is
the greater net balance of good over evil. An unflinch-
ing utilitarian will not hesitate to sacrifice some human beings for the sake of others if this is the only way
to achieve a superior total happiness. Utilitarianism
does not take seriously enough the question of human
rights rooted in the inherent value of persons. That
principle stands as an independent moral consideration

not subject to a pure calculation of quantities or qualities of consequential good. If there is ever a case in
which it would be preferable to sacrifice even a small
bit of total happiness for the sake of respecting the intrinsic worth and dignity of a person, then utilitarianism is shown, in principle, to be inadequate.

Imagine a married couple, Thelma and Sam, who are
content enough with their marriage to want it to continue.
Thelma has a violent feeling against infidelity and has
made it known to Sam that she would divorce him instantly
if he were ever unfaithful to her. Sam has a similarly
strong aversion to homosexuality. Enter Margie who begins a lesbian affair with Thelma and a heterosexual
affair with Sam. All three are made deliriously happy.
All three are utilitarians. What is wrong or bad about
this situation as long as neither Sam or Thelma finds out
about the other's relationship to Margie? Everybody it
seems is happy.

A utilitarian might make two responses. 1. Since
Sam knows how Thelma feels about infidelity and she knows
how he feels about homosexuality, neither could enjoy
the relationship with Margie. Honoring each other's
feelings is more likely to produce deeper and more meaningful satisfactions than ignoring the values of their
partners. 2. Rule utilitarians especially would respond that the affairs, if they ever began, would be unstable. All three would realize that they were lying
and cheating. In the long run, then, always following
the rule of fidelity in marriage is the more probable
means to the greater happiness than an affair. Lying
and cheating are to be avoided because they detract from
the general prospects of a lasting and desirable marriage.

But especially on act utilitarian grounds, why

would they not reason that "what you don't know doesn't
hurt you, and it helps me to have this relationship."
Isn't the value of truth that it generally promotes the
highest good? If truth in this case would produce less
total happiness, why should lying cause any discomfort
or cheating be thought of as wrong? Even if the whole
truth were known to all, why would Thelma and Sam condemn each other's actions on utilitarian grounds? Presumably Sam and Thelma as theorists approve of what the
other is doing as long as each keeps the secret. Yet
surely even though they might agree that lying and cheating are permissible, even required if the greater good is
being accomplished, existentially each would rather the
affair of the other were not happening. But why? A non-
utilitarian principle enters. A person has rights, by
which we may mean a claim on another's actions. This
claim arises out of the intrinsic value of a person.
In this case Sam and Thelma have a right to claim fidelity and truthfulness from each other. Each has promised
fidelity.

My thesis is that Sam and Thelma would cease to be
utilitarians if they knew the truth about each other.
They would rightly feel that their dignity and worth as
persons had been violated. Surely no one wants another
to practice that kind of utilitarianism on him or her.
The fact is that another independent principle is being
introduced that cannot be computed within the utilitarian calculus on a strictly means-end basis.

Imagine that the sheriff of a small town in the Old
West can prevent a riot that will result in perhaps a
hundred deaths only by framing and hanging a man he knows
to be completely innocent.[4] Would utilitarians agree
that the sheriff should sacrifice the man for the sake of
a larger good, especially if the knowledge that the

hanged man was innocent could be kept from the other
citizens of the town? If all the citizens are utilitarians, wouldn't they agree that the sheriff should frame
the innocent man and then keep the secret from them?
Were the secret out, of course, confidence in the justice of the system might be shaken with all sorts of unpredictable consequences -- cynicism, suspicion, fear of
being the next victim, etc. Not even the most convinced utilitarian can be happy with a theory that requires
one to do an unjust act for the sake of achieving the
largest good.[5] Let it be admitted at once, however,
that a deontological position also leads to a painful
dilemma. Should the choice be to refuse to frame the
innocent man and let dozens of people die (including
many innocent bystanders perhaps), this would give credence to the charge that deontology leads to more misery than a utilitarian view would have allowed.

Nevertheless, one feels the force of the claim that
in a society entirely made up of utilitarians (act utilitarians in particular), moral conventions like promise-
keeping and truth-telling would lose their credibil-
ity.[6] Anxiety would rise and mutual trust would tend to
break down. No one could ever be quite sure that someone was not lying and keeping the secret for the sake of
an increased general happiness. Rule utilitarians might
argue that this is a reason for always keeping promises,
telling the truth, refusing to frame an innocent person, etc. But another dilemma results. If no exceptions are made, then on some occasions the larger good
would not be achieved. The chances of a larger good
on the whole and in the long run might be increased,
though this is debatable, and certainly difficult to
calculate. How does one measure increased social confidence in the integrity of the social system in the long

run over against the loss of happiness in particular
cases, e.g., when a riot occurs killing many, a riot
which could have been prevented by framing one person?
If rule utilitarianism allows judicious exceptions for
cases like this in order to get the best advantage of
general rules plus exceptions, then it opens itself to
the same charges to some degree that can be levelled at
act utilitarianism.

Brand Blanshard takes up a case typically presented
by deontologists to show that teleological theories conceivably can result in doing an injustice for the sake
of a larger good. Should a judge -- the only person in
town who knows that the prisoner before him is absolutely innocent -- nevertheless convict the accused if
so doing would halt an epidemic of violence? W.D. Ross
had argued that a utilitarian would have to agree to
the condemnation if it produced a greater total good
than setting the prisoner free, even though it would
clearly be wrong to do so. No, says Blanshard. The
teleological principle itself forbids this proposed injustice. Condemning an innocent man would be a breach
of the whole fabric of social relationships upon which
the good of the community rests. It would disrupt the
plan of life that includes truth-telling, promise-keeping, and judicial integrity, and so on, all of which
are essential to social welfare. It is important to
stop a crime wave, but it is far more important to preserve the moral framework of society.

In his defense of utilitarianism Blanshard makes
reference to a well known distinction of John Rawls.
Rawls distinguishes between justifying a practice and
justifying an action that falls under this practice.
The latter involves summary rules based on the conclusions of past experiences in which the utility principle has been applied directly. Act utilitarianism

which allows summary rules based on empirical testing
is applicable in these cases. But the former involves
rules which define a practice, and exception is not to be
made to these rules. Rules of practice coordinate relationships and actions into a system or institution. The
practice itself is then subjected to the utility principle. Blanshard appeals in this instance to a rule of
practice and thus to a form of rule utilitarianism
which escapes the worst implications of act utilitarianism.

Let us grant this his defense is adequate to prevent
the punishment of an innocent man in this and in all similar cases. One cannot help but be struck by the fact
that in his appeal to the rules which are necessary for
social institutions (rules of practice -- Rawls), the man
himself has been pushed aside. Even if a utilitarian
reason can be found to save the poor wretch who stands
before the bar of justice, is there not another more
direct and simple appeal? It is wrong to condemn an innocent man, entirely apart from the consequences which
flow from this misdeed. However the wrongness might be
accounted for, the deontological moralist is surely on
firm ground in urging that the act in itself as directed
to the man himself is forbidden. In my version of deontology, condemning an innocent man violates his human
rights, assaults the inherent worth and dignity of his
humanity. Hence, while Blanshard may be able to arrive
at the right conclusion in this and all other cases on
teleological grounds, it does not follow that these are
the only grounds on which obligation can be established.
But does not even the position of the rule utilitarian
tell us something about the deficiency of this point of
view? Truth-telling, promise-keeping, and honoring
human rights are not neutral acts that take on moral

meaning only as means to achieve good ends. They have a
meaning, a value, a moral significance in themselves entirely apart from their use as means in the utilitarian
calculus. Else, why would telling a lie or breaking a
promise, or punishing an innocent man upset anybody at
all? These acts are an affront to the sense of worthiness we have as inherently valuable beings. Hence, a
non-utilitarian standard enters that has a grounding all
of its own quite apart from the principle of utility.
The rights and claims of one person on another do not
supplant the obligation to be benevolent and to seek the
largest possible social good. But the rights rooted in
the intrinsic worth of persons must be taken into account along with teleological principles if the rules
for moral decision-making are to be complete.

The same objections to utilitarianism can be seen
by looking at the problem of distributive justice.[8]
Imagine two distributions of similar goods and services,
producing equal amounts of total satisfaction. In each
case all the recipients are equally deserving (by whatever standards one would agree to). But in scheme one
the distribution is unbalanced with some receiving considerably more than others. In scheme two the distribution is nearly equal. A utilitarian will have no basis
for deciding between the two. It will not do to argue
that in most cases the more nearly equal distribution
will produce the greater satisfaction, for by hypothesis
in this instance we have ruled that out. But suppose
that in every case the principle of diminishing marginal
utility does actually work out in practice so that
making distributions more equal does increase satisfaction. Even so, this is a weak point since the wider
or even, conceivably, a just distribution would occur by
virtue of a happy fact or coincidence and not as a

result of the intrinsic excellence of utilitarianism as
a moral theory. The claim that an unequal distribution
to equally deserving recipients will create social unrest,
a breakdown of morale and motivation, or even violence
and so lead to a lesser good in the long run is a poor
defense of justice, even if it is factually true. If
the theme of the greatest number is stressed along with
the concern for the greatest good, then a second principle has been introduced. In this case utility is not
the only standard for measuring a given distribution.

This point is made more vivid if we imagine that in
scheme two (above), the good to be distributed is slight-
ly less than in scheme one but the division is completely equal to equally deserving recipients. Yet utilitarianism would have to prefer scheme one because it
achieves the greater good. Again, to argue that scheme
two is preferable is to introduce a notion of justice or
fairness which cannot be deduced from the utility principle. It is a consideration of a different sort.

Imagine a situation in which two equally wicked
recipients are to receive a share of goods. In scheme A
a small amount and in scheme B a large amount is divided
equally between them. The principle of the greatest good
(and even for the greatest number) is perfectly filled by
scheme B. If we have a distaste for the second option,
it is rooted in something other than the utilitarian
standard.

A further difficulty for utilitarianism arises when
the factor of efficiency is introduced. Suppose that two
groups -- X and Y -- are to receive a distribution of
goods and services. The two groups are equal in number,
merit, and in all other relevant aspects, except one to
be mentioned later. Justice would appear to require an
identical distribution of benefits to each group, D_1.

But it turns out that those in group X are much more
efficient in using their resources so that they achieve
much more satisfaction from the same amount of goods. On
utilitarian grounds a redistribution would be called for
in which group X is given more and group Y less, D_2. One
can imagine a situation in which the gains in satisfaction from superior efficiency now operating with more
resources would outweigh any losses that would be in-
curred resulting from group Y having less. Yet since the
groups are equal in every respect except efficiency, D_2
seems unfair when compared to D_1. Group Y has a claim
on half the total of the objective benefits, even if its
members are less efficient in the utilization of what is
rightfully theirs.

Finally, consider two acts, each of which on a
given occasion results in exactly the same amount of happiness for the same number of people. However, the first
act involves telling a lie, while the second does not.
Act utilitarianism, at least, would have no basis for
preferring one act to the other, since the net balance
of good over evil is the same. Rule utilitarianism
might argue that the act involving the lie is the worse
choice since it would have a tendency to debase social
confidence in the trustworthiness of people and thus
detract from utility in the long run. But here again
this is a weak defense of truth-telling. It results
from the unwarranted, unworkable, and unnecessary attempt to make the principle of utility do the whole
work of morality. In fact, teleology requires a deontological principle to complete the task of moral theor-
izing.

The considerations I have introduced do not apply
equally to rule and to act utilitarianism. I have indicated that rule utilitarianism, though finally inadequate alone, seems to offer a better protection of

justice and human rights. However, the debates between
act and rule utilitarianism sometimes get very complex
and subtle, leaving one exhausted and confused. An act
utilitarian could, of course, take into account the long
run consequences of a specific act of lying, promise-
breaking, infidelity, hanging an innocent person, and
so on. Hence, by taking into account the harm done to
future situations by the influence of a present act, one
might conclude that it is generally best to follow the
rule but that occasional, judicious exceptions would
maximize total good. But at any rate, the utility principle should be consulted directly in every situation
rather than acting upon a rule as such. However, a general utilitarian like M.G. Singer argues that it is not
sufficient merely to ask what is the total effect of this
particular act of mine on the future. Rather it is necessary to generalize and ask, "What if everybody did this
in these circumstances?" The utility principle is still
consulted directly but on a universal and not a particular basis.[9]

The debate it seems, though one can never be quite
sure until the next book or article appears, finally
comes down to this: Rule utilitarians argue that always keeping certain rules leads to greater universal
good in the long run, even though in some specific immediate situations less good might be accomplished
could have been possible by making an exception to the
rule. Act utilitarians argue that greater universal
good in the long run will result if the utility principle is consulted directly every time, even though the
outcome would frequently or generally result in the same
choice as following certain rules. An intermediate or
modified position would seek to combine nearly always
obeying certain rules with making rare and judicious
exceptions in special situations.

D

If utilitarianism is vulnerable to the charge of
using some people as means in order to achieve good ends
for others, deontological theories are open to the indictment of sometimes preferring obedience to rules or
to a principle or to some authority to the good of
people. This latter possibility arises because deontology does not make consequences for good or ill the decisive consideration in determining right action. Hence,
so the indictment runs, duty may on occasion conflict
with achieving the greatest good. Since this is the
opposite charge of the one directed at teleological
theories, some of the same examples or types of examples
would suffice to examine this potentially damaging attack on deontology. However, let us turn to some others.

Suppose Jerome is approached by a posse and is asked
the whereabouts of Thaddeus, whom they firmly believe to
be guilty of a murder. They intend to hang him at once.
Jerome knows where Thaddeus is but also knows absolutely
that he is innocent. If Jerome tells the truth, Thaddeus
will surely die for a crime he did not commit. A utilitarian has a ready answer -- the greater good will be
accomplished by telling a lie. Leaving aside a host of
complicating factors such as the possibility that the
posse learning of Jerome's perfidy may return and string
him up as well as finally hanging Thaddeus, the utilitarian response is persuasive. Confronted with a simple choice between telling the truth to a lawless posse
and preserving an innocent life, one clearly chooses the
latter alternative. Only a deontologist who allows no
exceptions to truth-telling is in danger of preferring
obedience to principle to serving human welfare. Given
a hierarchy of obligations and a distinction between

prima facie and actual duty, one can easily move on a
rule or an act basis to the conclusion that saving innocent life is preferable to telling truth to a posse
who has no right to the truth in this instance. In terms
of my own system, human worth is served in this case by
deceiving the would-be-hangmen.

A more difficult issue is posed by the kind of
standard question that used to be put to pacifists when
I was in seminary. Should we have let Hitler perpetrate
his horrors endlessly out of a commitment to non-viol-
ence? Surely the consequences of that are intolerable.
Or, we would say, suppose you are walking down the
street at night with your girl friend, sister, or mother
and you are attacked by a thug with a clear intent to
rob, rape, and do violence to your companion? Granted
that you are physically able to carry out a successful
defense and assuming that finally the rape and possible
murder can be prevented only by taking the life of the
attacker, is one really required to remain non-violent
in spite of the consequences? A deontological pacifist
with an absolute commitment to the prohibition against
taking another life regardless of circumstances and outcomes is bound to stop short of fatal measures. However, a deontologist with nonabsolutist principles can
argue that the prima facie injunction against killing
is superceded by the actual duty of defending the dignity of innocent life against a determined rapist or
murderer. Granted, a proportionate means to honor
human worth appropriate to the situation is required.
But the point is that deontological ethical theories do
not, in principle, lack resources for adjudicating conflicting duties.

A final dilemma may be worthy of examination.
Suppose that Horace who is married to Miranda has been

involved in an affair with Ramona. Full of regret under
the stricture of conscience, he has decided to tell
Ramona it is over, fully intending to commit himself
anew to his marriage with Miranda. On the very day
Horace is to carry out his resolve, accumulating evidence
prompts Miranda to ask him point blank if he has been unfaithful. What should Horace do? One might argue on
utilitarian grounds that it would be far better to deny
the allegation, supposing that the lie can be successfully defended. Telling the truth would do no one any
good. But should not a husband tell the truth to his
wife? A deontological theorist could agree that honoring her worth calls for a lie, truth in this case being
too cruel to her sense of dignity. This is the usual
reasoning of the advice columnists. Yet the counter
claim is that in withholding truth from his wife, Horace
is denying her information she needs and has a right to
for purposes of choosing how she will live in the future
with him. Horace is in full possession of the facts.
He can make his decision in that light. Unless he provides her with truth, she does not have the privilege.
Thus, by so denying her what she has a just claim to,
Horace is offending the intrinsic worth of a person to
whom he has promised fidelity. But if he did respond
with a full confession of the history of his recent life,
would not the consequences for ill be so great as to
overrule such considerations? Since misery can be avoided, is Horace not obligated to prevent such pain? What
good would the truth do?

The deontologist here, it seems to me, is in a
real dilemma. The considerations for and against lying
add up about equally on either side, while the utilitarian seems to have a clear answer (assuming that the lie
cannot be found out) that maximizes happiness and well-

being all around. One would, however, have to detract
the weight of the pain and remorse he might possibly
suffer by having to live with his lie and his unforgiven
infidelity. Nevertheless, one can at least see the possibility that deontological reasoning might lead to misery that could be prevented or to a lesser good than
might have been the case had the utility principle been
decisive. A Christian might contend that the deepest
exploration of the tragic and glorious potential of human
nature requires the risk of confession and the hope of
forgiveness and reconciliation in the light of truth
made possible by love. Otherwise, the relationship is
left clouded with ambiguity and demonic residue. The
conclusion to which all this leads is that whether
Horace should lie and seek forgiveness only with God or
tell the truth and seek reconciliation with Miranda as
well has to be settled contextually. It all depends on
their previous history together, the personality and tem-
perament of each, their announced wishes and agreed upon
ways of handling potentially destructive situations, and
so on.

I conclude that rule deontology which allows no
exceptions for specific rules may indeed lead to avoid-
able misery out of respect for such rules. Likewise,
act deontologists who make certain acts absolute taken
in and of themselves are likely to fall into the same
trap. However, rule deontological theories whose rules
can be superceded by superior rules and act theories
whose acts are determined contextually by intuition or
in the light of some higher principle have a guard
against such absolutism. My own position is that rules
and acts are derived from the single principle of honoring intrinsic worth. Hence, appropriate subordinate
rules or specific acts can be arrived at contextually.

Additional guard is provided if consequences for good
or ill are taken into account in deciding between conflicting deontological duties.

E

It follows from all this that teleological theories
may sometimes lead to a preference to a larger total
good achieved at the expense of violating the rights of
some. J.J.C. Smart protests that he is not happy with
this consequence. He admits that utilitarianism may in
some instances require one to do something unjust for the
sake of maximizing good.[10] Likewise, deontological theories may on occasion lead to miserable consequences that
a teleological ethic could have avoided or to a lesser
total good than utilitarianism could have achieved.
John Rawls, for example, admits that there is no reason
to think that just institutions, measured by deontological principles, will necessarily maximize the good.[11]
It would be a coincidence if such were the case. The
criticism of each type of theory by adherents of the
other points to a danger and to a tendency which may,
at times, lead to the results which opponents fear.
However, neither consequence is a flaw of sufficient
magnitude to undermine the ethical theory which produces
it. Rather, it indicates an unavoidable tension between
valid ethical orientations. Each type of theory is
needed to counterbalance the other.

In this situation three possible outcomes can be
imagined: (1) Sometimes ethical analysis may lead to a
stalemate with no preferable choice among two or more
alternatives. Teleological procedures or deontological
reasoning each employed to the exclusion of the other
could lead to this result. But sometimes deontology

may point to one action as most right while teleology
requires another in the same situation. When compared,
each may offset the comparative weight of the other,
leading to an equilibrium with the ethical pointer at
zero. (2) Sometimes it may be ethically advisable or
permissible to offend the dignity of some persons in the
interest of a significantly larger good for the total
community. News reports told of the plans of Detroit to
uproot a long existing Polish neighborhood causing
great anguish and offense. The reason is that this land
can be used by an automobile company with enormous alleged economic benefits for the whole city.[12] Or, as
already indicated, in matters of distributive justice it
may be morally right at times to seek a significantly
larger total social good even though this results in
significant inequalities in the sharing of the enlarged
bounty. This outcome is justified especially if the
larger good can only be had by generating these inequalities and even more so if those who are left worse off
are actually better off than they would have been under
a more equalitarian social arrangement. Certainly in
theory one would have to admit that there is some point
at which a potential good for nearly all moving toward
infinity would outweigh the countervailing weight of a
violation of the rights of a few moving toward zero.
(3) Sometimes a less bountiful total good must be fore-
gone in the interest of justice. This principle has
already been established in discussing distributive
justice. A smaller fund of goods distributed to
equally deserving claimants. The tradeoffs between
items (2) and (3) in this paragraph have to be decided
contextually with the help of all relevant facts, available measurements, moral insight, intuition, and a great
deal of muddling through ambiguous situations. One

cannot avoid some occasions when all is said and done in
arriving at the stalemate indicated in (1).

To summarize, teleology and deontology are two independent and relatively autonomous ways of reasoning.
Each has its own distinctive approach to moral questions.
Each has a validity that cannot be ignored in a complete
analysis of decision-making. They move toward each but
from a different but complementary center. Deontology
will tend to produce the highest good but not necessarily always. When it does not achieve the highest
good possible, it will be for a valid reason. Teleology
will tend to lead to the action that is most just but
not necessarily always. When it does not lead to the
action that most honors the rights and dignity of persons, it will be for a valid reason. Each is needed to
correct, complete, and balance the other.

For the most part deontological theories and teleological theories will overlap and lead to the same moral
choice. But a different grounding and rationale is involved in each case, and they may sometimes lead to conflicting conclusions which may be difficult if not impossible to resolve. What does one do when confronted
by two equally right actions or by a choice when what is
most right (deontologically) conflicts with what will
probably produce the most good? This is a potentially
tragic dimension of human life which requires a metaphysical explanation (unavoidable conflict between actualities and values in a pluralistic and interconnected
world) and a religious resolution (justification by grace
through faith).

Fortunately the moral choices that we face in our
daily lives can for the most part be decided on either
deontological or teleological grounds with the same
result (for a given individual at least). Ordinarily

we do A because it is intrinsically right or more right
or B because it produces better consequences, mixing
modes of reasoning intuitively or without sustained,
disciplined systematic reasoning. Rules of thumb, moral
conventions, habitual ways of acting, thinking and feeling, plus intuitive judgment and commonsense reasoning
provide us with a way to handle most situations without
great distress. But sometimes we are aware that some
choices involve conflicting obligations and values.
Moral philosophy may not always be able to resolve the
contradictions, but it may help us understand why there
is no system completely free of irresolvable conflicts
in the kind of world we live in. At any rate rational
coherence must not be forced at the expense of suppressing moral truths.

F

   Additional grounding must now be given to these
claims. What is meant by saying that deontology and
teleology have different but complementary bases in
moral reasoning? Deontology generates an order of obligations arising out of the inherent value of persons
(and all sentient beings). Teleology generates an order
of ends arising out of the possibilities of human
becoming (and that of all experiencing beings). Deontology is based on being and its inherent worth. Teleology is based on becoming and its fulfillment of potentiality. A person is a being with inherent worth,
dignity, value. A person has potentiality for satisfaction and enjoyment. Having intrinsic value, a person
has rights and prerogatives which other persons are
obligated to honor and respect. Having the potential
for pleasure and happiness (or however one wishes to

define the good), a person has privileges to seek fulfil-
ment which that person and others must honor and respect.[13]   Person A has equal rights and privileges to
that of Person B.[14] Moreover, person A has the duty to
respect, honor, and protect the inherent value of person B. Person A has a privilege to seek the good arising out of his or her potential but none superior to that
of person B. In principle, the potential of B has as
much moral claim on A as A's own. Hence, egoistic ethical theories have no grounding in truth. If every person's being and potential count for what they are, then
it is irrational (or at least eccentric and odd) and immoral for anyone to claim that only his or her worth and
happiness matter.

     Given the fact that a person has inherent value and
a potential for fulfillment, the basis is laid for both
deontological and teleological forms of moral reasoning.
Deontology develops an order of obligations which honors,
promotes, protects, enhances, and respects the worth of
persons. It spells out what we owe to each other as
beings with inherent value. If someone tells me a lie,
my sense of dignity and value is offended. We feel that
we are owed the truth even though in a particular instance the lie told us may do us little or no harm. It
is wrong to tell a lie, right to tell the truth, independently of the consequences that follow from a given
act. I believe it can be shown that the order of obligations usually thought to constitute right conduct can
be deduced from the faithfulness which people owe to each
other as persons with inherent worth. The priorities of
obligation are structured in accordance with this rationale. Hence, saving an innocent life takes precedence
over telling the truth to a deluded posse. The worth
and dignity of vigilantes under these circumstances do

not have the same claim on my duty as the inherent value
of the innocent life of the falsely accused suspect.
Right and wrong are measured by the relative degree to
which an act or rule honors or dishonors the status of
persons as persons. Being told a harmless lie by a
stranger is less offensive to the objective worth of
personhood and to the subjective sense of worthiness than
the infidelity of a spouse.

The hierarchy of obligations arising from deontological respect for inherent value is reinforced and
confirmed by the covenants people make with each to secure their rights. These agreements may be explicit and
formal or implicit and informal. Marriage vows are
taken in solemn ceremony in the presence of witnesses.
Each pledges fidelity and life-long commitment to the
well-being of the other. Friends implicitly assume and
give pledges of truth-telling, promise-keeping and loyalty to the worth each recognizes in the other. Such
agreements are implicit in casual and business dealings.
If I ask a stranger on the street the time of day, I
assume that he or she will inform me correctly. If I
buy peaches from a roadside stand, I expect that the
fruit in my basket will be as good as that displayed even
though no formal agreement has been made. Individuals
acquire both rights and obligations by being born into a
given society, even though no social contract is signed
upon attaining legal maturity. No society could function harmoniously without such assent to a basic integrity in social interactions. The pledges of allegiance
we make to each other are finally rooted in the recognition of the inherent value of each by the other. A covenant of fidelity assumes as a necessary ground the intrinsic value of the actuality and potentiality of persons. The more destructive an act is of this inherent

worth, the greater the wrong. The more an act affirms, enhances, respects, and is faithful to such value, the greater the moral weight it has.

Deontology viewed in this way may be especially powerful in creating a moral sensitivity to suffering. Hunger, oppression, denial of basic human rights to life, liberty, and the pursuit of happiness, and all such degradations are an offense to the worth of persons. A deontological ethic peculiarly obliges us to combat the worst evils of the moment. A sense of moral outrage at the wrongs done to a human being is the natural offspring of an orientation which focuses on what is fair and right. This may be particularly true when the crushing of the human spirit is the result of socially rooted violations of human rights and dignity. Social injustice is the special enemy of a developed deontological ethic. Witness the case of those well known non-utilitarians, the Old Testament prophets.

Teleology develops an order of ends and means which promotes the fulfillment of human potential. A person is a creative, self-determining purposive being. Human life is a process of becoming in which possibilities for enjoyment lure us forward and upward toward their attainment. A teleological ethic obligates us to act in such a way as to achieve the greatest good. Good is the fulfillment of human potential experienced as satisfaction. Pleasure, happiness, enjoyment are various ways of indicating the subjective experience which accompanies the objective actualization of human good. Whether one concludes that pushpin is as good as poetry (Jeremy Bentham) or agrees that it is better to be a dissatisfied Socrates than a satisfied pig (John Stuart Mill), the maximizing of the range, depth, complexity, and intensity of satisfying experiences is the goal of

life as viewed by the teleological system espoused. We
are obligated to strive for the good society, for that
social order which best enhances the maximum enjoyment of
individuals. A hierarchy of ends qualitatively evaluated is necessary in order to give priority to choice
and to resolve conflicts between competing but mutually exclusive goods. In particular instances, of course,
choice is dictated by which of the available alternatives, all relevant factors considered, is likely to
produce the greatest net balance of good over evil. Teleology, as well as deontology, prefers telling a lie to
a deluded posse if it will save an innocent life for this
very reason.

In principle, teleology is more likely to create
those conditions in which the full flowering of human
creativity in the long run can occur. Its basic tendency
is to enlarge the range and depth of satisfying experiences that accompany the actualization of all facets of
positive human possibilities. At least this is its potential. Moreover, teleological reasoning may have particular merit in times of unavoidable tragedy or crisis,
especially emergencies or accidents in which no injustice was involved in creating the situation. Consider
those bizarre and fortunately rare situations in which
a shipwrecked party finds itself on a desert island.
Suppose it is absolutely certain that all will die unless
some survive on the flesh of their companions with near
certainty of being rescued. The single-minded, pragmatic, calculating teleologist might readily, if sor-
rowfully, agree that for some to live is better than for
all to perish, and proposes a fair way to choose the
sacrificial saviors.[15]

G

One further step has to be taken to complete the
immediate analysis. What gives intrinsic value to persons? A short but more general inquiry into the nature
of being and value is required here. According to the
process philosophy I espouse, any entity has some degree
of intrinsic value if it is an experiencing subject with
potential that can be actualized. An experiencing subject is one which has a capacity for enjoyment. Experiencing and enjoyment are interdependent but not
strictly identical. Experiencing refers to the most inclusive fact of what is going on with a subject, while
enjoyment suggests a positive evaluation of what is going
on. One can experience what is not enjoyable (pain or
despair, e.g.), but one cannot enjoy without experiencing. Experience refers to the factual side while enjoyment refers to the value side of becoming. But they
are indissolubly connected. There can be no experiencing without the possibility of enjoyment (or its opposite). Experiencing aims at enjoyment. An experiencing subject capable of enjoyment is one with potentiality that can be actualized. Enjoyment is experienced when the potentiality of a subject is being actualized. To say the same thing differently, enjoyment occurs in the presence of healthy functioning in
an experiencing subject. Functioning is experienced.
Healthy functioning is enjoyed.

The concept of life or organism provides another
way of referring to this same configuration of meanings.
In the most general sense life is the process by which
a self-organizing system actualizes its own potentiality. Put more precisely, life is the complex ensemble
of processes by which an organism appropriates relevant

aspects of its environment and otherwise responds to the
impact of its surroundings in quest of internally guided
ends. The environment includes the past of the organism
and other historical conditions which establish its own
beginning, present environing circumstances, and future
possibilities. Think of an acorn that, given certain
conditions, grows into an oak tree. The Whiteheadian
description of life processes provides an instructive and
full accounting of how this takes place. Especially illuminating is his vision of the role God plays in providing relevant ideal possibilities for actualization
for each emerging occasion. However, whether one is persuaded by this particular metaphysics, life does present
itself phenomenologically as a process of actualization
in quest of internally guided ends. Reasoning by analogy
from our own human experience that objective actualization is accompanied by subjective enjoyment, one concludes that this principle holds for all life forms, at
least at the animal level.

It may be that the final real constitutents of the
world are life processes. If so, there are, strictly
speaking, no valueless entities.[16] In this most inclusive sense, an experiencing subject refers to a unified
system of internally directed functions with a history
in which its own inherent potentiality provided by its
past is at least partially actualized under the guiding
lure of relevant future possibilities. The fact of evolutionary emergence and the variety of life forms indicates
that the actuality-potentiality given from the past includes the possibility of self-transcendence by which
novelty and greater complexity of life functions are introduced into the stream of cosmic history.

But what about mere things such as stones, type-
writers, and the whole range of gross non-living

objects which appear to the senses? These apparently
are nothing more than aggregates with no self-determined
unity or identity, no self-constituted form, no self-
directed functions, no self-actualizing potential, and
no self-guided ends. They may be made up of organic
entities but they are themselves pure objects. The
possibility is that no clear and distinct line can be
drawn between mere things and life. Mere things as
such have only instrumental value. But even they have
the sum total of the intrinsic value possessed by their
component parts.

   In the most inclusive sense, then, all organisms
have some degree of intrinsic value. Ordinarily, however, we are accustomed to thinking that sentience,
awareness, feeling, or consciousness (however attenuated
or elementary) must be presupposed for something to be
an experiencing subject. In fact, experiencing and awareness, meaning some form of feeling by the subject of what
is happening to it, are nearly identical concepts. Where
the threshhold of awareness is, in this sense, no one
knows for sure. We usually associate it with animal life,
although some insist that plants have at least the begin-
nings of some primitive feelings. At any rate, it does
seem clear that it matters to a flourishing, growing
tree when it is cut down in a way that it does not matter to the stone when it is crushed. The tree as a whole
dies. The organic system ceases to function, and it
becomes a thing. It ceases to be what it was. The stone
is simply broken into small pieces of the same thing it
already was. In this sense, at least, the tree is an
experiencing subject with a capacity for enjoyment
(fulfillment of inherent self-directed potential). Presumably in some still further attenuated or simpler
sense this may apply to molecules, atoms, and subatomic

entities to the extent that they are living in the extended meaning of that term used here. For practical purposes, however, I shall identify sentience with animal
life.

Enjoyment in sentient organisms is the subjective
experience accompanying the objective fact of actualization. In non-sentient subjects (if indeed there are
any) enjoyment and experience merge and become identical
with the objective fact of organic functioning. Enjoyment in the subjective sense as found in animals is an
emergent fact that requires a certain complexity and
kind of molecular organization. The cosmos has a life-
producing capacity and tendency which has over vast periods of time elaborated a complex hierarchy of organisms
who in their higher forms at least can experience the
enjoyment and enjoy the experience of their own self-
organized functioning and fulfillment.[17]

There is a hierarchy of intrinsic value. The
greater the range, depth, intensity, and complexity of
the potential for enjoyment, the greater the inherent
worth of the subject. A being has rights commensurate
with worth and a claim to fulfillment commensurate with
potential for enjoyment. Hence, a person has more value
than an animal, and an animal more than a plant. But
all living beings have some degree of intrinsic value
and a corresponding set of rights and claims for self-
realization. Hence, not even a mosquito should be killed
or a weed pulled up without justification. All morality
begins with respect for life and its possibilities for
enjoyment. In the very nature of things, life is in
tragic conflict with itself. Organisms feed on other
organisms. Yet all life has intrinsic value so that
when life robs other life it can only be justified, if
at all, when the lower serves the higher.

All value is value for some experiencing subject.
This is clear by definition when we speak of instrumental
value. It is also true in cases when by extended meaning reference is made to intrinsic values, meaning that
they are sought for themselves and not as a means to
other goods.   Happiness or beauty is good because each
is good for some experiencing subject. Other goods may
be sought as means to others, as money is wanted because
of what it can buy or the power it can bring. But
whether intrinsic (sought for itself) or instrumental
(sought partly at least as a means to other goods), good
always means good for some subject. Where there is no
experience, there can be no value.

An experiencing subject with a capacity for enjoyment has intrinsic value. With this analysis in mind it
is possible to interpret the derivation of deontological
and teleological ethics. Deontology begins with the inherent value of an experiencing subject and produces an
ordering of obligations which devolve upon the self and
others to honor, protect, respect, and enhance this inherent worth. A being with inherent worth has rights
and claims commensurate with that worth. Teleology
begins with the potential for enjoyment of an experiencing
subject and produces a system of ends and means to actualize that potential to the fullest. The aim of moral
action is to maximize the good that is possible for a
given being and in the widest sense for the whole community of experiencing subjects. Deontology not only has
to provide a hierarchy of duties which resolve conflicts
for a given subject but also has to take into account the
fact that the claims of one subject are limited by the
rights of other subjects. Teleology not only has to
devise an appropriate compossible set of ends and means
for a particular subject (since not all good ends are

compatible or even possible to achieve in a finite setting) but also has to optimize the competing claims of
the whole community of experiencing subjects in quest
of maximum enjoyment.

The difference between the grounding for deontology
and teleology is real but relative. It is a matter of
focus but not of exclusive and entirely separate orientations. Deontology derives what is binding in human
conduct from the actuality of a person as a present
fact. Teleology focuses on potentiality as a future possibility. Deontology points to what a being has become
at the moment out of the total past which has created
it. Teleology looks ahead to what a being can become.
What it is and what it can be are, of course, interrelated facets of the total reality and process of an
experiencing subject. It must be granted that a part of
honoring intrinsic value is to meet the need and to fulfill the potential of a person. But the reason for
seeking good consequences from a deontological point of
view is that the intrinsic value of the person in question binds us to do it. It is not right exclusively because the good is increased. It must also be granted
that seeking to maximize the good of a person is a way
of honoring intrinsic value. But the reason that so
doing is right from a teleological point of view is that
the good is increased. Hence, these two orientations
move toward each other but from different starting
points.

So far I have declared that honoring intrinsic
value and promoting enjoyment are respectively the grounds
of deontological and teleological ethics. But I have
not argued for these assertions. They are part of a
total set of metaphysical convictions which include
theories about reality, value, and the character of the

world process. Neither the whole nor the parts of the
metaphysical system can be proven to be true by empirical
or rational methods or by a combination of them. It is
not self-evidently true. The most that can be claimed
is that it is a more or less likely description of the
nature of things based on good evidence and plausible
reasoning. Central to this philosophical orientation is
the correlation of being and value. It is good to be.
Whatever is is good, and it is good because it is. Hence,
I align myself with the broadly Platonic, more specifically Augustinian-Christian tradition, in Western
thought. Within this framework it appears self-evidently
true from my perspective that moral obligation is to be
grounded in this correlation of being and goodness. If
intrinsic value is not to be honored, preserved, and
respected, what is? If necessity in conduct does not
flow from the unity of being and value, from what could
it possibly come? If general and universal good experienced as enjoyment of being is not to be promoted, what is
to be? I can only claim that the ethical theory is organically connected with the total metaphysical system and
is consistent with its basic assumptions. In a culture
in which metaphysics as such is suspect, much less a
process philosophy, it is to be expected that demurrers
are to be raised from many quarters. Finally, this
ethical theory can only be presented and argued for as
a possibility for consideration by reasonable people
seeking sound grounding for moral actions. It is offered
neither as a self-evident set of necessary truths nor
as an arbitrary subjective creation with only enthusiasm
to recommend it. If such is possible, it is set forth
as a version of subjective objectivism or objective
subjectivism.

H

One controversy among contemporary moral philosophers needs to be examined to locate more precisely
the position being taken here. It is possible, I believe,
to move beyond either extreme position and recognize the
validity in the other by making some relevant distinctions.

The debate has to do with act versus rule. Both
deontology and teleology can be expressed in either version. The question is whether responsible action can be
specified in general rules or whether a decision has to
be made on each occasion in order to discern the act
that is right under a given set of circumstances. Obviously each has to have a way to account for what the
other position maintains. Hence, act ethicists usually
make or can make a positive place for general rules as
usually being right, as useful rules of thumb to save
time, as summaries, as rough guides, etc. but not binding if the situation calls for a different response.
Rule ethicists find it hard to deny that rules sometimes
conflict with other rules so that exceptions are inevitable in some cases. My own view is that a rule is implicit in any given act, whereas a rule must take into
account possible exceptions if it is to be complete.
Hence, act and rule theories move toward and disappear
in each other.

The maxim of any act implies a general rule that is
universally binding, but binding universally only when
just this set of circumstances obtains. But the rule
that is implicit is more than a useful summary of previous experiences or a rough guide that is usually re-
liable. Consider the following example. Suppose Edith
borrows $5 from Sue. Should she pay it back? Of course

she should. The next day she borrows $5 from Barbara.
Should she pay it back? The very same reasoning and
principle of action that would lead us to say "Repay
Sue!" leads us to say "Repay Barbara!" (there being no
other morally relevant factors involved in either case).
Rationality demands universality and equal treatment of
equals in equal circumstances. Hence, a universally
binding rule based on principle is implicit in every
act.

When a rule applies, it must hold for everybody.
But implicit in every general rule is the possibility
that an exception may sometimes be called for, thus requiring a specific rule to define the right act for that
occasion. A possible rule might be: Keep promises
(except in circumstances where a higher obligation or
good takes precedence). Suppose Kathy promises to meet
Bob at 4:00 PM to share a milkshake. On her way she
passes a pond in which a child is drowning, and Kathy
is a trained lifeguard. Should she break her promise
to meet Bob in order to rescue the child? Of course she
should. A complete rule would contain all the exceptions and indicate which responsiblities take priority
over others under all possible circumstances. Such a
rule book would be impossible to write and impractical
to use. Hence, judgment in the application of rules
is necessary. But surely act and rule ethicists (whether
acting on deontological or teleological grounds) would
agree that one should save a life in preference to keeping a promise to enjoy a milkshake with a friend. The
deontologist would conclude that the obligation to save
life is superior to the duty to keep a promise of this
sort. The teleologist would reason that saving a life
achieved a greater net balance of good over evil. In
either case the rule implicit in the act or the

exception to the rule called for in the act is based on
the principle that saving a life is a higher obligation
or achieves a greater good than keeping a promise.
Whether the principle is seen as operative only in that
particular act or in the exception to a general rule
that is usually valid does not seem to matter much. Act
ethics and rule ethics approach the same center of moral
reasoning from different points. Each stands for a valid
truth but needs the other to be adequate. Would not the
act ethicist give the same answer for the exact same situation every time? If not, rationality is abandoned. If
so, then it should be possible to incorporate the rationale for the answer in a general rule. Would not the
rule ethicist make exceptions to rules when situations
called for it? If not, rule ethics fails since no general rule with any degree of specificity can be adequate
for all possible situations. If so, then a complete set
of rules must specify the right act not only in general
but also for particular situations.

      This conjoining of act and rule ethics is, of course,
possible only by eliminating extreme forms of each as
being inadequate. An act ethics which takes each moral
choice as separate and independent, having no common
features with any other choice (extreme existentialism
or nominalism), seems clearly in error. A version of
act ethics which recognizes that there are some common
aspects that are present in different situations would
surely have to grant that these common aspects when
present can be covered by a binding rule and not merely
a rule of thumb. A rule ethics which affirms that the
differences between one situation and another are
contingencies which do not matter (extreme essential-
ism or realism) also seems clearly in error. To admit
that circumstances can alter cases is to recognize

that general rules must not be absolutely binding and
that exceptions must be allowed. I have illustrated
this pull of one on the other with particular reference
to the differences between act and rule utilitarianism.

The determination of what is right in a given
situation must be determined contextually, taking into
the total set of circumstances, possibilities, and
available alternatives. The rationale for what is determined to be actual duty can be formulated either in
act or in rule language. A rule can be stated which
includes both the general imperative and its relevant
exceptions by which one can determine priorities. The
rationale can be put in act terms if one appeals directly to the relevant generalized imperatives and then
makes a determination of their application in this instance, especially where conflicting prima facie duties
come into the picture. However, it must be remembered
that the maxim implied in the rationale which defines
the right act in this case can be generalized into an
appropriately qualified and complete rule. Also, the
determination of duty in a specific case on an act
basis is identical with spelling out the rule for that
occasion on an ad hoc basis.

One deontological imperative and one teleological
imperative admit no exceptions. It is always right to
honor the intrinsic worth of persons. It is always
right to promote the enjoyment (self-actualization) of
persons. From these universal rules may be derived a
number of others which have near universal applica-
bility and define prima facie duty. Tell the truth.
Keep promises. Pay your debts. Protect innocent life.
Usually the act that is to be done is specified by the
relevant rule. The exception occurs when a superior
rule takes precedence. Saving a drowning person has

priority over keeping a promise to have a milkshake
with a friend at 4:00 PM. But the determination of
which prima facie duty is to become actual duty must be
done contextually taking into account the specifics of
a particular case. One can consult the universal rule
directly. But in doing it will be found that the path
between the specific occasion and the ultimate imperative runs through a set of rules that mediate between
the universal and the particular. Hence, in deciding
what to do it is equally correct and appropriate to
say that one consults the absolute principle directly
or consults a more specific rule. The same path connects the universal with the particular via intermediate rules.

The principles by which acts can be related to
rules involve the tension between the universal and the
particular. As one moves toward universal relevance,
a rule must become more abstract and empty of specific
content. The imperative to honor intrinsic worth is
universal and admits no exceptions. However, it is abstract and, as such, does not indicate what must be
concretely done in a given case. The imperative to tell
the truth is more specific and relevant to situations
in which a lie might be told. However, it admits of exceptions. If in a given instance honoring intrinsic
human worth is better accomplished by telling a lie than
by telling the truth, then the falsehood becomes obligatory. Hence, the more concrete and specific rules
become, the less universal they are. The more universally relevant a rule is, the more abstract and empty
of specific guidance it is. Hence, some procedure must
be designed to mediate between universal rules and particular occasions. One can do this by writing complete
rules to cover all particulars. Or one can appeal

directly in a particular situation to the relevant
general imperatives (at some level of universality)
and move by intuition and casuistry or both to a determination of an act that is obligatory. But there is
one logic governing both procedures, and it unites act
and rule ethics into a comprehensive methodology for
determining what is right.

                              I

     Against this background of basic theory, questions
of metaethics may be addressed. The next chapter will
show that deontology and teleology are abstractions from
the total context in which moral actions occur. A more
comprehensive theory is required in which morality is
shown to be a response to actions upon us in a given
context. The ultimate Actor in the cosmic drama is God.
Right action, finally, is an attuning of our acts with
the intentions of an Ultimate Purpose. Hence, the category of "fitting response" to God's aims indicates the
larger framework in which the imperatives of deontology
and teleology need to be set. This also includes the
idea that morality must be grounded in religion and that
ethics must be connected to a theological base. The
following chapter will develop this thesis as the outcome of an inquiry into the standard metaethical questions posed in recent moral philosophy. (Readers who
wish to do so may continue with the line of argument
relating to normative ethics by proceeding directly to
sections F, H, I, and J of the next chapter).

CHAPTER III

ETHICS, METAETHICS AND RELIGION

A

Metaethics deals with the meaning of moral terms, the nature of moral judgments, and the justification of moral claims. It will lend further clarification to the Christian natural ethics being developed in these pages to take a position on these issues. It will also lead to a further unfolding and final statement of the normative principles of this version of process moral philosophy.

A central issue in metaethics is the debate sur-rounding cognitivism and definism. According to Garner and Rosen, the cognitivist affirms and the non-cogni-tivist denies the following:

1. Moral judgments are capable of being object-ively true.

1a. There is objective moral knowledge.[1]

Another distinction cuts across the issues related to cognitivism. The definist would affirm and the non-def-inist would deny the following proposition:

2. Any moral judgment (judgment in which "good" or "bad" or "right" and "wrong" is used in a moral sense) can be reduced or expanded by analysis or definition to another expression which has the same meaning but contains no moral terms.[2]

In addition to 1 and 1a referred to above, the cogni-tivist non-definist also affirms a third principle:

3. Moral knowledge is sometimes direct.[3]

This assertion follows from the previous ones. If moral knowledge is objective, and if it cannot be reduced to other forms of knowledge, it follows that it must some-times be direct. This position has usually been called intuitionism.

To begin with the proposition 3, there are

definitely intuitionistic features in the perspective
developed here in ways that will become clearer but
which will also distinguish my position from what is
often defined as intuitionism. I do believe, for example, that the nature of value, of the right and the
good, etc. are grasped in a direct and immediate insight that has the convincing power of self-evidence.
To have an intuition is even more like being grasped,
an experience in which a truth, a fact, a relationship
or whatever is disclosed. Once it is really seen, it
cannot be doubted. If the insight does not come with
direct and immediate clarity, then doubt cannot be
erased. In the last analysis, you either see it or
you don't. The set of intuitions and definitions
which make up the ethical perspective being developed
on these pages is grounded in a larger set of beliefs
about the nature of reality. Hence, ethics is a part
of metaphysics.

Again, non-cognitivists also contend for aspects
of the total truth that must be taken into account.
I believe that my ethical perspective is true and universally valid, objectively grounded in the nature of
things. But this is a belief that cannot be proven.
It cannot be demonstrated as logically or metaphysically necessary in ways that finally commend the assent of all who think clearly or see things aright.
Finally, in the strictest sense, all I can say is that
it is convincing to me. The intention is to affirm
objectively valid, universally relevant truth, but
the actual product is subjectively created, parochial,
limited, and persuasive only to those who see things as
I do. The ethics and metaphysics set forth here are
decidedly Western, Christian, modern, American, and
based on a particular version of process philosophy.

Hence, the resulting theory of obligation functions as
a set of subjective attitudes, recommendations, prescriptions, evaluations, decisions, commitments, and the
like about which I have strong feelings. Moreover,
while the ethical valuations that go with this perspective are organically connected with the metaphysical
beliefs in which they are grounded, it cannot be said
that the actual moral judgments that result logically
depend on this particular philosophical foundation.
The decision that it is preferable to save an innocent
life than to keep a promise to meet a friend would be
commonly agreed upon. Such a judgment can be justified
on many grounds and set within the context of a variety
of philosophical outlooks. Deontological and teleological perspectives certainly do not require just
those particular metaphysical assumptions which I have
asserted. The large degree of subjectivity and relativism which are present in all ethical theory are taken
account of in non-cognitivist theories. They err, however, in not appropriately recognizing that the aim of
ethics is (or should be) to affirm what is objectively
true, right, and good.

Hence, the position I take is definitely a form of
cognitivism, if that view is understood to mean that
there is an objective moral order about which it is possible to have justifiable knowledge. One, of course,
can be mistaken about what is the case as well as about
what is valuable or obligatory. Moral judgments are
capable of being true, but that does not mean that any
given person can have absolute and infallible knowledge of reality. Moral judgments, then, are not simply
subjective or arbitrary or lacking roots in reality.
Nevertheless, all knowledge is partially relative,
however much it intends correspondence with what is

objectively rooted in the nature of things. Moral
judgments do involve but are more than subjective preferences, attitudes, recommendations, prescriptions, and
the like. They are certainly not reducible merely to
strong feelings or commands. The subtleties and complications of moral beliefs cannot be reduced to any simple
formula. Not every contemporary view can be included in
one comprehensive theory. Yet it may not be too ambitious to suggest a position that recognizes validity in
both objectivist and subjectivist theories.

The issues surrounding definism are subtle and
complex. It is not easy to sort out all of the dimensions involved without falling into confusion. I wish
to insist on two points. 1. Moral judgments point to
a dimension of reality that cannot be reduced to factual
judgments purely and simply. In this sense ethical
statements cannot be reduced or translated into, or
strictly and logically deduced from, non-ethical ones.
2. Ought is connected with is, good is connected with
being, ethical statements are connected with non-ethical
ones, in organic ways. I mean that reality is value
impregnated. Hence, certain moral judgments inevitably
flow from that fact. Certain understandings of what is
right and good can be derived from an analysis of what
is objectively true. Ought and is, being and goodness,
hang together organically so that connections and tran-
sitions can be made from description to evaluation and
prescription which are rational and justifiable. If
definism denies point 1, then I am not a definist. If
definism is compatible with point 2, then in that sense
I am. I shall argue that when moral philosophy is put
in the widest possible context of metaphysics, neither
monism (identity) nor dualism (bifurcation) is the appropriate way to view the relation between moral judg-

ments and factual judgments.

Here let me pursue the point that obligation states
a claim of a different order which cannot ever be made
identical with any possible series of purely factual
statements, no matter how inclusive or complete. In any
such alleged series, there is a missing link which must
be supplied by a synthetic statement which introduces
the moral notion of ought into what otherwise remains a
set of descriptions.

This may be illustrated by reference to a contrary
claim made by John R. Searle.[4] The argument is that
the act by which Jones promises to pay Smith five dollars puts Jones under obligation, so that one must conclude that the money ought to be paid. Hence, one can
begin, proceed, and end with statements of fact, the
last of which contains an "ought" which is derived from
an "is" without the addition of any moral principles or
evaluative utterances. Uttering the words "I promise"
places one under obligation to do what is promised,
which is the equivalent of saying one ought to honor
the obligation. Yet closer examination shows that the
idea of ought in the moral sense is assumed or thrown
in or else it cannot be discovered as really being there
in the factual assertions. Granted that when genuinely
intended and made, a promise puts one under obligation
to keep it, nevertheless one can always ask why one
should do what one promised to do. Why should Jones
pay Smith just because he promised, unless one assumes
independently of the meaning of terms that promises
ought to be kept? If one insists that the very meaning
of a promise is to put oneself under obligation to
fulfill it, one can still persist in asking why one
should fulfill ones obligations. The only answer can
be that it is assumed or predicated that one ought to

do so. The moral ought cannot be produced by any set of
factual statements. It can only be introduced by a moral
statement although Searle comes very close to hiding the
point at which what he discovers is first placed there
from outside the set of statements in which it appears.
But no matter how much it seems to be the case (and the
appearance is deceiving indeed!), the factual ought cannot become a moral ought except on the basis of a moral
judgment. For no matter what Jones promised then, and
no matter what promising means then and now, Jones need
not accept the moral obligation to keep his factual promise now unless he accepts the moral premise that promises ought to be kept. This appears to involve an attitude and commitment of will in a personal and practical
sense, as well as a recognition of the objective claim
of duty that arises out of the very nature of things.

In a very useful article William Frankena has
delineated the issues that may help clarify the position being taken here. He invites us to consider four
statements:

1. Judgments of obligation and value (Oughts)
   are rationally justifiable, objectively
   valid, etc.

2. Judgments of obligation and value (Oughts)
   cannot be logically inferred from factual
   ones (Ises).

3. Judgments of obligation and value (Oughts)
   cannot be rationally justified, objectively valid, etc., unless they can be logi-
   čally inferred from factual ones (Ises).

4. Basic judgments of obligation and value
   are intuitive, self-evident, self-justi-
   fying.[5]

Three current positions may then be indicated as follows:

A. Cognitive definism or naturalism affirms 1 and
   3, while rejecting 2 and 4.

      B.   Intuitionism asserts 1, 2, and 4, while deny-
          ing 3.

      C.   A complex non-cognitive position not easily
          classified maintains 2 and 3, while denying 1
          and 4.

Frankena then announced a fourth point of view that affirms 1 and 2 but rejects 3 and 4. The heart of his
contention, as I understand it, is that there are other
ways than strict logical inference to derive "ought"
from or to connect it with "is." "Oughts" are generated
in the presence of some apprehension of fact toward
which we take a certain attitude or have some interest
in. The transition from "is" to "ought" is justified
or rational and will be so regarded by all who take a
similar outlook toward the facts involved. But this
transition does not depend on some suppressed "ought
premise" or on the intuition of some self-evident factor.
He illustrates the point with the following sequence"

      (a) I want to buy a new suit at a reasonable price.

      (b) There is a suit sale on downtown.

      (c) Therefore, I ought to go downtown today.[6]

Here an "ought" is derived from an "is." What makes the
transition rational and justifiable is the practical interest taken in connection with relevant facts. Frankena
believes that this principle applies to all kinds of
practical reasoning including morality. If by a commitment of will one decides to take a moral point of view,
then this decision in the presence of certain factual
considerations will generate an ought. The result
would appear to be a point of view which does not
strictly fit into either cognitivism or definism as these
are usually understood. Frankena classifies himself as
a "non-cognitivist of the post-emotive sort."[7] It seems
to me that John Searle needs to include the element of

practical interest by which we declare ourselves for or
against something to make valid his derivation of ought
from is. That is, granted a commitment to a moral
point of view, which would include the premise that
promises ought to be kept, everything Searle claims
would follow. But without that commitment in the background, the moral ought has no foundation and must be
slipped in by verbal magic.

The point of view I am developing would seem to be
very close in some respects to Frankena's fourth option.
A commitment to a moral point of view, a conative stance,
an underlying commitment does seem to be an ingredient
in morality which ethical theory must take into account.
This personal orientation provides a connecting link
between factual analysis and value judgments. The point
at which I apparently differ from Frankena is in stressing that the moral point of view itself is taken because it is in accord with reality. Is it our attitudes
or commitments that make it possible to derive some
"oughts" in a rational and justifiable way from the facts
("Ises")? Or do we have certain conative stances because we believe the "oughts" to have a rational and
justifiable connection with the facts? Frankena seems
to lean toward the former alternative, while I am
closer to the latter. I do agree that an act of will is
involved that cannot be reduced to an intellectual judgment. Nevertheless, I want to affirm a clear cognitive
view of moral judgments. However, I also recognize that
while we may intend to make moral (value) and intellectual (factual) judgments that correspond to reality,
there is a great deal of relativism and subjectivity
involved. In that light I can agree with the non-cognitivists that moral judgments do involve subjective
attitudes and commitments which are relative to a given

person or group without giving up the insistence that
our views about what is and what ought to be intend to
be responses to and reports of what is really there in
the nature of things. My position on these matters, as
Frankena's is ostensibly not, is rooted in a metaphysical vision in which a value principle operative in
reality provides the rational and justifiable basis
for value judgments that are appropriate in the light of
what is. I maintain that the fittingness is itself
rational and justifiable. We then decide whether we
will do in practice what is fitting.

B

Next, we turn to the question of the meaning of
moral terms and the justification of ethical claims.
Joe ought to keep his promise to play tennis with Martha.
Keeping his promise to play tennis with Martha would be
the right thing to do. What do the terms "right" and
"ought" mean in these sentences? When speaking in a
moral sense, "ought" appears to stand in a peculiar and
definitive relationship to "right." The connection
appears in the following sentence: We ought to do what
is right. Put otherwise, right is what we ought to do.
Ought recognizes that the nature of human life is such
that there are claims on our actions which we are not
at liberty to will away or avoid. Moral agents have
obligations, duties, responsibilities. These are categorical imperatives to which we are bound, not mere
conditional or hypothetical demands. Morality has reality, and this means that there are some things we ought
to do. Ought, then, recognizes the fact and validity
of moral claims. The limits, conditions, grounds, nature and justification of these obligations have yet to

be specified. Here it is only necessary to say that
when we use the term ought, we acknowledge the existence, authority, and authenticity of binding claims
upon our actions as moral agents. Ought tells only
that we have obligations. It does not tell us what
those obligations are.

     A first step in defining what acts ought to be done
consists in connecting ought with right. We ought to do
what is right. When we know what is right, we know
what we ought to do. Ought tells us _that_ we are obligated. Right tells _what_ we are obligated to do. What,
then, does right mean? Here, following W. D. Ross, we
need to distinguish between the essence of rightness and
the ground of rightness.[8] I propose that right be
understood to mean that which has a certain kind of fittingness or appropriateness or suitability. What is
fitting is a function of the total situation in which
moral agents find themselves under obligation. That
has yet to be specified. Here I only propose the stip-
ulative definition of right as that which fits the requirements and demands and possibilities of a moral situation. Since situations are frequently complex, the
determination of what is most suitable is difficult to
determine. Many claims may be present so that a process of weighing and calculating is necessary to determine which of many courses of action that would have
some degree of rightness (prima facie obligations --
W. D. Ross[9]) is the most appropriate response to the
total situation which becomes actually obligatory. We
ought to do what is most suitable given the circumstances and the available options.

     So far the essence of rightness, the meaning of
the term, has been set forth as a kind of fittingness.
But what is the ground of **rightness**? What makes an act

right or suitable? I have already indicated that there
are two gounds of appropriateness: (1) the deontological
imperative to honor the intrinsic worth of sentient
beings, and (2) the teleological imperative to promote
the enjoyment of sentient beings. To do right means to
do what is fitting in the situation. That which makes
an act right is that which honors intrinsic worth and
promotes enjoyment (maximizes the good). These are
right-making considerations. An act tends to be right
if it embodies or exhibits elements of one or both of
these right-making factors. An act is obligatory if it
is the most appropriate act (or equally appropriate to
any possible act) for the given situation when all the
relevant circumstances are taken into account. One may
substitute rule for act in the preceding sentence,
since I have already indicated that act and rule ethics
finally merge into each other. Here the assumption is
that finally what we do is an act (or series or cluster
of acts), whether in obedience to a rule or whether determined ab initio in a given context.

So far the term "good" has not been defined or related to the concepts of "right" and "ought". When this
is done, it should then be possible also to specify
what the subject matter of morality is. The term "good"
is many-faceted. An inventory of all possible uses is
not necessary here. The AMERICAN COLLEGE DICTIONARY
(1949) lists 27 different definitions. The root meaning is said to be fitting or suitable. Perhaps the
nearest we can come to a generic meaning is that the
term can be used in any setting in which something
merits (or is granted) approval for relevant reasons
specific to what is under consideration and is thus suitable or fitting or satisfactory. For the purposes of
this exposition all uses not finally related to moral-

ity may be eliminated. We may speak, for example, of a
good apple. Here the reference is to good of a kind.
Anything that exhibits certain criteria of excellence
pertinent to that class of things may be said to be
good. There is also a metaphysical meaning of the term
good. In this framework good designates the telic principle at work in the evolutionary process. Or we may
speak of the goodness and power of God who creates finite beings and directs them toward fulfillment (their
good). The metaphysical meaning of good is the underlying ground and final explanation of the meaning of
good in the moral sense. More must be said later about
this metaphysical foundation of morality.

Turning now to the moral sense of the word good, a
basic fact must be noted. The term good arises in relation to the being and experience of some sentient being, especially a person. Any adequate theory of value
must finally locate moral good either in or in relation
to an experiencing subject. Apart from the experience
of some sentient being the term good has no moral meaning or relevance. When philosophers speak of intrinsic
values, such as virtue, knowledge, or pleasure, do they
not mean finally that these are intrinsically valuable
for some person? Whether sought for themselves (intrinsic values) or as a means to achieve something else
(instrumental values), these good things have their goodness in relationship to experiencing beings.

I believe that all of the multidimensional complexity and subtlety involved in the legitimate moral
use of the term good can be systematized under two
headings. There is, first of all, a foundational meaning. The foundational meaning is that any being capable of experiencing good is intrinsically good. Experiencing good means the feeling of enjoyment that

occurs in the presence of the actualization of potential in a sentient being. Since all sentient beings can
experience enjoyment when their organic potential is
actualized, all sentient beings are intrinsically good.

From this basic fact there arise, in the second
place, a wide variety of interrelated derivative meanings of good. Two are especially important: A. There
are all those settings in which we speak of things that
are good for sentient beings. The reference is to whatever is sought for itself (intrinsic values) or sought
for the sake of something else (instrumental values).
In either sense whatever is good is good for or in relationship to some experiencing being. Means and ends
are related in a complex hierarchy in which ends become
new means to further other ends in an ensemble of interrelated goods. One may, for example, take a job to
earn money to get a college education in order to become an artist to earn money to buy food and pay rent.
The job is both instrumental and yet may be rewarding in
itself. The college education is instrumental to learning the history, theory, and practice of an art and yet
may be a joy apart from its consequences. The practice
of an artistic vocation may be an end in itself for some
people. Yet if paintings can be sold, they provide
money for other instrumental uses. Here the pragma-
tists have a valid point which may be recognized without concluding that all values are instruments. Unless
something has intrinsic value, then nothing can be instrumental. Yet what is instrumental in one setting and
in some aspects can be intrinsically valuable in another
setting and in other respects.

B. There are those settings in which the term
good refers to moral attributes of a person. The reference may be to virtuous actions such as kindness or

generosity. Or the references may be to inner characteristics of a person which are commendable, such as
attitudes, dispositions, motives, and the like. Together outward behavior and inner characteristics which
are approved make up what we call moral goodness.

Under category A we speak of that which contributes to or constitutes the good life. The good life
is made up of a complex of activities and states of being which maximize enjoyment. Under category B we
speak of the attributes of a good person. A good person is one whose inner dispositions lead to external
actions which honor the intrinsic worth and promote the
enjoyment of sentient beings. The foundational meaning and the derivative meanings can now be put together.
A sentient being capable of experiencing enjoyment is
intrinsically good, and intrinsically good because of
the capacity for experiencing good (enjoyment). The
ideal is a person who is intrinsically good living the
good life as a morally good person. If we add the
further idea of a good person living the good life in a
good society, we must say that a good society is one
that is so structured to promote the development of good
persons and of the good life.

                            C

The idea of good may now be related to the deontological and teleological imperatives. In so doing
good can be related to right and ought. If right refers
to what is morally fitting, and if it is fitting to hon-
or the worth and promote the enjoyment of sentient beings, then good can be shown to stand in an interdependent apposition with these ideas. Good is that
which it is fitting to honor and so promote. It is

right to honor what is intrinsically good and to promote (maximize) what is good. That is what we ought to
do. But note that it is beings that are intrinsically
good and therefore to be honored because they are good.
It is beings whose good is to be maximized. Goodness
and being are the final correlation. Goodness and being coinhere as a unity of apposites. Being is good,
and the good of beings is what ought to be.

     In the final analysis, then, the concepts of good
and right are interdependent. Right arises in a community of beings who are intrinsically good and who
are capable of actualizing their good. Right defines
those relations among beings which honor and actualize
the good of each in a community of interrelated and
interdependent beings. The highest ideal is the maximization of the mutual good of interacting persons
who honor the intrinsic good of each and promote the
good of all. Good arises when even a single sentient
being exists and moves toward the actualization of the
potential in the givenness of that organism. Right
arises when one other sentient being appears on the
scene. For now the good of each places claims on the
other. Right is the mutual honoring and promoting of
the good of other beings in a community of beings. Nothing else would be fitting or suitable or appropriate
in a community of intrinsically good beings in quest
of the good.

     At this point a further consequence emerges. Now
it becomes clear that deontology and teleology have a
single root, but neither perspective can be reduced
to the other. This single root is the fact that there
are beings who are good (intrinsically) who have a
good (an end which is enjoyment) that can be achieved
and who ought to be good (morally) to each other.

The various meanings which the term good takes on in
this sentence should now be clear. The idea of right
as binding duty whose rightness is not always or necessarily dependent on consequences (deontology) and the
idea of right as the obligation to promote the good as
judged by consequences (teleology) can be derived from
this single root. However, neither deontology or teleology can be reduced to the other. Deontologists can
show beyond any doubt other than that which is necessit-
ated by the desire to defend teleology that duty is not
solely determined by the obligation to maximize good.
Consequences are not the only determinant of duty.
Joe is bound to keep his promise to play tennis with
Martha because it is right to do so. And it is right
to do so because not to keep it would dishonor the
claims she has on Joe's actions because of the covenant
he made with her. And Joe should keep the covenant he
made because not to do so would dishonor the worth which
she possesses as a person. Not to keep the promise
might also result in a lesser good than keeping it, but
that is only a further reason for keeping the promise,
not the only sufficient reason. Deontology is less than
adequate, however, if it claims that obligation can
finally be justified apart from the goodness of beings
who have a good that they can achieve.

      Teleologists are right in urging that the good is
foundational for the concept of rightness. They are
also right in claiming that the potential of beings for
achieving the good is a basis for moral obligation which
cannot be ignored or merely subsumed under deontological
premises. Teleological theories are wrong in claiming
that consequences for producing the maximum net balance
of good over evil is the only determinant of duty.
"Act optimifically" is not the only moral principle.

Duty may be partly independent of consequences for good,
but duty is not finally independent of goodness.

D

A further step must now be taken to locate the
foundations of ethics in metaphysics. It is only in
this context that the language of morals can be fully
clarified. The meaning of ethical terms derives from
the realities they describe. Much moral philosophy,
especially within the schools of linguistic analysis,
focuses so much on language and its usage that its deeper referents are ignored. The ethical system proposed
in these pages presupposes a version of process philosophy in which the ultimate ingredients of the world
are organic entities. An organism is a system of mutually interdependent self-organizing parts that are
capable of functioning together in ways that sustain
its functions and achieve internally guided ends. An
organism is a living being. Life is the process by
which the potential of an organism is actualized. More
specifically, life is a structured process exhibiting
the capacity to interact selectively with its external
environment and to organize its internal parts as it
seeks to create, preserve, and fulfill itself, thus
realizing (experiencing) its inner telos.[10] Each being has a nature (essence) which defines its end (good).
Beings live in a community of beings. The meaning of
good and of right arises in this context. Good occurs
as beings fulfill their nature and experience satisfaction or enjoyment in the process. Good arises in a
setting in which beings who are good (intrinsically)
seek their good (enjoyment). Right has to do with the
relationship which such beings have to each other. It

defines the fitting relationship among beings who have a
good and who are or can be good for each other. Right
is a description/prescription of mutually beneficial
interactions among interdependent beings. Relationships
and interactions are fitting when they honor and promote the good which each embodies in fact and potential.

At this point some possible dangers of misunder-
standing must be cleared up. We must avoid thinking of
beings as static essences or things which move toward a
goal, which itself is a state that is reached at some
point in space and time. Beings are systems of activities who exist as processes in which a given potential
is being actualized. The end (good) of life is a pattern (ideal) characteristic of mature functioning. It
has a future reference in so far as sentient beings, in
particular persons, begin as a fertilized egg and grow
over a period of time toward adulthood. Moreover,
mature beings have a future as long as they live. The
good is achieved and being achieved in so far as an
actualizing of potential is taking place. The end of
life in so far as it is a goal achieved in adulthood
is a more or less continuous functioning in which the
powers, capacities, and potentials of maturity are exercised. The end is immanent in the process of development and in mature functioning. The model is that of
structured processes with an essence understood as an
ideal pattern of development and mature functioning
which makes an organism what it is. Good is nothing
more than this ideal pattern that leads to the fulfillment of potential and which characterizes mature
(creative) functioning.

E

More may now be said about the relationship of good
to enjoyment. In so doing it will be clearer how the definist claim is partially valid in a way that avoids the
definist fallacy. The end of life, the good that is
sought, is enjoyment. But what does this mean? It does
not mean that enjoyment and good are simply two different
ways of speaking about one and the same reality. One
term is not substitutable for the other. Yet there is a
sense in which they are identical. The essence of good
is not enjoyment, but enjoyment is the accompaniment and
the consequence of good. Good has an objective and a
subjective referent. In its objective sense good refers
to the actualization of potential. Life is the actualization of potential. Life is good. The subjective side
of good is enjoyment. The ground of good is the actualization of potential. The consequence of good is enjoyment. The essence of good is fittingness. The actualization of potential is fitting because it is expressive
of the very nature of things. It fits what is and can
be. That which makes it fitting is the actualization of
potential. The consequence of its achievement is enjoyment. The actualization of potential would not be good
if it were not enjoyable. It would not be enjoyable if
it were not the actualization of potential. What is
aimed at (the good) may be said to be actualization of
potential or enjoyment. The former points to the objective and the latter to the subjective side of good.
Either expression is correct, neither can be reduced
to the other, but neither can they be bifurcated.

If definism means the identity of goodness and some
non-moral term (enjoyment in my case), then it is wrong.
If non-definism means the bifurcation of goodness from

every non-moral term it is also wrong. The actualization
of potential experienced as enjoyment is good. Good refers to the unity which constitutes enjoyed actualization
or actualization enjoyed. If definism claims that good
can be defined, it is so far correct. But it is wrong
in claiming that good can be defined by or reduced to
something other than what it uniquely is and stands for.
Non-definism is right in insisting that good is something irreducible and unique. Good is what it is. Non-
definism is wrong in maintaining that it cannot be defined. There are terms which indicate its real meaning.
Good can be defined, just as any word can, by other
words. Good, however, is not as some claim a totally
disconnected quality or property, some non-natural entity existing in and of itself, which can only be known
by sheer intuition but which is not analyzable. It is
necessarily and universally associated with a real state
of affairs that is definable as actualization enjoyed or
enjoyed actualization. Good, however, does refer to a
value dimension existing in organic connection with
what is but not reducible as such to facts or states of
affairs.

F

One final look may be taken at this point at the
metaethical questions surrounding definism. Consider
the statement: Good is actualization enjoyed or enjoyed
actualization. Is this a synthetic or an analytical
statement? I venture to say that it has the peculiar
characteristic of being, in some respects, both. Perhaps this can be made clearer by the recognition that
good is the inevitable, universal, and necessary accompaniment of the actualization of potential. So close

is this connection that one can say that good is identical with this state of affairs. Enjoyment is good.
Good is enjoyment. In this sense, these statements seem
to be analytic. Nevertheless, it is also the case that
good points to a value dimension that has a unique meaning of its own. Thus, by indicating that enjoyment is
good, something additional is being said about it.
Moreover, if enjoyment is identified as good, then that
definition is useful for making moral decisions about
what ought to be promoted only if one has already accepted the judgment that enjoyment is good. In this sense
the statement that enjoyment is good is synthetic.

Here I am following Frankena who goes on to say:

> If this is so, in effect, what looks
> like a definition is tantamount to a
> value principle, and, if this is so, then
> we are still left with the problem of its
> justification and, in particular, of its
> relation to beliefs about what is. [11]

It seems that it is still necessary to say why the enjoyment of actualization is good, even if the definition
and meaning of good are correct. This pushes us toward
a higher level of analysis. Here it would appear that
the final justification of the meaning of good is in
the apprehension of a value factor present in reality
which gives to the evolutionary process its telos. Good
does, as Plato said, transcend being and it is the final
explanatory principle. Observing the working out of
this telic principle in nature gives us the clue to
what good is as it is embodied in fact, that is, in emerging sentient beings. In this framework the end of existence does seem to be the objective actualization of
potential which generates a subjective feeling of enjoyment. This is good because it appears to be what good
aims at or does. Hence, there is a sense in which good

stands out beyond being or process where it is simply
grasped by an intuitive insight. There is another
sense in which it is immanent in process as its internal principle. The intuitionists are impressed by the
former aspects, while the definists are convinced by
the latter. The former implies that no series of factual statements can ever account for the apprehension
of good. The latter does allow for the translation
of ethical into non-ethical statements.

Moral statements are neither completely independent of statements of fact nor identical with certain
of them. Value and fact are interdependent and organically united to each other. Ought is connected with
is. As I see it, the problem for metaethics is to discern the nature of this connection. The position I defend is that there is a set of moral obligations that
are appropriate or fitting in the light of the facts of
existence, including the ultimate metaphysical situation. The stronger case is that a certain way of
viewing normative ethics follows from and is even required by what is ultimately the case. At the ultimate
level it may be said that ought can be derived from is.
I mean that when the total set of metaphysical facts is
taken into consideration, it follows that certain moral
and value principles have a unique fittingness to that
situation and hence must be affirmed as uniquely valid
and true. Ought and is ultimately hang together in a
comprehensive organic unity which constitutes the totality of what has to be taken into account in ethics and
metaphysics. Value and fact have a relatively autonomous standing in relation to each other but are finally interdependent in a larger unity of things which
includes them both. Hence, neither is uniquely or
unilaterally explanatory of or reducible to the other.

Let me spell this out briefly, albeit at a high level
of abstraction.

G

In a previous work I set forth the hypothesis that
the ultimate metaphysical situation can be described as
the possible becoming actual under the lure of the
good.[12] My intuition is that possibility, actuality,
and ideality (value, the good) are the ultimate factors
to which metaphysical analysis must make reference in
accounting for reality. The evolutionary process exhibits the pattern I have asserted. Over long periods
of time more complex forms of life have emerged. Complexity of structure is associated with complexity of
function and a greater range and depth of experience
and enjoyment. I believe that the appearance of suc-
cessively higher forms of life can best be accounted
for by the fact that there is a purposive factor at work
in the evolutionary process. There is purpose in nature. To say it differently, there is at the base of all
things a Creative Power and Purpose which accounts for
emergent evolution. God is the Ground of Process, the
Source of Good. God's creative work in the world by
which sentient beings with potential for enjoyment
emerge is described abstractly as a process by which
the possible (beings capable of experiencing good) becomes actual (the evolutionary process in fact) under
the lure of the good (the purpose of God to create) by
actualizing the potential of the universe and thus experiencing satisfaction (God's enjoyment). This is what
is meant by asserting that the possible becomes actual
under the lure of the good. In this context the main
point to be noted is the belief that there is an

intentionality in the very nature of things which aims
at the production of beings capable of enjoyment. Such
beings are intrinsically valuable (good) and are capable of experiencing good (enjoyment). Hence, a value
principle is operative in reality.

Moral philosophy is driven finally to connect its
theory of obligation to the three metaphysical ultimates
of possibility, actuality, and the good. The basic
principle of deontological theory is loyalty to the intrinsic value of actuality, of experiencing subjects.
The central theme of teleological theory is the promotion of enjoyment (actualizing the possibilities of
good) in experiencing subjects (actuality). Seen in
this light the concept of right can be derived from a
vision of reality at the ultimate level. Derivation,
however, refers to the discovery of a moral correlate
required by the structure of existence. But since the
structure of existence is value impregnated, certain
statements about good, right, and ought in human life inevitably flow from statements of fact. Put differently,
value coinheres with existence so that ethical statements
about obligation and metaphysical statements about what
is have a deep intrinsic connectedness. Hence, morality
is rooted in reality and exhibits a fittingness to reality. Moral living is attuning oneself to the character
and aims of the universe. Morality is a response to
activities and intentions ingredient in the very nature
of things.

                               H

What I have intended to do is to affirm a close
correlation between ought and is, value and fact, which
recognizes organic connectedness and interdependence but

denies identity. In this way I hope to avoid what
William Frankena has called the definist fallacy.[13]
G.E. Moore had introduced the notion of the naturalistic
fallacy, which in some way ends up by defining or trans-
lating ethical terms into non-ethical terms. Frankena
argues that the generic error underlying what Moore
objected to is the fallacy of identifying or confusing
one property with another. The motto of Moore's
PRINCIPIA ETHICA was taken from Bishop Butler: "Everything is what it is, and not another thing." To con-
fuse something with something else is always an error,
but it is not clear, as Frankena shows lucidly, that it
is a fallacy in any logical sense. The issue finally
comes down to a question of fact. Are certain ethical
statements analytic, tautologous, or true by definition?
Or are they synthetic? The definists take the former
view, the non-definists (sometimes called intuitionists)
take the latter view.

   What we appear to have in the final analysis is a
series of statements relating fact and value which are
relatively autonomous but which depend on the others for
the completion of their meaning. They are defined in
mutual dependence on each other. All together they
form a system of interdependent parts which mutually
define and sustain each other. Neither is complete
without the other. Consider the following. Good is
what God intends in creating the universe. What God
intends is good. God is good. What God creates is
good. What God creates is living beings with potential
which can be actualized. Actualization of potential
is accompanied by enjoyment. Enjoyment is good. Good
is enjoyment accompanying fulfillment of potential.
Beings with potential for enjoyment are intrinsically
good. Whatever contributes to the actualization of

of potential and enjoyment is good. Right defines the
relationships appropriate among beings who are intrinsically good and who have a good to be actualized.
Whatever honors the intrinsic good of sentient beings
and is instrumental to actualization of their enjoyment
is right. We ought to do what is right, because right
defines what is appropriate or fitting in a situation
of good beings with a potential for good. To do what is
right is to take a moral point of view. One ought to
take a moral point of view because it is fitting in a
two-fold sense. It fulfills the nature (essence) of
humanity, and it is to live in tune with the basic patterns and processes of the universe and the intentionality of God. It is good to live in harmony with ultimate reality. All of these sentences form an interrelated whole made up of interdependent parts.

     In this system of assertions good is foundational
for the understanding of right relationships and right
actions, that is, of moral actions. As such right defines what we ought to do. We ought to do what is right
because right defines what is fitting in the situation
of beings who are good with a good. So the concepts
of good, right, and ought also form a moral triunity
of interdependent concepts. Good and ought stand out in
particular with a kind of ultimacy, while right mediates
ought and good. Good is discerned at the center of an
intellectual vision of the mind. Ought emerges as a
practical commitment of the will. Both mind and will
are driven by eros. Eros drives the mind toward the
true, while eros drives the will toward the good. In
this situation an occasion arises which involves both
an intellectual discernment and a practical commitment.
My own view is that intellectual vision grasps the
presence of the principle or fact of good as a constituent

feature of what is (the true). The ultimately real is a
process of becoming by which actuality is driven and
drawn toward its ideal possibility (the good). Good is
the ideal possibility which draws beings toward their
actualization, while eros drives beings forward toward
their good. Beings naturally seek their own good.
They are driven and drawn toward it. Right emerges when
beings confront each other. Beings have rights to seek
their own good which create binding claims on other beings to honor and to promote that good. It is at this
point that a decision confronts the will. Will one do
what one ought? One ought to do what is right, what is
fitting. It is fitting for the will to do what it
ought and to commit itself to the right which honors and
promotes the good of the community of beings who are
driven and drawn toward their ideal possibility (good).
The creative becoming of finite beings reflects the ultimate fact of a Cosmic Process in which the possible
becomes actual under the lure of the good, that is, in
which all beings are driven and drawn toward their ideal
possibility.

Good (as ideal possibility or inherent worth) is
transcendent to the being which the mind knows. Likewise, right (the fitting), and ought (as the demand to
do the fitting) stand out from action which the will
chooses. Good as ideal possibility confronts the mind
as end or goal which ought to be. Ought is the demand
to do the fitting, that is to honor the inherent goodness and promote the potential good of beings. Right
unites what is with what ought to be. It is at this
point that the intuitionists are on to something that
must be acknowledged. They see some unique, indefin-
able quality of good, or they see principles of right
action or duty, or they see that there are some oughts

that bind us. These qualities, principles, relationships, these "oughts" and "duties" are self-evident.
They are real and just there in fact and are either
seen or not seen. Good, right, and ought are irreducible to anything else. Yet it is only in relation to
states of affairs, to structures of being, to what is,
that good, right , and ought take on specific and definitive meaning. Apart from this incarnation into and
their relationship to what is, these terms are bare,
empty and abstract.

It seems to me that the intuitionists are pointing to the apartness and irreducibility of terms like
good, right, and ought, while the definists (whether
naturalistic or metaphysical) are contending for the
definitions and meanings that these terms take on in
relationship to descriptive statements about what is
actually the case. Hence, the definists hold that certain propositions containing ethical terms are analytic, tautologous, or true by definition, while intuitionists hold them to be synthetic. According to
Frankena:

> What underlies this difference of opinion is
> that the intuitionists claim to have at least
> a dim awareness of a simple unique quality or
> relation of goodness or rightness which ap-
> pears in the region in which our ethical terms
> roughly indicate, whereas the definists claim
> to have no awareness of any such quality or
> relation in that region, which is different
> from all other qualities and relations which
> belong to the same context but are designated
> by words other than "good" or "right" and
> their obvious synonyms. The definists are in
> all honesty claiming to find but one charac-
> teristic where the intuitionists claim to
> find two . . . .[14]

Good, right, and ought refer, I claim, to dimensions
that are neither reducible to nor separable from descriptions and meanings and definitions of what is.

Hence, both the intuitionists and definists have a
point, though neither would appear to have the whole
truth.

Morality, then, appears to arise in a double context. This first involves the discernment of value
principles which create an order of obligations. The
second is a commitment of the will to live in accordance with them. This should not be taken to mean an
assertion of the primacy of the intellect over will.
It is true to say that the will enacts what the intellect has discerned to be good and right. But it is
equally true to say that the will is engaged in actions
related to the good and right, while the intellect
serves the will by discriminating and critically reflecting upon choices. Intellect and will are relatively autonomous but interdependent and mutually supporting
activities of the total self. Nevertheless, the
intellectual discernment of the good and the volitional
commitment to doing the right establish the framework
within which moral discourse takes place. Discernment
and commitment are involved at every level and step.
Without moral discernment ought never emerges in the
objective sense, and without commitment the objective
ought never becomes subjectively owned. In short, an
intellectual intuition or vision establishes the fact
and meaning of good and of the right which we ought to
do. But a practical commitment of will is necessary
to establish the validity of the ought by which we determine to live in accordance with what is objectively
fitting (the right). In this way one becomes committed
to a moral point of view.

I

One final metaethical question can now be addressed. Suppose someone asks, "Why should I be moral?
Why should I do what I ought instead of what I want?"
The first priority is to decide just what is meant by
such queries. Let us assume that the question is
whether one should take a moral point of view. I have
already indicated that to take a moral point of view is
to acknowledge that there are binding claims on actions
toward other beings arising out of some valid interpretation of what is right and good. Within this framework, it would make no sense to ask why should I do what
I ought. The only consideration is to determine what is
right. Once that is discerned, it follows that one
ought to do what is right. Within a moral framework, it
is self-contradictory to ask why one should do what one
ought, since one obviously ought to do what one ought to
do. It is the very notion of oughtness that is being
questioned. What are the grounds for asserting that
there are right and wrong actions which place persons
under obligation? Can reasons be given to justify or at
least support the idea of moral oughtness? If I take a
moral point of view, I ought to do what is right. But
why ought I take a moral point of view? Is there a
basis for the oughtness of a moral ought?

There cannot be a moral reason for taking a moral
point of view. Morality assumes it. If there is a
justification, it must be trans-moral or metaethical.
Morality is a realm of discourse within which concepts
of right and wrong, good and bad, obligation and oughtness are the presuppositions of discussion. The oughtness of moral oughtness can adequately only be established on metaphysical grounds. More precisely, the

ultimate grounding of the validity of morality is religious. Morality is a penultimate question. Religion
deals with ultimate questions, ultimate concerns, ultimate reality, ultimate value.

The religious answer to the question of moral
oughtness is that it is right to do right. Right has
the same formal meaning in this religious framework as
it has in the moral framework. It suggests what is fitting, suitable, appropriate. One should take a moral
point of view because it is fitting to do so. If moral
rightness defines what ought to be done in the relationships of sentient beings who are intrinsically good and
who have a good they can actualize, religious rightness
defines what is a fitting relationship between beings
and the ultimate ground of their being and value. This
does not imply that there is anything arbitrary about
moral oughtness. It is true but not sufficient to say
that one ought to be moral because God commands it. It
is equally true to say that God commands it because it
is right.[15] The religious ground of moral rightness defines an ultimate fittingness. To live morally is to
live in tune with reality, to fit ones life into a
structure and a pattern which is rooted in the ultimate
nature of things. It is to harmonize ones own being and
actions with what one discerns to be the structures,
dynamics, and goals embodied in the universe. We are
born into a world of beings who act upon us and into a
situation which requires a response in light of some
interpretation of what is going on. Morality is defined
by some interpretation or vision of life informed by
some images or patterns which are thought to be appropriate to the situation in which we find ourselves.[16]

To take a moral point of view is to respond in a
fitting way to the world as it impinges on us and offers

us options. Morality rests upon some religious vision
when it presses its questions far enough. This does not
necessarily imply a supernaturalistic or even theistic
religion. Religion in the largest sense refers to the
way people respond to whatever is regarded as ultimate
in being or value, to what is believed to determine life
and destiny, to be of most importance in the nature of
things. When no objective (religious) basis for taking
a moral point of view is found, the alternative is to
ground morality in some subjective (human) commitment,
decision, or preference which has no justification outside itself. One can on humanistic grounds, of course,
affirm the intrinsic value of persons, thus giving some
objective reference to subjective commitment. However,
such a grounding is inadequate, I maintain, unless it is
connected to a base in the ultimate nature of things.

The vision elaborated here assumes that there is a
creative process at work in the cosmos which gives rise
to beings with a potential for enjoyment. These beings
are intrinsically good because they have a capacity for
experiencing good (enjoyment). The appropriate response to this creative activity at the basis of all
things is to honor the intrinsic value of sentient beings and to promote their enjoyment. Not to respond
in this way is to act out of harmony with what is most
real, to ignore the nature of things. To use different
language, it is to be estranged from ones essence and
from God. In religious language such missing the mark
may be seen as rebellion against God, as disobedience,
as sin. It is finally to miss ones own true good.

Why should I be moral? The only reason is that it
is fitting to do so. If a person does not care to be
in tune, to relate ones own being and action to the
deepest realities and purposes of the universe, then

there is no reason to take a moral point of view by
making a decision to do so in light of the belief that
it is fitting to do so. It is fitting to do so because
of the way things finally are in a universe impregnated
with a telic principle.

     In light of the foregoing, it is possible to give
a revised and final statement of the moral imperative.
In so doing, morality can be shown to have a single
ground. Ethical theory is now seen to arise out of a
perception that reality is value impregnated. Ethics
defines what is fitting for human beings to do in light
of the way things ultimately are. The single ground of
morality is the imperative to respond appropriately to
the creativity present in the cosmic process which both
gives us being and determines the context in which
moral action takes place. That context is a world in
which emergent evolution has produced a wide variety of
sentient beings with the capacity for enjoyment. There
is an intentionality in the very nature of things which
has created beings who are intrinsically good and who
seek the good. The imperative to respond to cosmic
creativity in a fitting way is both a description of
appropriateness and a prescription of obligation. At
this ultimate point ethics and metaphysics are united.
In like manner, morality and religion are united.
Finally, deontology and teleology are seen to grow from
a single root.

     Morality arises only where there is freedom of
choice. Human beings must decide how they will live,
how they will order their own lives and how they will
relate to other human beings and the whole natural and
living environment. Morality takes its form and content as a description of what is fitting in light of an
interpretation of the total situation in which human

consciousness emerges. Morality bids us to respond appropriately, to act in a way that is fitting given the
facts and the potentials of life in all its forms. To
act appropriately is to be in tune with the ultimate
fact of a cosmic creativity whose intentionality is to
create living beings and to actualize their potential.
To live otherwise is to act contrary to our own nature,
to nature, and to nature's God.

    With this philosophical orientation in mind, the
ethical vision so far elaborated can now be related to
the specific and normative source of Christian ethics,
namely, the Bible, especially the New Testament.

                            J

    Before proceeding to an examination of New Test-
ament ethics, however, the connection between the philosophical and the theological stances assumed on these
pages needs to be further clarified. Part of my polemic
has been that philosophical ethics as generally prac-
ticed in American universities tends to be truncated
and superficial. The attempt to sever morality from
religion and to regard ethics as an autonomous discipline free of metaphysical grounding (except for some
anthropological analysis of such issues as human freedom) breaks asunder what in reality is a unified whole.
The interpretation of ethics thus far developed has led
to a number of points where humanistic rationalism falls
short. Enumerating these will serve to clarify the
methodology of Christian natural ethics as well as high-
lighting the content of the normative and metaethical
vision that is being elaborated on these pages.

    The insufficiency of autonomous secular ethics in-
volves the interplay of metaphysics and religion.

Metaphysics deals with theoretical questions having to
do with the nature of reality as a whole, while religion
refers to existential or practical questions arising
out of the human quest for meaning and fulfillment in
relation to ultimate realities and values. Meaning depends on being, and the nature of being has implications
for morality. Hence, religion and metaphysics are interconnected. The following issues will illustrate my
claim:

    a. An ethical theory not grounded in metaphysics
is superficial, lacking anchor in bedrock reality. Obligation has a source in the ultimate nature of things
beyond human choice or even human nature. Those non-
cognitivists who see moral judgments as only prescrib-
ing or recommending a way of life that presumably has
justification in subjective (even if rational) choice
are abstracting human and moral reality from the ultimate foundations in which duty, goodness, virtue, and
obligation are grounded. One can choose to bracket off
these metaphysical-religious considerations, but that
does not negate them. I have argued also that the
justification for taking a moral point at all has to be
transmoral, that is, a religious decision rooted in
metaphysical fact.

    b. Humanistic ethics is insufficient to deal
with the incompatibility of competing values and the
reality of the tragic. This point can be illustrated
in a variety of ways. It has already been noted that
sometimes ethical analysis may lead to a stalemate
between two or more available courses of action. More
serious is the fact that sometimes, for example, a
larger good for all may be purchased only at the expense of creating greater inequalities. Or one has a
choice between a smaller flow of goods divided equally

to equally deserving persons or a larger fund of benefits divided more unequally. Put more generally, doing
the right (deontologically) may limit the good (teleo-
logically). A morally serious person must surely experience anguish given these unavoidable conflicts,
ambiguities, dilemmas, and stalemates.

     More serious and more anguishing are instances in
which persons are caught up in the predicament of what
can be called tragic choice. Consider the following
examples:

> A teen-age girl is seduced, deceived, and
> finally abandoned by a boy friend who leaves
> her pregnant, and she chooses an abortion
> as the lesser of the evils available to her.

> A farm boy is drafted and dies in a war that
> he does not understand and had nothing to do
> with causing, and yet goes into it because
> the leaders of his country tell him that it
> is his duty to do so.

> A couple married for twenty-five years are
> divorced at the husband's insistence and over
> his wife's protests -- a split which is argu-
> ably better for him and worse for her than
> the conflicted marriage.

Here are choices which are morally defensible as perhaps
the best among available choices. Yet unavoidably they
involve tragic disvalues and negative consequences.
Once again, a secular ethics without recourse to a
transmoral resolution is metaphysically shallow and existentially inadequate. Where, as a matter of fact, in
most textbooks of philosophical ethics does one even

find an acknowledgement of the reality of tragic
choice, much less an attempt at working out a solution?

My claim is that the Christian vision provides a
rationally persuasive resolution of these anguishing
elements in the moral situation. Immanuel Kant argued
that immortality (and, hence, God) must be postulated
to insure that the inexhaustible demands of the categorical imperative could be carried out and so that virtue
finally would be joined to happiness. Likewise, I contend that a religious resolution of the metaphysically-
based moral predicament is called for.[17] In this
framework the contraditions in finite reality are accepted in the context of what Christians call grace.
Grace refers to the unconditional love of an Ultimate
Beneficence experienced by human beings which allows
them to accept themselves and the situation in which
they find themselves tragically and sinfully involved.[18]
The existential consequence is that those who have such
an experience are freed from the burden of being morally perfect and from the weight of assuming that moral
responsibility itself can resolve the human predicament.
Grace also enables persons to be morally responsible
without falling into either complacency or despair.
Finally, the Cross symbolizes the fact that God suffers with us in our tragic anguish in a companionship
of supportive love.

c. Secular rationalism, which takes the scienti-
fically knowable human and natural worlds as the sum
total of reality, has no adequate resources for dealing with the failure of persons to live up to their obligations. What does one do with one's moral failure?
How do we deal with each other's transgressions
against duty and the wounds we mutually inflict? Theologians call it sin, but by whatever name failure to

honor intrinsic worth and promote universal enjoyment
is real. Is it just ignored as of no consequence?
Forgiveness of persons of each other solves part of the
problem, but if obligation is rooted in ultimate conditions, then reconciliation with the Ground of the
Cosmic Process is essential to adequate resolution. If
there is a Universal Love at the heart of the cosmos,
then grace, mercy, and forgiveness may be real, and, if
they are, they constitute the only final resolution of
the predicament of moral failure.

     d. Humanistic morality lacks the resources of the-
istic religion for providing motivation that bridges
the gap between the moral demand and the moral act.
Here I agree with Paul Lehmann.[19] Obligation toward
others is felt as an alien pressure, as a demand that
conflicts with desire for self-gratification. Or in
many cases it does, particularly when the ethical demand
is rigorous and unrelenting, calling for reverence for
all life and universal beneficence. A religious orientation which involves gratitude for the gift of being
and the promise of enjoyment, reinforced by the grace
of God which relieves us of the heavy burden of our
moral failures and the tragic dimension of moral ambiguity, can transform the felt pressure of demand into
spontaneous and joyful service of the neighbor and of
universal good. Love of Universal Being engendered in
deep religious response to being loved is the most adequate basis of moral motivation by which duty is transformed into the free expression of a life in tune with
Ultimate Purpose. In this context obligation states
not only what we ought to do (imperative) but what we
will do when rightly attuned to reality (indicative).
A conversion of egocentric will into God-centered will
is the prerequisite of this spontaneous honoring of

intrinsic value and the promotion of universal good.
Faith evoked in response to the experience of Unconditional Love and Creative Purpose as the source of finite life and its possibilities is the most powerful
ground and description of such a conversion.

It may appear that a shift has been made in this
last section from a philosophical to a theological
stance, thus violating the methodology of Christian
natural ethics. This breach disappears when the foregoing points illustrating the insufficiency of a secular
autonomous ethical rationalism are taken as questions
posed by a theistically grounded philosophical ethics,
to which a Christian theology of creation and redemption centering on the love of God would be an answer.
This answer while anticipated and stated in the preceding paragraphs depends factually and initially on the
special insights of Christian revelation for its source
and grounding. Yet, presupposed, the answers it provides for the moral predicaments I have listed are rationally convincing, as are the claims of Christian
revelation itself. The convincing power of Christian
claims is found in their capacity to make sense out of
life taken as a whole when rationally clarified by an
appropriate philosophical analysis.

Put more precisely, an appropriate philosophical
analysis shows the insufficiency of humanistic rationalism and poses questions which require answers based
on some clarifying insight into the human and metaphysical situation. For a Christian this clarifying insight is provided by the Scriptural witness to Jesus as
the Christ, the Logos of God. It must be granted that
this correlation of philosophical analysis and theological claim arises out of a total perspective which
includes a Christian commitment which informs the

philosophical work and a commitment to a theistic process philosophy which informs the Christian vision.
Hence, it must be acknowledged that the assertion of
the insufficiency of secular autonomous ethics reflects
the Christian background of the polemicist, yet the
polemic itself appeals to no criteria foreign to philosophy.

This procedure is in keeping with the method
stated in Chapter I. A philosophical stance assumed by
a self in the world and a theological stance assumed by
a believer in the church mutually transform each other
until an equilibrium is reached. At this point there
is a mutually supporting interdependence and a correlation of claims which make up a unified totality which
can be viewed as contained by an ellipse with two foci
as previously specified. The claim is that a philosophical ethics emerges which can be judged by rational
criteria of philosophy. A further claim is that the
ethical perspective thus produced is not inharmonious
with the essence of Christian ethics and, in fact,
coincides with its norms and presuppositions.

In this respect, the method I employ resembles
that of Paul Tillich, who correlates questions raised by
philosophical analysis with answers provided by the
Christian theological tradition.[19] However, I have
emphasized that this final correlation emerges out of
a mutually transforming dialectic between "reason" and
"revelation." The philosophical questions are raised
by one who anticipates Christian answers, and the
Christian answers presuppose the form and content of
the philosophical questions, or so I believe. Those
assumptions are at work in the text of my discussion
at this point. A further clarification is that I work
with the notion that both philosophy and theology

provide questions _and_ answers. Both contribute to a
mutually transforming dialogue which results finally in
a unified, total perspective involving both description
and prescription, analysis and resolution of issues.

                           K

     The transition to Christian ethics proper can be
made complete with one final summary which reviews the
resultant ethical theory as it has developed to this
point. Beginning, as is customary in philosophical
circles, with a comparison and interpretation of deontological and teleological perspectives, the following
chapter of metaethics showed that taken alone they were
abstract and incomplete unless incorporated into a comprehensive religious and metaphysical scheme. This is
necessary in order to ground morality in bedrock reality.
In particular, it was shown that a comprehensive view
requires the uniting of morality and religion. As a
part of this larger picture, the further claim advanced
was that moral action needs to be seen as a response to
the totality of the actions, circumstances, and possibilities which constitute the setting in which obligation arises. This environment includes supremely the
activity and will of God. Morality is, in essence, an
alignment of human activity with Cosmic Purpose, a response to an Intentionality which harmoniously links
human aims with God's. Deontological and teleological
interpretations of moral obligation need to be set within this larger setting. Honoring the intrinsic worth
of persons and promoting their self-actualization is an
appropriate response to Ultimate Reality and Purpose.
Hence, to ask what is morally right is equivalent to
asking how in a given situation human action may most

appropriately align itself with the Creative Intentionality which undergirds not only human existence but that
of the cosmos itself. It is within this framework that
deontological and teleological ways of determining moral
responsibility become concrete and complete. And it
is at this very point that the transition from philosophical to Christian ethics can be made. The next
chapter takes up this task with a normative statement
of a morality based on the New Testament.

CHAPTER IV

AN ETHIC OF SACRIFICIAL-EQUALITARIAN LOVE

A

H. Richard Niebuhr taught a generation of theologians that in addition to deontological and teleological
ethics, there is a third form of moral reasoning worthy
of attention. This neglected way of viewing ethical
theory he calls dialogical ethics. In Niebuhr's words,
deontology uses the political image of a citizen whose
duty is to be law-abiding. Teleology uses the image of
the self as a maker who creates means to achieve the
good life. Dialogical ethics uses the image of answer-
er or responder. The moral life is a response to actions upon the self in the light of an interpretation
of that action. Response ethics asks not what is my
duty nor what is my chief end, but what is going on?
And what is a fitting response to what is happening, to
what is acting upon me?[1]

The ethical perspective I have developed embodies
a set of assumptions about what is going on in the
world that sets the context for moral response. Process metaphysics claims that there is at work in the
world a creative purpose which brings into being experiencing subjects who have intrinsic worth and a potential for enjoyment. To put it in standard Christian
terms, God creates life and directs it toward salvation. In this interpretation of what is going on in
the world, the fitting response to the creative-redemp-
tive activity of God is to honor the intrinsic worth
of living beings and to promote the fulfillment of
their potential.

H. Richard Niebuhr is surely right when he claims
that moral action in the Bible is prominently seen as

human response to divine action. There follows a brief
interpretation of Biblical ethics along these lines.
The thesis is that the viewpoint previously developed
on philosophical grounds coincides with Christian ethics
based on the New Testament.

In THE ETHICS OF ENJOYMENT I claimed that in the
Biblical witness THE WILL OF GOD IS TO MAKE HEAVEN REAL.[2]
God is at work in the world creating a royal and loyal
people and directing them toward a good future. In the
coming Society (Kingdom) the joy of life will be complete in a perfected community. Joined by bonds of love
to each other and having their unity in the praise of
God, the heavenly inhabitants enjoy the supreme bliss of
a completely fulfilled life. The theme of a good future
takes many forms throughout the Bible. In the beginning Abraham is promised that his descendants will have
many children and that they will bless the world. In
the end John is given a magnificent vision of the New
Jerusalem coming down out of heaven in all its radiant
splendor. In between are varying conceptions of the good
future that God has promised. But throughout them all
runs the idea that the will of God is to make heaven
real.

Moral action is the fitting response of human beings
to the work of God in the world to make heaven real by
which life is created and directed toward fulfillment.
In his study of New Testament ethics, C.H. Dodd claims
that the moral imperative can be stated like this:
REPRODUCE IN YOUR ACTIONS TOWARD OTHERS THE QUALITY AND
THE DIRECTION OF THE SAVING ACTS OF GOD TOWARD YOU.[3]
The quality of God's action is love. Hence, we should
love each other as God has loved us. The agape of God
toward us becomes the norm of the agape that we show
toward others. The direction or aim of God's action is

the coming of the Society of God on earth. Hence, the
coming of the Society is to be the supreme goal of our
action. Put in the philosophical language of Christian
natural ethics, to love one's neighbor is to reverence
the intrinsic value of every person. To seek the Society of God is to promote the fulfillment of the potential for enjoyment of all persons in community. The
moral imperative, then, can be put in two sets of language, which coincide in meaning. Stated philosophically the principle is this: Respond to the creation
of life in the evolutionary process by honoring the intrinsic value of living beings and by promoting the
fulfillment of their potential. Stated theologically,
the principle is this: Respond to the action of God in
creation and redemption by loving others as God has
loved you and by actualizing the Society of God on
earth.

The question as to whether dialogical ethics constitutes a third form of moral reasoning is problematic.
It could be so understood and developed. But primarily
it adds an essential dimension frequently neglected in
ethical theory. It states that as a matter of fact
moral action takes place in a concrete context in which
we act as beings who are also acted upon by other beings.
Hence, inevitably and factually we do the right and seek
the good as a response to what is happening in light of
our interpretation of how we are constituted and shaped
by what is going on in the world. The statement that
we are to reproduce in our actions the quality and aim
of God's prior action on us sounds like a deontological
imperative. It is better understood, I think, as an
acknowledgement and description of the fact that moral
action takes place in a system of activities which
create and mold us and which require some interpretation

of the total social and ontological situation in which
moral action occurs. Moral action _is_ a response. How
we respond depends on how we understand the bases of
obligation (deontological) and aspiration (teleological)
within the factual framework within which we live and
act. This means that, in one sense, all ethics is contextual ethics. A complete ethical theory will interpret the context of moral action, that is, its ultimate
ontological setting which determines what the right and
the good are. Niebuhr's contribution, then, is in calling attention to a neglected dimension of ethical theory
rather than stating an independent and separate form of
moral reasoning in addition to deontological and teleological ethical theories. The more precise statement of
the moral imperative I have derived from C.H. Dodd, then,
would read as follows: When you respond to what is
happening to you and in the world (as you will inevitably
and factually do), the fitting way of response is to do
the right (love) and seek the good (the Society of God)
by reproducing the pattern of God's action toward you.
In so doing you will be aligning yourself with reality,
for the truth is that God loves us and our neighbors and
seeks the good of us all.

B

Christian love, of course, finds its source, its
inspiration, and the definition of its nature in the New
Testament interpretation of Jesus. The life of service
which led to a sacrificial death is the measure of the
heights to which agape rises. "Greater love has no man
than this, that he lay down his life for his friends"
(John 15:13 RSV). The prodigality of this love poured
out for sinners, for enemies, for the neighbor in need

is boundless. It is rooted in grace and comes spontaneously and unmotivated to us from God to become the pattern and norm of our responsibility toward others.
Agape in the New Testament is grounded in a religious
vision of a gracious, merciful God whose love for us is
unconditional, extravagant, marvelous, and mysterious.
It evokes faith and answering love in us which accepts
the gracious forgiveness offered us. The gratitude felt
in the believer for this unmerited favor expresses itself in spontaneous and joyful service of the neighbor
modelled after the self-giving which led Jesus to the
cross.

The boundlessness of such love, its heedlessness of
self, its prodigality in pouring itself out for the
neighbor without counting the costs is undeniable as we
read its character on the pages of the New Testament.
The question is how we should understand the ethics of
agape in the 20th century. In particular, does the
sacrificial self-giving which is so prominent in the New
Testament rule out a legitimate love of self - a defense of its just interests, and a quest for its own fulfillment? The New Testament does not explicitly settle this issue on textual grounds. No systematic definition of terms appears. The questions we raise in the
midst of complexities, ambiguities, compromises, conflicting obligations, and unavoidable trade-offs simply
were not addressed by the New Testament writers.

Generated in the hot fervor of apocalyptic expectations and motivated by an appeal to religious absolutes, the New Testament states an unconditional ethical ideal without regard to it practicality in a continuing society for which one takes responsibility. But
we must deal with its practical application. When we
translate the ethics of Jesus and of the New Testament

into a workable guide for living in a contemporary society, a congruence arises with the morality I have developed in the form of a Christian natural ethics.
Christian love is agape. I maintain that there is a
correspondence, if not identity, between agape and the
philosophical claim that we are obligated to honor the
intrinsic worth of every person.

In a study of the interpretation of agape in recent
theological literature, Gene Outka concludes that the
normative content most often accorded to that term is
equal regard.[4] Agape is regard for the neighbor as a
person independently of the special qualities or moral
merit of a given individual. Following Karl Barth,
Outka defines agape as identification with the interests
of the neighbor in utter disregard of the other person's
attractiveness. The Christian moral imperative requires
the believer to meet the needs and promote the welfare
of persons as persons. Hence, every individual, qua
human existent, is equal to every other. Agape is act-
tive concern for the other which is permanent and unal-
terable. Nothing the neighbor can do, be, or become can
erase the fundamental obligation on the part of the believer to be attentive to the needs and welfare of the
other as a person. Agape is unconditional active concern for other human beings. It does not ask whether
the other is deserving or whether the love shown is returned or acknowledged in any way. It is not withheld
even from the enemy or from those who hate the lover.

In all these ways I see an identity between agape
and the moral norm I have proposed on philosophical
grounds. I have argued that every person has intrinsic
worth and that we are obligated to honor that worth.
This is another way of saying that one should have equal
regard for all persons as persons in the meanings that

Outka has associated with agape. Christian love is, of
course, set within the context of the Christian vision
of reality and the proclamation of the Gospel. However, there is a coincidence of normative content between agape and the philosophical imperative to reverence the intrinsic worth of persons.

C

Likewise, I believe there is a congruence between
the New Testament norm of promoting the Society of God
and actualizing the human potential for enjoyment. The
idea of the good future that God will bring into being
suggests an ideal society in which all the needs of the
body and of the spirit are met. It implies a complete
triumph of good over evil. It is a community in which
the wholeness and fullness of life are completely actualized so that joy reigns supreme. The idea of the
coming End in which the people of God will inherit the
destiny God intends for them undergoes a long period of
development and takes a variety of forms. Not all of
these can be reconciled with each other. In the New
Testament the hope for the coming Society is set within
an apocalyptic context in which the New Age is to be
brought into being by a direct and sudden divine intervention. The Society of God is to be instituted by a
cosmic miracle in which all sin and evil are conquered
absolutely and forever.

The New Testament picture of the end of history cannot be taken literally, for things did not actually work
out that way. History still continues. When the New
Testament idea of the Society is demythologized and
translated into contemporary language that is both
credible and relevant, it is congruent with the ethical

imperative to maximize the enjoyment that accompanies
the fulfillment of human potential. The Society comes
in so far as the potential for enjoyment is actualized
in individuals living in community with others. Just as
with the New Testament idea of agape, the conception of
the Society of God is set within a framework of theological assumptions and claims. But the ethical implications of a contemporary reconstruction of that ideal
society coincide with the philosophically based norm of
enjoyment as the supreme good of life.

Likewise, in both cases there is close connection
between the Biblical affirmation of a Creator and Redeemer whose will is to make heaven real and the philosophical assertion of a creativity in nature which has
elaborated an increasingly complex hierarchy of life
forms. These life forms are driven and drawn toward the
enjoyment-producing fulfillment of their potential.
Moreover, these experiencing subjects have intrinsic
value which moral beings are obligated to respect.
Whether seen Biblically or philosophically, human life
arises in a context of value-producing activities rooted
in the depths of reality. We are acted upon by other
beings and by the Ultimate Source of our being and of
all beings. In that framework we have to respond to
what is going on around us in the light of some interpretation of the meaning and direction of the cosmic
process which gave us birth and being. Biblically and
philosophically my claim is that we live in a goal-directed system of activities in which experiencing subjects find satisfaction by mutually-supportive relationships with persons and other living forms in the universal quest for fulfillment. Hence, not only is there a
convergence of claims at the ethical level between the
philosophical and Biblical sources of the vision being

set forth here, but it holds also at the cosmic level of
interpretation. God the Creator and Redeemer seeking to
make heaven real -- a creative cosmos evolving ever higher forms of enjoyment seeking living beings: these are
alternative ways of approaching one central truth about
reality and morality.

Stating the moral imperative in contemporary terms
must account for the New Testament idea that the Society
comes primarily as a gift. Jesus and the early church
expected the end of the Old Age to come soon and suddenly
by direct action of God. The Society is an objective
reality that is coming. The idea is not that if people
repent of their sins and love their neighbors, the Society will come. Rather the message is that the Society
is coming, therefore the only appropriate thing to do is
repent and obey. Nevertheless, the Society has already
begun to come in the ministry of Jesus. It is present
wherever the power of God is at work casting out demons,
healing the sick, forgiving sins, and making life whole.
The response of the believer in loving actions is a
public and visible manifestation of the presence of the
Society. By reproducing the quality and direction of
God's action, the community of the faithful become co-
creators of the Society. How can this apocalyptic
version of the Society which proved to be untrue in any
literal sense be reinterpreted for persons living 2000
years later in the expectation that history will continue indefinitely without being ended suddenly by a
cosmic transformation?

We awaken into consciousness in a world that is
prior to us and which we did not create. Life comes to
us as a gift in all its complexity and with all its
marvelous potential for enjoyment. Over billions of
years an incredible adventure has taken place. Some

creativity at the base of things has brought life into
being out of simple matter-energy. Human beings have
emerged from a long process. We inherit the gift of life
with its persistent drive toward fulfillment in all of
its myriad forms. We can plant and we can water but
only as God gives the increase of growth and harvest.
It happens by itself when we cultivate. We can engage
in sexual intercourse but the production of new life in
the most fundamental sense is not our act. The processes
by which a fertilized egg becomes a healthy baby at
birth occur by themselves. They happen apart from our
will. So it is with all the satisfactions and pleasures
we experience. The potentiality that is actualized by
our cooperative action is a given and the enjoyment we
experience is a gift. Moreover, there is a drive in the
cosmic process toward the production and fulfillment of
ever higher forms of life. Evolution is future-oriented
and goal-directed. It pushes toward the perfection of
its possibilities by creating more complex living beings
with greater ranges and depths of experience and enjoyment.

     The Biblical theme of the Society of God points to
the intention of God to create a people and to bring
that community into a perfected future. The most productive framework for a contemporary reinterpretation of
this motif is the theory of emergent evolution by which
a creative purpose at work in the cosmos has produced
an ascending order of life forms of increasing complexity culminating on earth with the appearance of human
beings. The promise of the Society's coming in all its
fulness has not yet been realized and the ultimate
future of the evolutionary adventure on earth is hidden
in mystery. Yet in both perspectives human beings live
a life of response to the givenness of creation and the

potential of the future. They can enter creatively into
the unfolding of the human quest for justice and joy, but
they do so in cooperation with realities and possibilities that confront them as a gift with promise. My claim
is that the fitting response to the action of God upon
us in the evolutionary process is to love our neighbors
by honoring their intrinsic value as persons and to
promote the coming of the Society by actualizing the potential for enjoyment in community.

D

Love-fulfilling and Society-of-God-promoting actions are interdependent and complementary. They require
and presuppose each other. Love of neighbor expresses
the reality of the Society. Society-promoting actions
manifest a love of neighbor. Deontological obligation
incarnate in loving service of the neighbor is joined
to teleological aspiration embodied in Society-seeking
strategies. If not pressed too far, a distinction in
orientation may be useful in seeing the relationship
between love and the Society. Love begins with a focus
on the nearest neighbor here and now. It directs attention to immediate needs. It compels us to attack the
worst evils of the moment. However, in order to meet
the needs of our neighbors and to relieve human misery
here and now, it is necessary for ethical action to take
account of present social structures and future possibilities. The social order must be transformed in accordance with the imperatives of justice. In this way love
moves toward the concerns growing out of the quest of
the Society. Promoting the Society of God on earth
directs attention to the social order and to its ideal
possibilities. It has a future orientation which takes

the whole of society into acount. Society of God ethics
obligates us to create the kind of social order that is
most likely to increase human welfare and promote the
enjoyment of all. From that vantage point, it proceeds
toward meeting the needs and enhancing the welfare of
individuals in the present. Hence, each orientation
moves toward and merges with the other.

     In connection with the interdependence and comple-
mentarity of love-fulfilling and Society-of-God-promoting actions, love should not be interpreted strictly in
either deontological or teleological terms. Reinhold
Niebuhr and Paul Ramsey interpret love as a deontological
imperative.[5] Joseph Fletcher and William Frankena give
the love ethic a teleological meaning.[6] Both points of
view are plausible. The law of love should be taken in
the most comprehensive sense to mean that one should
honor the intrinsic worth and promote the welfare of the
neighbor. Likewise, the imperative to actualize the
Society obligates one to meet the neighbor's need here
and now. The Society is manifest where the hungry are
fed and the sick are healed at the moment. In this way
a deontological element is added to the teleological
quest for future actualization of Society possibilities
in the more universal and long range sense. Hence, if
love is given some deontological primacy, that does not
mean that a teleological element is not present. One
might, following W. D. Ross, argue that among the obligations which bind conduct is that of promoting valuable consequences.[7] In this case, the valuable consequence which love seeks is the good of the neighbor.
This would amount to a kind of impure or mixed deontology.

E

Immediately upon considering the meaning of agape
in the New Testament, a number of characteristic problems come into view. Prominent among them is the relationship of self-love to neighbor-love. Does agape
allow a person to protect, promote, and otherwise further his or her own interests, needs, and goals or must
they be subordinate to serving the other? What does it
mean to love ones neighbor as one loves oneself? There
would appear to be three main ways of relating self-
love to neighbor-love that can claim to be a legitimate
contemporary interpretation of New Testament thought.

    1. The first negates self-love and calls for a
purely sacrificial view of agape. In much Protestant
theology of the last generation agape is said to be
heedless of the interests of the self. It is self-giving love that expends itself in behalf of the other
with no thought of reward or reciprocity. It is sacrificial love in that the self and its interest are completely put aside so that the neighbor might be served.
Self-love is excluded. Agape is based on the forgiving
love of God received in faith which overcomes anxiety
about the self so that the believer is liberated to
express the gratitude felt to God by serving the neighbor.

    Anders Nygren has provided the terms of the conver-
sation about the meaning of agape since the publication
of his seminal work AGAPE AND EROS.[8] In his view agape
is spontaneous. It is not motivated by the intrinsic
worth of persons but flows out to the neighbor because
it is the nature of agape to do so. It is indifferent
to value in that the worthiness of the other person is
utterly irrelevant. Agape is shown to sinners and right-

eous alike, just as the sun rises on the just and on the
unjust.   Its character is most plainly seen when it is
recognized that God's agape is shown toward us in that
while we were yet sinners Christ died for us (Romans
5:8).   Agape is creative.   It does not recognize value.
It bestows value in that persons who had no worth acquire worth by being loved.[9]

Reinhold Niebuhr defines agape as sacrificial love
and contrasts it with mutual love.[10]   The latter is said
to be the highest form of morality based on rational considerations.   This form of love counts the good of the
self equal to that of the neighbor and seeks a harmony
of interest in which all are fulfilled.   It is based on
the hope of a loving response from the other.   Agape, by
contrast, is heedless of the self's interests as it seeks
only to serve the other.   The sacrifice of Jesus on the
cross is the epitome of agape.   But it is not rationally
justified by its results in actual life.   Agape does not
always win a response of love in return.   Hence, there
is a tragic dimension to history.   Love suffers as it
waits for a final victory beyond this life.   Moreover,
agape transcends the welter of claims and counterclaims
that must be ambiguously balanced in the quest for justice.   Mutual love, however, is not sufficient by itself.   It cannot be maintained if it is the intended
goal.   The fear that it will not be returned corrupts it
and makes it too timid to be effective alone.   Unless
mutual love is constantly initiated and nourished by
sacrificial love, it will degenerate into an anxiety-
based calculation to see if the costs outweigh the benefits to the self.   This anxiety and selfish motivation
can be overcome only by trust in a transcendent Power
and Love which will triumph eschatologically but not
always or ultimately in history.   Without this

religious grounding in a faith which transcends historical hopes and possibilities, egocentric motives will
inevitably and eventually predominate, so that the
neighbor cannot be loved for his/her own sake. Hence,
mutuality dies.

Niebuhr's view leads to an interpretation of
sacrificial love as the "impossible possibility."[11]
Agape is both transcendent to historical reality and
possibility and yet relevant to every situation. It
functions as an absolute demand that both judges every
level of present achievement that falls short of what
is possible and points the way toward a fuller embodiment of the perfect ideal. The gap between the absolute
demand and the flawed achievement is bridged by divine
mercy expressed in the forgiveness of sins. Hence, we
are saved by grace, but the demand that flows from
faith which receives grace continually functions to
transform the more imperfect to the less imperfect embodiment of the transcendent ideal.

This means that in everyday life and in social
context we must make moral judgments under the guidance
of unconditional, self-sacrificing love that are full
of compromise and ambiguity. The complexities of actual
life prevent the perfect harmony of self with others and
permit only a proximate and ambiguous justice. The per-
versity of our wills introduces self-seeking motives
into moral actions so that self-interest and other-
regarding motives are mixed in a thousand configurations.
Hence, the heedless self-giving which pure love demands
is a rare and occasional achievement even in the most
intimate person to person relationships. Nevertheless,
the impossible possibility of unconditional love functions as a transcendent ideal that is always relevant to
actual fact as judge and guide.

Niebuhr's interpretation is compelling, except
that what is essential can be preserved on the basis of
making the neighbor's need equal to our own and without
negating the inherent value of the self. An equal giving and receiving in mutual self-realization is an ideal
that transcends most personal and social relationships,
not a failure nor an inherently unstable possibility.
If mutual love does not sustain itself, that is a failure of will rooted in a collapse of religious faith in
the efficacy of Ultimate Love, not a defect in the ideal
of mutual self-realization. However, if one defines
mutual love to begin with in pragmatic, calculating
terms as requiring equal return for its ministrations
or else, then of course it is inferior to agape. But
one need not think of it that way. Niebuhr's own definitions of mutual love are not always clear or consistent. In any case, sacrificial love also requires a
faithful lover to enact it in ways that persevere in the
face of rebuff, attack, or some other form of non-
reciprocal response on the part of other persons.
We are talking about people who love, who do or do not
persist in living by their ideals, whether that norm
be equalitarian (mutual) or sacrificial love.

Since the formulations of Reinhold Niebuhr have
been so influential in American Protestantism during the
last generation, a briefly extended comment may be useful. Niebuhr's analysis would benefit from a more discriminating distinction between the "impossibility" that
springs from finitude and that which springs from sin.
The simultaneous actualization of all possible human
values is not possible, whether for self or for self in
relation to others. Every good sought or realized eliminates some others that might have been chosen. Moreover, even the best justice possible in complex social

situations will be shot through with compromise, ambiguity, and limitations imposed by the mutual exclusive-
ness of finite actualization. It is not factually possible for all persons to achieve the full realization
of all their potential enjoyments due to social as well
as metaphysical limitations, no matter how self-sacrificing each is willing to be in preference to the other.
Heaven is, in that sense, not possible on earth.
Niebuhr is well aware of all this. Presumably he does
not hold persons accountable for achieving the metaphysically impossible through heroic moral efforts of
self-sacrificing love. Then is the impossibility of
which he speaks a failure of moral will? Is it impossible for us to be as loving as we ought because we are
persistent and irreformable sinners? What is not factually possible is not morally required. What is factually possible and morally required may be highly unlikely and improbable because we are sinners, but not
strictly impossible. There is no need to violate
Pelagian logic in order to preserve what is essential
to Augustinian insight.

One can see merit in simply stating that sacrificial love as an "impossible possibility" is a transcendent but always relevant norm. However, in practical
terms can one avoid pushing for further clarification
of what this norm actually obligates us to do in real
life? If the "impossible possibility" terminology is
more than a rhetorical device and not simply a logical
absurdity, one has to ask where in actual conduct the
possible that I can do becomes the impossible that I
cannot do and am not morally required to do. How self-
sacrificing is one supposed to be? If I stop short of
total self-renunciation and absolute abandonment of
self-actualization, am I a sinner? How far am I

supposed to go morally? Where does legitimate accom-
modation to the sheer limits of human frailty and an
appropriate quest for self-realization become sinful
compromise with self-interest? The phrase -- "impossible possibility" -- itself gives aid and comfort to
those who suspect that a paradox may just be a contradiction when used by a theologian!

　　　Niebuhr never worked out a comprehensive and systematic conception of mutual love that would have allowed the precise analysis that might be most useful.
Sometimes he defined it in factual or descriptive
terms as disinterested concern for the other which is
reciprocated. At other times mutual love refers to a
relationship to others calculated to achieve the self's
own happiness or one predicated on the self's need of
others. Perhaps Niebuhr's views can be made coherent
if we recognize that he apparently thinks of mutual
love in two contexts. 1. Mutual love is the wonder-
ful but unintended consequence and product of agape
which sometimes does occur in fact. Agape (sacrificial love) is the source and sustainer of the normative relationship of disinterested concern for the
neighbor. It is unconditional and heedless of self.
It is concerned only with the good of the neighbor
and persists whether the neighbor responds lovingly
or not. Agape becomes or is manifested as or takes
the form of mutual love when the other does recipro-
cate. When mutuality occurs, the highest possibility
for history is reached. The fact of mutuality so
achieved defines the moral content of history. Since
agape is not always reciprocated, there is a tragic
dimension to history. Therefore, agape cannot be
rationally justified in terms of its historical consequences. Sacrificial love requires grounding in a

supernatural or superhistorical or eschatological faith
which depends for its justification on a fulfillment
beyond history. 2. Mutual love, however, is sometimes
thought of as a form of love independent of agape --
an autonomous, historically-justifiable and rationally-
based concern for others. Conceived in this way, mutual love seeks and requires reciprocity. It is love
which intends the good of the self equally with the
good of the other. As conditional, this form of love
depends on a loving response on the part of the other.
Thus, it is inherently unstable and infested with anxiety. It is insufficient on its own. Unless it is initiated and sustained by sacrificial love, it tends to
degenerate into a calculating, pragmatic orientation
designed to protect the self. Sometimes Niebuhr seems
to be thinking of mutual love in the first context and
sometimes in the second. Unless one makes the necessary shifts between the two as required by the text and
context of his discussion, confusion and inconsistency
result. Or so I read him.

Actually, it appears that three kinds of distinctions need to be made in order to clarify the idea
of mutual love. The first is between mutuality as a
condition and mutuality as a goal or operating norm.
Clearly, if reciprocity is made a condition of love,
then it is unstable. But if mutuality is a goal, the
situation may be quite different. The second distinction is between the philosophical interpretation of a
goal or norm and the psychological capacity to live in
accordance with it. Beliefs about reality and values
do influence actions. Nevertheless, one may firmly
embrace an ideal and not always practice it. Inability
consistently to live up to the ideal does not necessarily invalidate the ideal itself. The third distinction

closely related to and blending in with the first, is
between conditional and unconditional love. Niebuhr's
criticisms tend to envisage mutuality or reciprocity
as a condition of an initial or of a continued relationship. Hence, such love is unstable, as well as
theologically inadequate as an interpretation of
agape. However, one can conceive of an unconditional
love which views mutuality or community as a norm, an
ideal which is psychologically possible. Such an interpretation is theologically compatible with the New
Testament conception of agape, or so I believe.

     I agree with Niebuhr that unconditional love re-
quires grounding in a religious faith that can sustain
hope and commitment to the neighbor when reciprocity
is lacking. The difference is that I believe that love
which seeks mutual self-realization can endure as well
as purely sacrificial love, whereas Niebuhr does not
entertain that possibility. He typically understands
mutuality in a way that undercuts or eliminates uncon-
ditionality. These two elements need to be distinguished, but they need not be incompatible. Moreover,
I assert that the defense or promotion of the equal
claims of the self in relation to the neighbor is necessary to the preservation of justice, not a failure
or contradiction of love. My view is that love contains a justice dimension which includes the self,
whereas Niebuhr takes the essence of agape to be sacrificial in ways that exclude the self from the calculations of justice. Both Niebuhr and I affirm that
love involves heedlessness of the self. The difference
is that I see sacrifice as arising contextually only
when the needs of the neighbor exceed the needs of the
self or when the larger good of the community requires
it, not as the primary or essential trait of agape. I

find the writings of Reinhold Niebuhr to be endlessly
fascinating, insightful, and provocative. My contention is simply that there may be ways of conceiving of
agape that are no more problem-filled than his, while
having some advantages in preserving a better balance
between self-realization and self-sacrifice in the
pursuit of universal fulfillment.

The primary difference between us is that we locate the vital center of the moral norm at different
points. Hence, a different Gestalt or paradigm forms
around that core concept. Niebuhr finds the heart of
the matter in the sacrificial dimension of agape which
nourishes, sustains, transcends, and transforms mutuality. I find the controlling center in the quest for an
equal (or functionally, contextually appropriate) giving and receiving which aims at mutual self-realization
in community. At this vital core love and justice
unite. I agree with Niebuhr that the moral norm involves a sacrificial and an unconditional element and
that agape as defined by the New Testament focuses on
this dimension. This risking, outgoing, persistent
concern for the neighbor is essential to the creation
and preservation of right relationships. Where I differ is that I insist that the moral norm includes at
the other pole a concern for universality which includes the self equally with all relevant others. This
is the justice dimension of the moral norm. Niebuhr
would doubtless see this as a rationalistic compromise
which vitiates the genius and essence of New Testament
ethics -- its transhistorical, eschatological, even
otherworldly or supernatural dimension which marks it
off from secular alternatives and makes it offensive to
philosophical reason. Niebuhr's version speaks pro-
phetically to the strong, the aggressive, the powerful,

the privileged, and the oppressors. My version, I
believe, can also challenge the proud and the mighty,
but has the advantage of speaking directly without mod-
ification to the poor, the weak, the timid, the outcasts, the downtrodden, and the oppressed. For these
individuals and groups the idea that the essence of
moral responsibility is self-sacrifice is neither good
news nor good ethics, neither Gospel nor law.

F

2. Self-love may be regarded as a derivative of
neighbor love. If service of the neighbor requires attention to my own needs or interests, then self regard
not only is allowable but mandatory, but only for the
sake of the other and not for the self. Outka lists
three possibilities that various interpreters have proposed.[12] a. If others are treading on me, then it may
be necessary for me to stand up for my own rights and
welfare, lest others be encouraged to neglect the conditions which are necessary for a just community. Not
only will others be better off if they are forced to
respect me, but if they do not, it is impossible for a
good society to be achieved. b. The interests of
third parties may require me to protect my own interests
in the act of protecting those who are dependent on me
or whose cause I take up. If an attacker breaks into
my home, I may restrain him/her for the sake of my
sleeping but endangered family, although in resisting
I may save my own life as well. c. I may be required
to look after my own welfare in order not to become a
burden to others. A job that pays for my rent and food
keeps me off the welfare rolls.

Beyond this, of course, is the general fact that

service to others may require me to be healthy, wealthy,
and wise. In order to heal the sick, I may seek a medical education at the best school, which incidentally
may result in my earning a good salary, which I can
also use to benefit others. This is a position argued
for by Paul Ramsey.[13] The case is a strong one.

In neither position 1 or 2 is self-love admitted
on the ground floor. While both views do gain support
from some New Testament texts, nevertheless they involve rational difficulties which are unnecessary to
defend what is essential to Christian love lived out in
the complicated world.

In a practical sense it would not seem to matter
much in terms of behavior after all, for Paul Ramsey,
at least, allows me to do for myself what is genuinely
necessary to equip me to serve my neighbor. Since I
have many neighbors, there is no end to the rationalizations or even authentic reasons that I may produce
to justify doing for myself all sorts of things either
for my own sake or for the sake of my neighbor. But
suppose I have no neighbors? Suppose I find myself
stranded for a lifetime on a desert isle fortunately
abounding in readily available food and shelter. May
I now eat to satisfy my hunger or drink to quench my
thirst for my own sake? Or must I now die, since I
have neither a neighbor to serve nor any ground for loving myself for my own sake? It would seem strange indeed to say that only in this extreme and unlikely case
can I love myself as a proper object. But if I may be
permitted to eat some fruit for my own enjoyment and
health in my splendid isolation, then on what basis
does it become immoral for me to eat a piece of fruit
just for my own sake alone in the presence of others
(assuming that there is no near neighbor whose need in

that moment takes precedence over mine)?

It is difficult to avoid the conclusion that we
are involved in a shell game when we try to think
through the systematic implications of the notion that
love of self is forbidden entirely or only as a derivative of neighbor love. It is my duty, I am told, to
take care of myself for my neighbor's sake. It is my
duty to love my neighbor for my neighbor's sake. Presumably, my neighbor may (ought) love me for my sake.
But now in what appears to be a mysterious sleight of
hand, I am told that I may not love myself for my own
sake. Understandably, I ask, "Why not?"

W.D. Ross may be right in arguing that we are
conscious of a duty to promote the good of others but
not to promote our own good. Suppose we admit with
Ross that, at most, we can say that seeking pleasure
for oneself is "morally entirely colorless,"[14] neither
praiseworthy or blameworthy, except when it involves
the omission of a duty to others. Even so, love of
self is at least permissible. Members of the Nygren-
Niebuhr-Ramsey school frequently point out that by nature we love ourselves; that is a given, but it is a
fact which is to be overcome by ethical will. The
Christian imperative, they say, is that we should love
our neighbors as we naturally and inevitably love ourselves, yet not equally with ourselves but instead of
ourselves. This interpretive reversal by which self-
love is forbidden, I claim, is an excessive overkill
set forth to overcome the self-centered gravitational
pull of eros, aided and abetted by a pride-inflamed
will which stubbornly and sinfully exalts self-interest
to the neglect of others. Is it not enough to make
neighbor love equal with self-love?

Moreover, against Ross do we not have to urge

that sometimes we are conscious of a duty to ourselves, or at least that others should take their own self-worth and self-interest more seriously? Persons who think so poorly of themselves that they allow others to dominate them need to develop a proper self-respect, self-esteem, love of themselves. In this case, if we cannot speak of a duty of self-love, at least we can urge those who do not affirm their own worth to take advantage of their privilege of asserting their full claims as a person. If it is a sin against God and neighbor to pursue self-advantage to the detriment of others, is it not a sin against God and oneself not to claim ones full right as a person who counts just as much as any other? Women, blacks, homosexuals, and all who suffer oppression need to hear a self-affirming word. It is not sinful for those who are in bondage to join together to throw off their chains, both for them-selves and others. In fact, may it not be their moral duty to do so?

This does not deny that sometimes a sacrifice of self and of self-interest may become obligatory as a part of duty. Nygrenites like to stress that the na-ture of agape is seen most fully in that while we were yet sinners, Christ died for us (Romans 5:8). Their point is that we are unworthy of such beneficence. But surely our unworthiness lies in our sin not in our personhood as such, in our behavior not our being. Theologians need to beware that in exalting grace they do not offend the goodness of creation. Jesus urged that sparrows are valuable, but that human beings are much more precious (Matthew 5:26, 10:29-31). Presum-ably, this is because of something in our personhood as compared to sparrowhood and not simply in an arbitrary attribution by God of superior worth to people in relation to birds.

The New Testament does sometimes call for an extreme renunciation of self. Consider the "hard" sayings of Jesus. Go the second mile, resist no one who is evil, give to every one who would borrow, give cloak as well as coat, turn the other cheek, and so on (Matthew 5:38-48). These are baffling and difficult injunctions with which Christians have wrestled for centuries. If taken literally, they present insuperable theoretical as well as practical obstacles. It will not suffice to regard them as involving an apocalytic suspension of the ethical. Not the mere possibility but only the absolute certainty that the world will end very soon would free a person from the obligations to other neighbors to allow her/him to sacrifice self totally in the service of the neighbor in question. Suppose that I am on my way with life saving medicine to a village struck by an epidemic. If a Roman soldier accosts me to assist him with his belongings for a mile, I ought surely forego going the second in order to carry out my mission of mercy. Only if I knew that the end would come before I could reach the stricken village would I be free from this obligation to expend an extreme measure of devotion to the soldier in going the extra distance. But, presumably, if I had such knowledge of the imminent collapse of history, I would not have begun my rescue trip in the first place. The mere likelihood that the end will come at any time does not relieve me of my obligation to the dying if I have the possibility of reaching them before the final moment arrives. Only the certainty that this was literally the last hour or day would sustain such an apocalyptic or ethical obligation.

But perhaps there is a clue in this very example

which will let us remain literally true to Jesus without literally doing what he says. Suppose we assume
that Jesus is telling us what we must do when there are
no other neighbors in the picture for whom we have responsibility.[15] Having only ourselves to think of, we
can freely serve the neighbor before us in total heedlessness of self and resist not, go the second mile,
etc. But once other neighbors are near and needy, our
responsibility to them must be taken into account.
Then we can hold back from extreme measures to any one
of them and seek a just distribution of our services
among them all. This is true as far as it goes. Certainly, it would be irresponsible to do a work of extreme charity for a Roman soldier in relieving his minor
burden for a second mile if I could save many lives in
a nearby town by delivering medicine to them.

The text itself gives us no warrant for inserting
either apocalytic imminence or duties to other neighbors
into the picture. However legitimate it may be to introduce these contingencies (and I have allowed the
second but disowned the first), let us assume for the
moment that only the Roman soldier and I are involved and
apocalyptic time is not a factor. Am I obligated to obey
literally these hard injunctions in absolute disregard
for my own interests, needs, and goals? To assume an
unqualified sacrificial view of agape raises insuperable rational, ethical, and existential problems. To do
so potentially invents a neo-golden rule which bids us
do unto others as they would have us do unto them. If
there are no independent grounds of moral judgment in
the inherent worth of the self to which the self can
appeal, there are no limits to which the self can be subject to the aggrandizement of any wanton bully or next
door neighbor who happens to come along. If agape is by

nature self-sacrificial, there is no guard against the
"blank check" by which the self can be tyrannized without
limit. Suppose the Roman soldier compels me to go the
third mile after I have freely gone the second, shall I
voluntarily go the fourth? Suppose he compels me to be
his servant for a year, shall I by choice make myself
his slave for a lifetime? The consequences of agape when
seen as totally sacrificial of the worth, the needs, the
rights, and the just claims of the self are intolerable.

Is a person with greater need to sacrifice indefinitely for the person with less need, the poor for the rich,
the weak for the strong, the sick for the healthy, the
oppressed for the oppressor, the helpless widow for her
cruel landlord? Are there no safeguards based on the
integrity and worth of the self to limit such exploitation? If not, love turns out not to be a guardian and
higher reference for justice, but actually to be a source
of injustice. Sacrificial love in these instances is
less "moral" than rational-equalitarian justice. If
agape as heedless of self only indicates a direction, is
taken as an illuminative rather than as a prescriptive
norm, then what is to be the operating standard of obligation? Sacrificial love as an illuminative directional
signal works very well when directed to the well-advan-
taged, the proud, the aggressive encroacher on others'
rights -- a typical sinner in classical Protestant theology. But sacrificial love as a directive to outcasts,
the weak, the helpless, the exploited is morally inferior
to the injunction to seek justice for all, including the
self.

It may be objected that these criticisms, if directed
against Reinhold Niebuhr, fail because they do not take
into account the dialectical relationship between agape
and mutual love that was intended. Perhaps, but where

does Niebuhr tell us that the self as self has rights
over against the neighbor, that agape has a justice component when the self as self is involved? For the dialectic between sacrificial love and mutual love to work,
the latter must have some independent standing ground of
its own in relation to the heedlessness of agape, and
the norm must be seen as arising in the dialectical engagement of agape and mutuality. But this does not seem
to be Niebuhr's fundamental position. Indeed, it is the
position that I am arguing against Niebuhr.

To define justice independently is just what
Niebuhr does not and cannot do, according to Gordon
Harland.[16] Justice arises as love seeks embodiment in
the world in relative structures and ambiguous situations.
But if justice has no independent reality or definition
of its own, how can love be in dialectical relationship
with it? It would appear that the dialectic is between
agape and some context, so that justice arises out of an
engagement of love with some concrete situation. Actually, Niebuhr does sometimes acknowledge that justice
has some independent status of its own, just as mutual
love does. Moreover, some formal ingredients essential
to justice can be identified by intuition and/or rational
analysis - freedom, order and equality, for example.
Reason in its search for universal principles derivable
from an inquiry into human nature and the historical
search for fulfillment can discern and validate these
elements of justice. Hence, his position has some af-
finities with classical natural law theory, although he
is critical of such theories because they typically
claim absoluteness and universality for historically
relative and contingent values and norms. His more
characteristic view, however, is that love itself is the
only essential or normative principle, itself implicitly

and partially, if not clearly and universally, apprehended in reason's own search for ultimates. In that
case, justice as the balancing of claims, needs, and interests refers to those more or less permanent or universal features which arise as love engages concrete situations. On that assumption, principles of justice
are generated from within agape. But, again, the dialectic appears not to be between love and justice but
between love and the situation which generates ideas of
justice. I prefer to see the dialectic also as an internal one between the love (sacrificial) and justice
(equalitarian) elements of what is one unified, organic
norm constituted by the tension between its polar apposites. Alternatively, in Niebuhr's defense, we might
argue that a distinction needs to be made between agape
as the absolute, illuminative norm and the contextual,
prescriptive functioning norm that arises dialectically
in specific instances. But this seems a needless com-
plication made necessary only by a deficient conception
of agape to begin with. As for Ramsey's view that any
provision made by the self is justified only if necessary
for the service of the neighbor, that may be pragmatically
and operationally a sufficient basis for the self to take
care of its own needs. But it is theoretically inadequate.

But how, then, are the "hard" sayings of Jesus to
be understood? They can be seen as the most uncomprom-
ising statement possible of the fact that nothing the
other person can do can eliminate the free, spontaneous
and unconditional affirmation of that person's inherent
worth. Neither the compulsion of the Roman soldier's
sword, the threat of the intruding attacker, the law-
suit of the coat-seeking prosecutor, nor the hatred of
the enemy can relieve us of the obligation to continue

to affirm the humanity, the value, and the welfare of
those who have no similar regard for our own personhood
-- an obligation which agape transforms into a freely
bestowed gift of benevolence and service. The overflowing compassion and boundless ministrations of love to
friend and enemy alike are stated with hyperbole -- and
even shocking exaggeration. These sayings point in a
direction but are not literal injunctions to be obeyed
without regard to circumstance or consequence. The interpreter is left to make the best of it and to apply
these utterances to the practicalities of life in light
of some intuited essence which appears to inform them.
Perhaps the best we can say is that agape creates a glad
willingness to give all and surrender all for the sake
of the neighbor in utter disregard of self, were it best
and fitting to do so given the circumstances. Jesus the
religious visionary leaves the systematic philosopher
and the ordinary believer with a perfectionist vision
of a form of love which leaves absolutely no room for the
slightest abatement of unconditional concern, unqualified regard, and unbounded beneficence toward other human beings regardless of who they are and what they do.
Its heart is not sacrifice of self but service of the
other. Hyperbole must be allowed to make its point
without leading to self-contradictory outcomes.

In the text itself the "second mile" sayings are
presented in contrast to the morality of the old order
in which the rule is "an eye for an eye and a tooth for
a tooth." Instead, in the new order one cannot return
evil for evil but must repay evil with good. The point
is that no matter what the other person does, the citizen of the coming Society of God cannot cease to honor
the worth and promote the welfare of that person. The
demand to love the other is unconditional, absolute,

unfailing, without exception. In any given situation
that might or might not require that one literally would
go the second mile, be utterly non-resistant to attack,
and so on. Whatever one might literally do must be an
expression of love in service of the needs and the true
good of the other.

G

3. Finally, agape may be seen as counting the needs
and the good of the neighbor equal to ones own. Theologians who view the essence of love in sacrificial terms
would find the congruence I have proposed between moral
philosophy and New Testament ethics offensive. I have
claimed exactly what Nygren and others reject. My argument is that the neighbor is to be loved because persons
are intrinsically valuable. I have supported this with
metaphysical assertions based on rational grounds. The
implication is that I as a human being am of equal value
with my neighbor. Moreover, my just claims can be defended even by myself. For Nygren, Niebuhr, Ramsey, and
others in that general camp an interpretation of love
based on the metaphysical assertion of the equal worth
of self and neighbor undercuts what is distinctively
Christian. A love which counts the good of the self
equal to that of the neighbor negates the sacrificial
love revealed on the cross, which is the norm of Christian behavior.

Perhaps there is no interpretion of agape that does
not leave rough edges not easily assimilable into some
systematic scheme. The heart of the problem is to interpret sacrificial love in a way that does not negate
the self and equalitarian love in a way that does not
compromise the sacrifice of self essential to the New

Testament vision. To see love as in principle sacrificial involves consequences which destroy the very substance, spirit, and aim of love. A self which gives itself without limit to the needs and interests of others
subjects the self to a potential degradation which contradicts what love seeks. Love values persons and seeks
their fulfillment. Sacrificial love with no defense of
the self for the sake of the self allows the self to be
devalued. Sacrifice is for the sake of the other but
when it results in the indiscriminate, even if voluntary,
subjugation of the self to the tyranny of others, it
runs the risk of losing for the self what it seeks for
the other. Hence, there must be limits put on sacrifice, however much it may be a vocational necessity under
some circumstances or a spontaneous outpouring of affec-
tionate affirmation.

Moreover, the interpretation of agape in sacrificial terms has the strange consequence that such a norm
should not always be actually applied in real life because of its destructive consequences. Reinhold Niebuhr
suggests that when the life and interests of others become involved in an action or policy which also affects
the self, the sacrifice of self may actually be a betray-
al of the welfare of others. Hence, agape must be abandoned as a norm in favor of the criteria of relative
justice and mutual love.[17] Agape, of course, remains
relevant as a transcendent ideal, the "impossible possibility," which does lead us to the right policy.
Perhaps what is wrong is the strange claim that the defense of a just interest is a violation of agape because
it is undertaken by the self for itself rather than for
others. But if this direction is taken, will not equalitarian love compromise the norm of the cross and the
heedlessness of self which Jesus both taught and

illustrated in his life and death?

H

An interpretation of love can be formulated which
includes the sacrificial quality that is essential to
agape without negating the self and its just claims to a
good of its own. First of all, the model of selfhood
that is envisaged is not that of isolated, independent
individuals confronting each other as completely autonomous selves whose welfare is private to each. In this
view social relations have a secondary reality. Institutions like the state and church arise on the basis of
a contractual arrangement among individuals. Even on
this individualistic conception sacrifice of self is
called for by equalitarian love when the neighbor's need
exceeds that of the self. Social nominalism, however,
is not an adequate rendering of the facts. Nor is it the
best basis for grounding the moral norm of agape.

The alternative view is that the self is both autonomous and related in its essence. We are distinct individuals, particular and specific. If I drop a stone on
my toe, only I feel the pain in the strictest and proper
sense, however much others may sympathize and even cry
with me. We have to believe and to die for ourselves.
"You gotta' walk that lonesome valley. No one else can
walk it for you. You gotta' walk it by yourself." Yet
we are also organically related to others biologically
and socially. Indeed, from the biological point of view
we are literally connected by organic bonds to the whole
web of life on the planet and to its complex history of
billions of years of evolutionary development. The salt
content in our blood mirrors our origin in the sea. The
very processes by which life is sustained and nourished

are dependent on the sun. More immediately, we are the
product of the union of a mother and father whose traits
live on in us. We are driven by the same sexual forces
that produced us to a union of love with another like but
different from ourselves. The fit of penis and vagina
illustrates the complementarity of male and female and
the need of another to make ourselves whole persons.
The highest fulfillment of selfhood is found in loving
and being loved in a reciprocity of giving and receiving
in which while remaining ourselves we become one with
another. In the language of Paul Tillich, selfhood --
like all beings -- is characterized by both individuality and participation.[18] We exist as individuals but in
and for community. We are born as a particular human being, but we exist in interdependence with others until
we die. We are shaped by languages, cultures, moral-
ities, philosophies, and religions which are products of
a long history of social interaction. All these mold us
before we can think for ourselves. When we learn to
think, we do so only with tools provided by our social
past, however much by our own efforts we may transcend
them and create novel futures.

Against the background of this organic understanding
of the self as both autonomous and related, we can see
why agape is a fitting ethic. Also, we can see how agape
must include both sacrificial and equalitarian elements.
Given the fact that we are discrete individuals, there
is a sense in which we do have and can enjoy a good of
our own. And if we are selfish, we can seek that good
disproportionately to the disadvantage of others. But
if we are also members one of another, there are metaphysical limits to selfishness. The highest good of the
self cannot be achieved privately but only in union with
others. Hence, agape is not an arbitrary standard

imposed externally by alien authority. Agape fits the nature and destiny of the self. Moreover, while it is indeed the will of God for humanity, the obligation to love is not an arbitrary divine command. Here, too, agape reflects the very nature and aim of an Ultimate Creative Purpose. An agape ethic is appropriate for human beings in an organic and metaphysical sense, for it is in fact, "the way, the truth, and the life." Life in love with others is the destiny for which we were made and the description of the path to the highest good.

However, if agape is to be a fitting ethic, it must include both sacrificial and equalitarian elements. As real individuals, we do have a good of our own. We have rights growing out of the intrinsic worth of our human-ity. The good and rights of each are equal to those of any other individual. But if our true and highest good requires community, then not only is selfishness out-lawed but sacrifice may be required by the risk-taking involved in reaching out to establish community with others. The ideal is a mutuality of self-actualization in loving union with another and others in which there is a reciprocity of giving and receiving, of responsibility and benefits. But sacrifice of the immediate or strictly individual good of the self may be required by the obli-gation to regard the other's good equal to one's own or to secure the larger good of the community by which one is ultimately sustained. Sacrifice grows out of the com-munal nature of the self and the obligation to meet the greater need of the neighbor, while equality is estab-lished by the fact of individuality. Yet what appears from one perspective as a sacrifice of self for the sake of community is actually an expression of the true self whose relatedness to others is integral to its own nature and essential to the self's own fulfillment. Hence, it

is metaphysically and ethically true that those who lose
life actually find life. Part of our own fulfillment is
contributing to the good of others, and the joy is not
decreased even when we may willingly give up something
that we might have justly claimed for ourselves. Hence,
sacrifice and self-realization are not always mutually
exclusive, but sometimes the former may actually be the
means toward the latter.

The same point can be made by noting with Daniel
Day Williams that the self is both social and temporal.[19]
The social nature of the self means that the self is
truly fulfilled only in loving relations with others in
community. Moreover, the self has a history in which
maturity is attained only through growth and sometimes
painful transformation. Viewed in this light, sacrifice
will inevitably come into play in the life of selves inspired by the spirit of agape which seeks the good of the
self in a community in which each gives and receives in
ways that promote the fulfillment of all. The self will
frequently find it necessary to sacrifice some present
satisfaction for the sake of future good to be enjoyed
by the self or others.

More importantly, agape requires us to give up our
exaggerated estimate of our needs and to give fully equal
consideration to the deprivations of others. The self is
obligated by love to surrender whatever it is that blocks
the full participation in the quest for justice and goodness in society. Sometimes the good of the whole may
require the sacrifice of life itself, if there is to be
a community at all. Survival and justice may be so
threatened that only the sacrifice of some can preserve
the life of the rest. However, what is usually required
is not that we give our lives but only that we give up
what is selfish, distorted, or neurotic. In intimate

relations we may need to overcome some need to dominate
or control or to learn to deal with anger forthrightly
rather than in passively aggressive ways in which we
preserve a superficial niceness. Growth toward maturity
and full sharing requires constant transformation of our
shriveled, unhealthy selves with their egocentrism and
greed. Our main problem is not that self-sacrificing
love does not often enough transcend the quest for a
mutual good. Rather it is that our selfish love seldom
rises to the heights of genuine giving and receiving in
which self and other are mutually benefited.

   Nevertheless, in the relations of individuals to
each other and in community, it must certainly be said
that abstractly the worth and welfare of the one is equal
to the other. Else neither has a sufficient basis for
serving the needs of the other. If I am not a human being who is intrinsically valuable, why should my neighbor give me food or bind up my wounds? Likewise, why
should I minister to my neighbor unless she or he is of
great worth? To say that agape does what it does because of its own nature or that agape expresses the virtue or character for the agent independently of the object provides no reason why mosquitos should not be
cared for as having equal value with human beings. If
the example is the standard one of two persons with two
available apples where only enjoyment and not survival
or nutrition is at stake, would not love as well as justice suggest that each take one apple? Enthusiastic
love might well willingly or joyously surrender its
claim for the sake of the other, but on what basis could
one argue that it had no claim to enjoy but only an obligation to give up?

I

The example of the cross can be seen as the overflowing of love so great, so rich, so full, so pure that
it willingly sacrifices all, even life itself, for the
sake of the beloved. Or it can be seen as a vocational
necessity required of Jesus because no lesser means than
the sacrifice of life could have been the instrument of
salvation for the community. The nature of agape is expressed in either interpretation. But neither removes
the equal claim of all persons for fulfillment, nor does
it eliminate the equal obligation of all to serve the
greater good of the community, even at the expense of
the sacrifice of the self when no other way will suffice
under extreme conditions. But surely the ideal good
which God wills is the fulfillment of all in a society
in which each gives equally and receives fully. Amid
the complexities, ambiguities, and contradictions of
the actual world riddled with injustice and tragedy, the
sacrifice of some for the sake of the larger good of the
community is an instrumental necessity freely chosen by
love.

Love when it is fully mature overflows with self-
giving even to the point of surrendering all for the
sake of the loved one. But this does not undermine the
claim of the self to equal regard nor does it forbid
self-seeking that is compatible with mutuality in community. Indeed, a person who was only self-sacrificing
and never sought self-realization would be lacking in
full humanity. To require as a moral obligation that
the interests of the self be universally and absolutely
sacrificed to the needs of the neighbor defeats the very
intention of divine love itself, namely, the fullest
possible realization of the potential of human beings --

all human beings -- for enjoyment, for salvation in the
Society of God.

When agape reaches the height of overflowing affec-
tion which freely bestows all gifts at whatever cost to
the self, ethics is transcended by ecstasy. Joyous enthusiasm which dances in the presence of the beloved
takes the place of rational calculation and measuring of
obligations. All talk about rules, claims, counterclaims, and comparative judgments about benefits given
and benefits received seem out of place. At this level
self-giving is not experienced by the lover as a sacrifice but as a spontaneous, unmotivated willing of the
other's good which is served in an atmosphere of rejoic-
ing. The thought of counting the costs does not arise.

At the point at which ecstatic affirmation of the
other in unrestricted gift giving flows into the ethical
realm, it merges into the felt obligation to serve the
good of the community even to the point of sacrifice of
self-realization when circumstances require it. However, love need not be thought of as sacrificial in its
ethical essence, although it may become so in vocational
service. At its center agape is equal regard for all
human beings, including the self, as of intrinsic value
whose needs and welfare lay an obligation on all who
take a moral point of view. But surely love may be
thought to transcend thought of the self at its ecstatic heights and to require sacrifice of self for the
sake of the larger good of the community without requiring that we think of love in its essence as forbidding
self-love and an equal claim of the self for fulfillment.

Indeed on its other side love may not only permit
but require the self to stand for its own rights and its
own needs even when the self has to fight for them.

Are blacks, women, Jews, Hispanics, homosexuals, and others subject to prejudice allowed by love to defend the dignity only of their fellow sufferers but never their own? If the nature of agape requires a "yes" answer, then surely a morality that would bid oppressed individuals to protect themselves for their own sake is superior because it honors justice more fully. Sacrificial love, it appears, may sometimes do less and not more than justice requires. Would agape invariably forbid a daughter who is the last remaining child of a large family from leaving home to marry and pursue her own life, even though this might deny pleasure and companionship to aging and protesting parents? Would not a union member be right in fighting for a just raise in pay, even though he or she would personally benefit from the victory? Would not some parents who consistently sacrifice their own needs and pleasures in order to assist their children be advised on the authority of agape itself to think more highly of themselves and to spend something on their enjoyment for a change? Agape does not require that we give a blank check to others that enables them to draw on our account of time, money, talent, and energy until the entire treasure is exhausted. Discrimination must be made between the exploitative whims of others and their legitimate needs. Only the latter are to be served, and not even these to the indeterminate neglect of our own welfare and desire. Agape does not demand the abandonment of dignity, self-affirmation, self-esteem, and self-worth. Nor must the service of self be justified derivatively as a secondary consequence of the obligation to serve the neighbor. My teeth are worth brushing for the sake of my health and not just so that I can have a beautiful smile for somebody else.

Love is a many splendored virtue. It is multidimensional. Around its core concern to honor the worth
of persons taken as equal bearers of human dignity form
various strategies which enable it to do its work. At
its best it is directed by creative imagination which
makes the task of serving human need and welfare into
an artistic expression of compassionate beauty. Today
it may serve the other with forgetful abandon and no
thought of reward. Tomorrow it may say, "It's your
turn, my feet hurt." Today it may show boundless compassion for the wounded, the weak, and the helpless.
Tomorrow it may angrily knock a few heads together for
the sake of social justice. It cannot be reduced to a
set of rules or to any simple formula. It is, in fact,
in its mature expressions rightfully careless about the
rules while joyfully serving the loved one in spontaneous and creative ways that do more and not less than
the rules require. What it does do in myriad ways is
to seek to knit together the human community in imaginative ways that enable potential to flower and flourish
in all human beings. It is willing to sacrifice where
necessary for the sake of the larger good, but it may
insist that the self as well as others be taken into
account when benefits are distributed.

Frequently, it must find its way where no clear
answers are available and where compromise and ambiguity
reign. Trade-offs are inevitable. Some gains must be
made at the cost of other values. Love does its best,
the best that can be done under the circumstances, and
sometimes that may not be very good. It can and may do
everything in pursuit of human welfare, justice, and
joy. What it cannot do is cease to regard any human being as worthy of its ministrations. Agape may be spoil-
ed by too much definition, by too much attempt at

precision. Yet clarity of thought about its nature may
also serve the purpose of honoring human worth in self
and others. What is clear is that the person who holds
on to private claims too tightly out of fear and inse-
curity will never discover the heights and depths and
richness of love. In self-abandonment without ceasing
to love the self, the way to the fulfillment of the
larger self is realized.

It would be tempting at this point to appeal to the
paradox of self-realization through self-sacrifice.
Jesus promised that whoever lost life for his sake and
the Gospel's would find life. Finding life through losing it can mean that the anxious, self-centered, timid
self dies to be reborn as a trusting, outgoing, bold
self who finds the fullness of joy in the praise of God
and love of neighbor. Life in the Society of God means
losing the narrow, constricted, defensive, and aggressive self that pursues material, temporal, and parochial values so that a new self can be born whose peace
and happiness are found in the grateful adoration of
God and in loving union with others in mutual giving and
receiving. This aspect of the total truth must not be
neglected. Self-giving may be done joyously with no
sense of sacrifice but only of happy reward. Mutuality
in giving and receiving may discover far deeper satisfactions than selfish living. In this way, experience
confirms the promise in the paradox of dying to the old
selfish self in order to live with greater joy in the
Society of God.

Yet there is a tragic dimension to life found in
the inescapable fact that serving some ends eliminates
others. Certain value pursuits are incompatible with
others. It is not always true that the highest good of
the self is coincident with service of others.

Self-interest and other-interest frequently exclude one
another. The young daughter mentioned previously cannot
both stay at home to comfort her parents in their old
age and pursue her own fulfillment in a career for which
she has gifts. The soldier who dies for his country in
a just war cannot live to become the poet his soul longs
to be. Jesus cannot die on the cross and live to an old
age to enjoy the blessings of earthly pleasure and human
companionship. Sacrifice of self is not always the road
to self-realization in every sense of the word, even if
the sacrifice is gladly made and supreme satisfaction is
taken in being of service to others. Sometimes a choice
has to be made between seeking the fulfillment of the
self and promoting the good of another. All that I
claim is that agape does not always rule out the former
and require the latter as a matter of principle. Unfortunately, there is no rule or formula which tells us how
to adjudicate these conflicts, tensions, and contradictions. A variety of different patterns of giving equal
due to self and neighbor present themselves. Choice requires creativity and compromise under the unyielding
norm of sacrificial-equalitarian love.

     This leads to the recognition that Paul Lehmann is
on the mark in claiming the Gospel is not so much concerned with morality as with maturity.[20] The Christian
ideal is not primarily that of a person bound to rules
and principles, even those that may be generated by the
law of love. Rules and principles are necessary to give
structure. Rules may guide, but beyond that is the goal
of a mature self motivated by gratitude for being loved
that moves out in spontaneous expression of concern for
others. Such maturity is both a gift and an achievement. When accomplished it manifests itself in a
creative pattern of living which catches up as many of

the varied possibilities for fulfillment as it can and
weaves them into the most productive network of total
human happiness as is possible for a particular person
to achieve for self and others given whatever vision and
abilities he or she has. Such a path will move through many
ambiguities and compromises on its way to seeking fulfillment for self in a community of mutual giving and
receiving in which the mature person must often make the
first move and be content with unrequited overtures of
helpfulness and love. Self-sacrifice and self-realization will find a different balance for one than another even when each is guided by the ideal of taking the
neighbor as seriously as self. Life is too complicated
and too shaped by luck, circumstance, and chance for
any general promise or prediction to hold about the possibilities of knitting together the interests of self in
a fabric that also regards every other human being of
equal worth.

What agape calls for is not the negation of the just
interests of the self or its rights to defend those interests when they are threatened. All that it forbids
is the opposite of itself -- hate, cruelty, neglect, in-
difference, selfishness. All that it requires is that
the needs and welfare of the other person are always to
be taken fully into account and never put aside. Its
essence is an unconditional, absolute, and universal
concern for other persons as having intrinsic worth and
whose claims can not be nullified either by the behavior
of the other or by the will of the agent. The imperative
of love is to do just what love requires in a given situation. In itself it is not heedless of self or sacrificial or suffering or mutual or self-seeking. It honors the worth of all persons, including the self, but
never under any circumstances excludes the neighbor

regardless of how hateful or cruel or indifferent the
neighbor is. The situation may call for sacrifice of
self or it may call for the self to defend itself
against the exploitation of others. In some cases love
may be reciprocated. In some cases it may not. In any
case love only requires what love requires.

J

It is possible to schematize the main ways relating self-love to other-love under three headings:

PURELY SELFISH LOVE	SACRIFICIAL-EQUALITARIAN LOVE	PURELY SACRIFICIAL LOVE
Love self instead of neighbor.	Love neighbor and self equally.	Love neighbor instead of self.
Self is object of love.	Self and neighbor are equally objects of love.	Neighbor is object of love.
Neighbor love is derivative and instrumental to good of self.	Sacrificial love is instrumental to mutuality and good of community.	Self love is derivative and instrumental to good of the neighbor.

The middle view, I contend, is the correct one.
The model can be further clarified by noting that the
dynamic, vital center of the model is identical with the
ideal of unconditional mutual love. This norm is contrasted with conditional mutual love, as already indicated, under the discussion of Reinhold Niebuhr's views.
Conditional mutual love is a promise to enter into a
covenant of equal giving and receiving on the condition
that the other responds in like manner. "I will love you
only and if and to the degree and as long as you love me
in a relationship of equal responsibility and benefits."

Unconditional mutual love seeks community with the other
and regards the needs and welfare of the other equal to
ones own regardless of whether the other reciprocates or
not. "I will love you and seek community with you un-
conditionally. I will stand ready to sacrifice for the
sake of that ideal without ceasing come what may. What
I seek is mutual self-realization in a fellowship of
giving and receiving in which responsibility and benefits are shared. But I will keep my part of the bargain
whether you keep yours or not. I will count your needs
equal to mine and will sacrifice my own interests for
the sake of meeting your greater needs. But I will not
cease to count my own needs as worthy of equal attention and will guard my own rights and my own just access
to my own good."

The important point here is two-fold: (1) At the
center is an ideal of a community of selves enjoying
mutual self-realization joined organically by bonds of
unconditional love in which an equality of giving and
receiving leads to the highest fulfillment possible for
each. (2) The sacrificial and the equalitarian elements
can be seen as guarding that vital center from destruction from either side. The sacrificial dimension of
love enters when the larger good of the community or the
greater need of some call for the disproportionate contribution of self-giving from others. "To each according to need, from each according to ability" is an appropriate statement of this dimension of the norm. The
equalitarian dimension of love enters when the ideal is
threatened by injustice which endangers the rights of
the self or others.

Some clarification is needed at this point. The
norm may be stated ideally and abstractly as equality
of giving and receiving designed to promote mutual

self-actualization. This assumes members of a community
and situations that are equal in every respect. Since
this is not the case, it must be said that operationally
and concretely the norm is giving and receiving appropriate to particular persons in specific contexts. Abilities and needs differ, and the relationship between them
changes with circumstances and situations. An outfield
slugger who bats .400 and frequently hits home runs will
contribute more to winning ball games than the second
baseman whose average is .250 and seldom gets more than
a single. But in no sense does the superior batter
sacrifice self-interest in contributing more to the team
than others. However, a healthy person may be required
to give up something for self in order to meet the needs
of a chronically sick or handicapped family member.
Even if this self-sacrifice is done willingly and not
thought of as a "sacrifice," nevertheless time and energy devoted to the weaker member inevitably means some
loss of enjoyment that might have resulted from seeking
self-actualization more directly. Hence, the ideal community may exhibit functional inequalities growing out
of particular situations. Love only requires that these
inequalities be appropriate modifications of the abstract
ideal of equal reciprocity of giving and receiving in the
quest for mutual self-realization. Responsibilities and
benefits are apportioned according to abilities, needs,
circumstances, context. Disproportionate giving may or
may not involve self-sacrifice. Everyone is called on
to do his/her best in the light of the ideal of equal
reciprocity.

This model may be illustrated as follows:

THE SACRIFICIAL DIMENSION	UNCONDITIONAL MUTUAL LOVE	THE EQUALITARIAN DIMENSION
Unequal self-giving instrumental to fullest self-actualization of community and meeting of unequal needs.	The ideal of mutual self-realization in a community of reciprocal giving and receiving and appropriately shared responsibilities and benefits.	Equality of rights for self and others instrumental to justice by which each person's claim to self-realization is maintained.

Another way to put this is that at the heart is an ideal which unites love and justice. Love especially indicates the unbounded self-giving for the sake of the other. Justice especially indicates the worth of every person which establishes freedom to seek self-realization equal to that of the other. In the encounter of self with the neighbor, there is a love element which leads to self-sacrifice, and there is a justice element which leads to equal regard for the self. Informing both is the will to community which generates risk taking and creative initiatives to achieve the ideal of mutual giving and receiving but which is resistant to the destruction or neglect of any. The model can be illustrated as follows:

LOVE		JUSTICE
Sacrifice of self.	Ideal of appropriately reciprocal giving and receiving in a community of mutual fulfillment.	Regard for self.

Without the sacrificial element love runs risk of falling into a calculation of cost-benefits and a balancing of accounts in which self interest subverts the interests of the neighbor and finally destroys mutuality.
Without equal regard for self love runs the risk of falling into an unjust degradation of self. Love includes
a justice element, and justice includes a love element.
They coinhere in a unity of apposites.

                              K

     The norm of Christian love implies that whenever I
am confronted with a need greater than my own, I am
called up to sacrifice my own interest in effort to meet
it. Such a view strictly insisted upon might be called
fanatical, unrelenting, and oppressive. A similar
charge has been made against act utilitarianism. If
one is obligated in every moral situation to do what
maximizes general or universal welfare, then little
freedom for self-actualization is left. Every act is
momentous. No finite set of obligations can ever be
discharged so that one can say that duty has been done.
Similarly, the love ethic of the New Testament seems to
generate a similar agenda of impossible demands so that
the self is smothered under an unbearable burden. Is it
possible to reconcile this radical ethics with a life of
adventure and joy in quest of creative self-actualization? Can one enter into a career of robust enjoyment,
seeking the full and zestful actualization of all the
rich variety of human pleasures, satisfactions, and ac-
complishments and still be a morally responsible person? Or does one have a choice between the joyful pursuit of self-actualization and burdensome moral duty to
the poor and oppressed and needy who are always with us?

This is probably the greatest dilemma of an agape
ethic. Life was given to be enjoyed, and yet in the
midst of so much misery can one be happy in ones own
success and enjoyment? A theology of creation points
one way, while the recognition of injustice and evil
leads in the opposite direction, while we wait and work
in hope for universal blessedness. The victory of
grace over law seems the most promising theological
approach by which one may preserve the integrity of
moral obligation and yet live in joyful gratitude, free
to be and to enjoy life as an accepted and acceptable
child of God. Yet, in Niebuhr's terms, where does the
possible that I can and ought to do become the impossible that I cannot morally and factually accomplish?
However much one may appeal to the grace which covers
all our sins and frees us to live in serenity and joy
in pursuit of reasonable pleasures for ourselves, that
tension which calls us into a ministry to suffering
people remains. Some neighbor somewhere is always worse
off than myself.

Is there any alternative but to mark out a clear-
ing under the umbrella of grace where we can pursue life
with joyful abandon in an adventurous quest of the richest and fullest possible enjoyments? Claiming such
space is grounded in the created goodness and inherent
worth of ones own life given and acknowledged by God.
It is permissible and necessary because of our sheer
finiteness and our limited responsibility for causing
and curing the tragedy and misery which preceded us and
now surrounds us. This recognition frees us from the
unbearable burden of taking all the world's ills upon
ourselves. Life in grace is freedom to be, to enjoy, to
pursue happiness within ones own space. Else what good

is forgiveness for sin if life is perpetually weighted
down by the enslaving power of unrelenting moral obligation? Surely part of the liberating work of grace is
freedom from the bondage of infinite moral duty! My
argument, however, is that justice and merit themselves
create some circle around us in which we can have a life
of our own in pursuit of our own self-realization.

     Yet the task of relating grace to law is never
done. How large a space shall we claim? What are the
boundaries of this freedom to be ourselves in a zestful
quest of our own self-actualization? How far shall we
distance ourselves from the anguished cries of hungry
children? How far shall we go in benign neglect in
avoiding responsibility for relieving the misery of our
neighbors that grace may abound? Where does the gift of
grace end and the demand for obedience to the heavenly
vision begin?

     Perhaps no more can be said than that the dialectic
of grace and law becomes operational in human existence
in the tension between complacency and despair. Those
who are enslaved by the despair of never being able to
complete the moral task of obedience need to hear the
freeing word of grace which clears them out a space to
live and be in peace. Those who are busy with their own
selfish preoccupations or at ease in Zion in the complacency of cheap and misunderstood grace need to hear the
demand to be about the business of meeting the need of
those who suffer. The gift of grace frees us from despair. The demand of the law undercuts complacency.
Life is lived in responsible freedom between these poles
in the creative tension that preserves our space without
setting up an inviolable territory of selfish preoccupation. The other dialectic is that related to the
growth in grace toward Christian maturity by which

obligation is transformed into free, grateful, and
spontaneous loving in which what we do expresses what we
have become. The process never ends and the questions
are never fully answered. Nevertheless, in the dialectic between grace and law one may find a way to combine
a zestful quest for joy abundant and a life of moral
responsibility in a continuing quest of maturity.

Beyond establishing this basic orientation, some
additional comments further clarify the implications of
a sacrificial-equalitarian ethic for individual responsibility and public policy. The fact is that unless I
belong to the very worst off group in society, there
are always many neighbors whose need greatly exceeds my
own. Does this mean that I can never proceed to better
my own condition as long as any person is less well off
than myself? Can I never provide music lessons or a
college education for my children while a neighbor's
offspring lack food and shelter? Would a society devoted to Christian principles never build a park or tennis
court while some of its members were starving? It would
appear that agape as the principle of life for individuals in society results in acts and policies strictly
oriented to serving the worst off groups in society.
The consequence would be a one way vector which would
direct moral action toward those with the greatest deprivation. The implication is a levelling off at the
lowest level of human fulfillment. Equality for all before excellence for any is the outcome of unqualified
love.

Many of the questions raised by the equalizing
directive of love must await the development of a theory
of justice. Here it can only be said that agape does
create a bias and direction which favors the claims of
the neediest. Yet it cannot be said that all moral

action without exception is to be guided by an absolute
equalitarian policy. Some of the factors which must be
taken into account can only be listed with a promise of
further treatment later.

First, there is the tension between seeking the fulfillment of the nearest with less deprivation and the
neediest who may be far away. The nearest not only includes those in geographical proximity but those close
neighbors for whom we have a special responsibility given
our chosen roles and our natural destiny. We have immediate responsibilities as parents, spouses, and children, for example. A full account of duty would include
a vocational ethic specifying our responsibilities in
these naturally occuring lots as well as in the offices
and roles we play as workers and citizens in society.
Finally, there are those shared commitments we have in
the voluntary associations to which we belong in pursuit of the common good and social justice.

Second, there is the tension between the essential needs of survival, security and health and those
enriching values which add quality and breadth to welfare. Food is essential to life but good music may
add great meaning and joy. Sometimes the latter benefit for some must be purchased at the expense of the
former for others. To take a simple (and inadequate)
example, a rich benefactor might face the choice between endowing a symphony orchestra and giving an equal
amount to relieve immediate starvation in Africa.
(This assumes the problematic fact that in a society
guided by agape there would be rich benefactors!)

Third, tension arises between short-term and long-
term investments in human welfare. The same benefactor
might choose between giving a million dollars to buy
food in the midst of a famine in Ethiopia or sponsoring

a rural agricultural development project in Bangladesh
which would not have a pay off for nearly a decade.

Fourth, qualifications are introduced by the principle of merit, achievement, and effort. The New Testament itself contains the admonition that those who do
not work do not eat (II Thessalonians 3:6-12). At some
point love ceases giving to the lazy and insists on a
principle of justice in which each receives in accordance with contribution or merit.

Love cannot do its proper work without the assistance of creative imagination and intelligent weighing
of competing claims. It must make many compromises and
endure many trade-offs in its attempt to weave the tan-
gled threads of human possibility and need into a tap-
estry exhibiting the greatest harmony and richest fulfillment of the whole community of individuals. Love
stands beyond most human achievements as a lure and demand for a more ideal organization of human interactions
that would be more creative and more fulfilling than
the status quo. It demands more and better from us in
behalf of others than our selfish preoccupations and
skillful rationalizations of our own interests generally
produce. The heights of sacrificial-equalitarian love
are seldom reached except in a few saints or in occasional moments of intimate interaction with those nearest
and dearest to us. Agape draws us away from ourselves
to the neighbor's good. Love is a principle of continuing transformation in the lives of those open to its
influence and imperatives. It never lets us go. But
creative intelligence must guide its generous and overflowing bounty of other directed beneficence which
obstruct ideal harmonies and perfect fulfillment of all.

L

So far I have used the language of agape to explain
the meaning of Christian love. But what about eros?
Does it have any positive place in the discussion of
Christian ethics? Eros is a given fact in human life
and in all life. It is the hunger for what satisfies,
for what is good for the organism. In this form of love
the good of the self is by definition at the center.
Nygren defines eros as being by its very nature acquisitive. Granted that such love is a given in human life,
can it be Christianized? Or must it be overcome by
agape? I shall argue that eros is the natural basis for
the quest of enjoyment. Moreover, it is the ally and
counterpart of agape when it is properly understood and
transformed.

Eros is the drive for actualization of potential in
an organism. It is the energy of life that seeks survival and fulfillment. It may be identified with what
Alfred North Whitehead called the three-fold urge present in all life: to live, to live well, and to live
better. [21] It can also be identified with the characteristics of life I noted in a previous work: the drive
for self-creation, self-preservation, self-transcendence,
and self-enjoyment. It is rooted in the genetic makeup
of an organism. Living beings are born with it. It has
a biological foundation that is to be located in the
evolutionary history of life on earth. Eros is a multidimensional and variable energy that is as extensive and
broadranged as life itself. In human existence it has
physical, emotional, and spiritual aspects. It is at
one level the desire of the sexes to unite with each
other in coitus and companionship. It brings groups together in common enterprise, and it is the urge in

individuals for private ecstasy. It is the longing for
the true, the good, and the beautiful and for the vision
of God in mystical union. In short, it is the manifestation in all of its forms towards the actualization of
the potential given in the genetic materials of every
organism at conception.[22] In that sense, it is the
vitality which seeks the good, i.e., the actualization
of organismic potential. In this foundational meaning
eros is a universal fact.[23]

    However, eros may take on different historical man-
ifestation under given circumstances. Human beings interpret their existence and devise ways of life to express the vital energies present in their bodies and
spirits. They organize and direct the drive of life in
accordance with their historically-created visions of
the true, the good, and the beautiful. Civilizations
embody some characteristic Gestalt, a pattern of ideals,
values, and goals which serve as a normative guide to
living. Ethical systems, religions, and philosophies
of life lift up possible and recommended ways of directing the drive of life toward fulfillment. Agape may be
regarded as one of these historically-created visions.
As such it embodies a distinctive understanding of
human existence before God, and it results in a peculiar style of life which counts the neighbor's need
equal to ones own. Agape as human love is a willed and
spontaneous response to the goodness and grace of God
which reproduces toward the neighbor the quality of
God's action toward the self.

    How, then, do agape and eros relate to each other?
Eros is not in its essence selfish, although left to
itself it does gravitate in that direction. It is the
drive for actualization which is experienced as enjoyment (good). In that sense it is self-centered in

seeking as such the good of a particular organism or
self. This gives credence to the definition of eros as
self-regarding or acquisitive that is so prominent in
those theological interpretations which seek to contrast
eros with agape. Eros does have this tendency. Its
gravitational pull is in the direction of self-actualization, seeking the good of the self in which its energies are present and driving. However, in so far as
there is a need for community, a desire for sexual and
family relations, a quest for friendship, companionship,
common endeavors, etc., eros leads the self toward
others in a variety of ways which need not be essentially
or exclusively selfish. The energies which urge us
toward self-actualization may be sublimated and transformed in an indefinite variety of interactions which
may range from simply using others for selfish purposes
to the total negation of the self in some act of supreme
sacrifice. Eros, then, is a variable and complex drive
which may unite self-regard and other-regard based simply
on its natural and given tendencies. Certainly in sexual relations there are varying degrees of natural af-
fection and ecstatic joy in the presence of the other
person. Genetically rooted erotic urges are not necessarily wholly selfish. Sexual love takes us beyond ourselves toward the other in joyful union in which the
partner may be cherished and spontaneously affirmed.
Naturally-based human loves may in indeterminate degrees
value the neighbor as companion, friend, and fellow
sufferer. A sense of mutual need and spontaneous af-
fection based on eros itself may unite persons to each
other in healthy giving and receiving.

Human intellect, feeling, and will always intervene to direct, sublimate, transform, and otherwise
organize the natural drives of sex and hunger as well as

all the other vitalities of human life, including the
spiritual quest for union with God. The interposition
of will may corrupt the natural vitality which is eros
and direct it into a wholly self-centered style of
relating to others. Or it may elevate eros into a quest
for universal values and mutual fulfillment in which the
other takes an equal place with the self in the good
that is sought and shared. Agape may be regarded as
that transformation or organization of eros which, motivated by gratitude to the boundless benevolence of God,
reaches out toward the neighbor with unconditional regard. Agape, then, is not so much the contrary of eros
or its negation as it is a possible transformation or
organizing principle of eros. Agape redirects the
gravitational pull of eros toward self-centered self-
actualization so that the human drive for fulfillment is
constrained by the love of God manifest in Christ and
thus channeled into a way of life which counts the
neighbor's good equal to one's own.

    If with respect to agape the question is whether
the love of others excludes love of self, the issue regarding eros is whether actualization of the self's
potential includes others. Is eros irredeemably selfish? Surely, Augustine is right when he claims that the
answer depends on the object of eros. If the good of
the self is sought in what is objectively and absolutely
good, namely God, then that is in fact salvation. To
seek the good of the self in the self is the meaning
of sin. So teaches Augustine. I would argue in a
similar fashion. If the self is made for community and
for fellowship with God, then eros which has the Society
of God as its aim includes the good of the self in the
good of all in which the self shares equally but not
selfishly. Self-realization in community is indeed a

philosophical statement of the norm of the just and
good society which the theological concept of the
Society of God requires. This theme will be developed
further in succeeding chapters.

     In short, then, two ways of looking at love come to
the same point. Agape directs the self to have equal
regard for the good of the neighbor. Its distinctive
quality is that at its ecstatic heights it is heedless
of the interests of the self, although in principle the
good of the self is equal to that of the neighbor.
Eros is the natural drive which, when ethicized, bids
the self to seek its good in community with others in
the quest of mutual fulfillment. Self-interest is included without being selfish or eliminating the obligation to sacrifice self when the true good of the self
and others linked to community welfare is fundamentally
threatened.

     Using the language of eros and agape, I have argued
that agape is other-regarding without negating the self.
Transformed or ideal eros is self-regarding without negating others. The reason is that the obligation to
honor the intrinsic worth of other persons includes per-
mission if not the obligation to honor it in myself.
The directive to seek self-realization in community rests
on the assumption that the self's real good is social
and not private. At their center the good of the self
and of the other are on an equal footing. However, at
the heights of each, rational calculation gives way to
ecstatic spontaneity in which love overflows into sacrificial actions in which cost counting has no place.
Agape is a human possibility rooted theologically in the
goodness of creation and the imago dei. It fulfills
the essence or nature with which we are born. We are
made for community, for mutuality, for agape, in the

sense that its realization is the highest good of human
life. But its enactment is also a historical achievement
in life as the ideal itself is a historical product of
the Hebrew-Christian religion. When fully achieved in
an individual life, it is experienced as a gift before
it becomes a work of will. In its ideal form what is
divinely commanded and humanly willed is spontaneously
expressed. Duty becomes a joyous manifestation of con-
verted character. A good tree brings forth good fruit
as its natural product.

The assumption underlying this synthesis is that in
God Eros and Agape are identical.[24] In the divine life
Eros is the urge toward universal realization or self-
realization, that is, the actualization of all compossible (logically compatible) ideal ends over endless
time. Since the self-realization of God includes the
self-realization of all finite creatures, God's self-
love (Eros) is identical with universal love of the
cosmos and all particular individuals within it (Agape).
The Agape of God wills what the Eros of God naturally
desires. The cosmos metaphorically is God's body. The
entertainment of all ideal possibilities organized into compossible configurations for actualization during
a given cosmic epoch may be thought of as the mind of
God. Even more speculatively, one might imagine Eros
weaving a world on the frame of Space-Time in its
quest of the Good (ideal ends). The ultimate elements
which constitute the Primordial Situation would then
be Eros, Space-Time (primordial actuality), and the
good (ideal possibility). From these primal elements
arise the presently actual world still driven toward
future actualization under the drive of Eros. Eros,
as God's self-love, is identical with love of the world
and a quest for universal realization and thus is

describable as Agape. The idea of Eros weaving a world
on the primordial frame of Space-Time in quest of the
Good is identical with two previous statements. The
first is the claim in the previous chapter that the
ultimate metaphysical situation is characterized as the
possible becoming actual under the lure of the good.
The third identical statement is the one with which
this chapter began to the effect that The Will of God
is to make heaven real. All point to what is the imaginatively assumed ultimate foundation of the ethical
orientation centering around sacrificial-equalitarian
love.[25]

M

The final result of this chapter is a conception
of love which synthesizes agape and eros. The attempt
has been to point to a vital center constituted by a
dynamic balance of elements which are relatively autonomous but coinhere in a unity of apposites. Three
sets of interrelated and mutually-involving polarities
(apposites in dynamic tension) have been enumerated.
(1) One is the pull exerted between agape and eros.
Agape refers to the unbounded self-giving of persons
toward others which arises in spontaneous gratitude for
the unconditional grace and beneficence of God toward
humanity. Eros is that dynamic urge toward self-realization in persons which drives them toward sublimity
and excellence. When transformed by agape, eros becomes
a desire for union with others in a community of mutual
self-realization. Love as eros-agape becomes the ideal
and essence of normative love.
(2) A second pair of apposites creates the continuum between the religious-ecstatic and the rational-

ethical dimensions of love. Eros-agape at its heights
involves an ecstatic union with God which expresses itself in free and spontaneous outpouring of unbounded
benevolence toward others which gives unsparingly without counting the costs. Human love toward God is expressed as adoration, praise, and joyous ecstasy in the
presence of pure goodness. However, when resources are
limited in comparison to need or when the interests of
some are threatened by the selfish aggrandizement of
others, or when tragic incompatibility arises between
competing positive values, rational calculation is necessary to enable love to express its character as justice.

     (3) Cutting across and dynamically intertwined with
the first two is the tension between the sacrificial and
the equalitarian dimensions of love. Every person as
person has equal intrinsic worth and an equal claim to
self-realization. This equalitarian element is the
basis for justice. It is in balance with the sacrificial dimension of religiously inspired ecstatic agape
which serves the other in joyous abandon heedless of
self. Hence, when issues of justice have to be adjudi-
cated in the light of finite possibility and limited resources, ecstasy gives way to rational-ethical calculation. Love is just love. But its vital center is
located where its polar elements unite in a dynamic
balance of coinhering apposites.

The following diagram shows the relationship of
these three polar apposites:

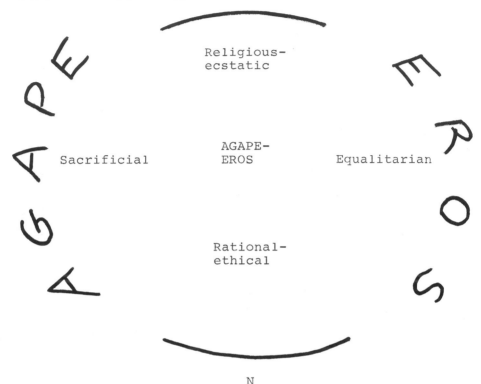

Religious-
ecstatic

Sacrificial   AGAPE-   Equalitarian
                        EROS

Rational-
ethical

N

This chapter has elaborated a conception of love
based on the New Testament. It must be admitted that
the product is an imaginative construction which creates
a <u>Gestalt</u> which unites a subjective <u>Gestalt</u> of perception
with the objective <u>Gestalt</u> of New Testament data. The
model itself is a philosophical synthesis based on a
reading of the various New Testament documents. While
I have not engaged in detailed exegesis of particular
passages, the claim is that the resulting synthesis is
not alien to the spirit of those writings and indeed
captures something integral to its essence, in so far
as such diverse materials may be said to contain an
essence at all. Without listing all the passages that

have ethical content or implications, it may be said
that in addition to the passages already discussed in
the text, the following especially contain relevant material for discussing the New Testament witness to right
conduct: Mark 1:14-15, 12:28-34; Matthew 5:1-7:28,
25:31-46; Luke 4:16-21, 10:25-37; John 15:14, 17:20-23;
Romans 12:1-15:7; I Corinthians 5:1-10:31, 12:4-31,
13:1-13; Galatians 3:1-6,10; Ephesians 4:1-6:20; Philippians 2:1-4:20; Colossians 3:1-4:6; I Thessalonians
4:1-12, 5:12-22; II Thessalonians 3:1-12; James 1:26-
2:26; I Peter 2:1-3:12; I John 4:7-21.   These ethical
passages (didache) are, of course, set within the proclamation of the kerygma, God's gracious redemption
through Jesus Christ.   They follow as describing the
ethical manifestations of faith which arises in response
to God's love toward us.   The pattern is, as I have indicated, that human love should reproduce the quality
and aim of divine love.

Several comments are in order in justifying the
model I have abstracted from the totality of the New
Testament vision.   The first is that the New Testament
does indeed stress the agapaic, the religious-ecstatic
and the sacrificial dimensions of love.   I have argued
that a systematic and comprehensive model of love has
to include also the dynamically apposite elements which
I have designated as the erotic, rational-ethical, and
equalitarian dimensions of love.   Agape love touches
and unites with these polar elements at its center but
does stand in a particular way for certain distinctive
qualities.   If it can be argued successfully that by
this synthesis I have joined together what should forever remain asunder, then I can only confess that I
stand at the boundary of Christ and culture, theology
and philosophy, revelation and reason, church and world.

My position in this regard is akin to that of Paul
Tillich, who argues that the concrete personalism of
Biblical religion has to be united with the transper-
sonal elements of the doctrine of God which arise in
the search for ultimate reality.[26]

A second observation is that many of the listed
passages do contain the elements that I have incorporated into the model of unconditional love which seeks
mutuality of self-realization in community. Organic
and corporate images pervade the New Testament. The
Society of God is a community of the faithful existing
in the complete blessedness of body and spirit in the
unity of love. In addition, Romans 12:4-8 and I Corinthians 12:12-31 are typical of the organic imagery used
to describe the ideal community. The church is a body
with many members, each with a role to play that contributes to the functioning of the whole. Reciprocal
and proportionate responsibilities are urged upon members of the body. Incarnating the mind of Christ means
considering the other as well as oneself (Phil. 2:4).
Believers are urged to love one another as Jesus loved
them (John 14:12), to bear one another's burdens (Galatians 6:2), and to bear their own load (Galatians 6:5).
Mutuality and reciprocity in community are the rule,
while at the same time a sacrificial spirit is urged
with each preferring to please the other (Romans 15:1-3,
Philippians 2:3, I Corinthians 10:24), doing all for
the sake of mutual upbuilding (Romans 14:19), assisting
the weak, needy, and immature (Romans 14:1-15). A concern for justice and merit is seen when it is said that
those who do not work should not eat (II Thessalonians
3:6-12). All of this is caught up in the model I have
elaborated which includes both sacrifice and reciprocity, self-giving and mutual helpfulness, cross bearing
and justice.

A third reflection is that not everything in the
New Testament itself conforms to the heights of agape.
I mention three items in particular: (1) while there
are equalitarian themes and passages (Galatians 3:23-28),
generally women are subordinated to men in a fashion
that agape and justice forbid (I Corinthians 14:34-35;
I Timothy 2:8-14, Ephesians 4:22-24, I Peter 3:1-7);
(2) there is a tolerance of slavery which has to be
criticized (Philemon; Ephesians 6:5-9; Colossians 3:
22-4:1); and (3) sometimes the state is assigned an
authority which is not universally justified (Romans
13:1-7, II Peter 2:13-17). Unless it can be shown that
these compromises were necessary (best under the circumstances) for contextual reasons, then it must be
said plainly that the concrete insights of the New Testament sometimes fall short of its universal norms. The
passages themselves suggest a non-contextual universality which must be questioned, although the contrary
position could perhaps be argued on good exegetical
grounds.

A final comment is that the New Testament is not
explicit about its methodology; nor does it present a
systematic model. The authors just tell us what Jesus
said, or they offer their own conclusions with little
methodological clarification as to how they relate norm
to context, agape to natural law, and so on, although
there is some concrete material in which such reasoning
is presupposed. Neither is there much guidance as to
how love and justice are to be related in the context of
an ongoing society with all the complexities, ambiguities, and compromises that entails. We are left on our
own. I can only claim that my way of doing what the
New Testament does not explicitly do has some New Testament warrant though not absolute justification as the

one and only authentic method. This is all anyone who
does not violate bounds of humility can claim, even if
some may actually be closer to the spirit of New Testament religion than others. But who is closer, and who
shall judge? And by what criteria that are themselves
not adulterated with subjectivity and relativity?

        This final comment suggests that in the strictest
sense the New Testament itself is not the norm but that
it contains the norm or witnesses to the norm. Hence,
we need to press beneath and behind the documents of the
New Testament to locate the central truth to which these
documents give witness. This central truth is that God
and the way of salvation are normatively revealed in
Jesus as the Christ. This revelatory and redemptive activity as apprehended by the Apostles and the early church
is the center and core of the Christian vision. The
New Testament is the authentic and authoritative witness
to this normative saving act. We encounter this activity and the norm of life given in it by discerning
what is the core of the New Testament witness. So, in-
directly, the New Testament is itself normative, even
though we have to discern in particular instances where
that norm is and is not being correctly interpreted by
the New Testament community and authors themselves. But
we can know the norm by which we criticize their witness
only on the basis of their core witness to the norm.
Strictly speaking, then, we imaginatively attempt to
place ourselves in the setting of the original community
itself with the indispensable aid of the New Testament.
In encounter with the normative revelation itself (the
redemptive act of God in Christ), we then interpret and
live out the meaning of Christian discipleship in the
concrete contexts of our own lives. In so doing, we
reenact the methods and procedures of the early community

itself which produced the New Testament in the first
place. But we are dependent, as they were not, on the
written deposit in which the primal revelation is auth-
entically presented to us. However much it may be the
case that the community of faith today remembers in a
vivid way those original events as transmitted through
the continuous life of the church, we are nevertheless
fundamentally dependent on that original document to
refresh our memory and, especially, to correct it again
and again.[27]

This chapter has dealt basically with interpersonal
relationships -- the moral norm as believers deal with
one or more neighbors primarily within established
structures of society. The following chapter turns to
the question of justice -- the moral norm as believers
seek for that ordering of the community that most appropriately adjudicates relationships and makes distributions among persons and groups with competing but
valid claims. This discussion has already been partly
anticipated in that love contains a justice element
even in one to one encounters while justice is the social
and structural expression of love. The next chapter
will elaborate the form and dynamics of the latter dimension of the love-justice norm.

This can be put another way. The chapter just
concluded examines the moral life mainly from the point
of view of the response of believers to the love of
God -- the quality of God's actions toward them. The
next section examines the implications of the response
of believers to the gift and promise of the Society of
God on earth -- the aim or direction of God's actions
toward them. Love and the Society of God form the two
foci of Christian ethics. Each element presupposes and
requires the other. They are interdependent apposites.

It has been a matter of convenience to develop the ethics
of love primarily in the present chapter and the ethics
of the Society of God in the one to follow. The effort
to develop the latter complements the view of justice as
communal love. The norms of the just and good society
will be elaborated as a Christian natural ethics which
develops the ideal of self-realization in community. To
show the correlation of justice, communal love, self-
realization in community, and the ethics of the Society
of God is the task that lies ahead.

CHAPTER V

THE JUST AND GOOD SOCIETY:
A First Approximation

A

Justice stands directly in the path that leads from Christian love to social policy. But what is justice? The common answer is that it is giving to everyone what is due. But what determines "what is due"? The clues to the answer that is appropriate for this essay have already been stated. Justice is communal love. This conception arises out of the fact that love contains a justice element, and justice contains a love element. Love and justice coinhere organically at a center which unites them both in a dynamic balance. The preceding chapter developed the love dimension of justice. The task now is to articulate the justice side of love with particular reference to society and the principles of social policy.

We may begin by further specifying the elements in the ethical norm arising from the dynamic tendencies of love and justice respectively. The following diagram suggests the phenomenological pattern:

LOVE	JUSTICE
Love is spirit.	Justice is structure.
Love is ecstatic.	Justice is rational.
Love is sacrificial.	Justice is equalitarian. (impartial between self and others)
Love is spontaneous and "instinctive"	Justice is calculating and deliberate.
Love transcends order and overflows rules	Justice generates and honors rules in quest of order.

Love has a latent	Justice is universal.
tendency toward	
partiality and	
particularity.	

When love and justice are viewed as a unity in dynamic tension, an answer is provided to the question as
to whether love does more or the same as justice. It is
typically said that love does more, for love and justice
are usually considered separately, with love having the
attributes listed in the left column above, while justice is made up of the elements in the right column.
But to separate them is to limit them and to deprive
both of dynamic tendencies by which they mutually complete each other.

Imagine four different situations. In the first
case identical twins come rushing into the house after
play and ask their mother for a snack. She pours them
each a glass of milk and divides the four remaining
cookies equally between them. Here love and justice
come to the same point. Love can do no more than justice, and justice can do no less than love. To give
one child three cookies would be a violation of both
love and justice. The same principle would hold if
mother were not home and the twins are left to divide
the cookies between them. Granted equal nutritional
needs and physical health, would love require that the
one twin give up one or both cookies to the other? I
have said "no" on the basis of an unconditional love
which includes an equalitarian element of justice. One
twin out of love for the other could voluntarily give
up one or both cookies to the other. But would those
who hold that the essence of agape is sacrificial
insist that one was required by that criterion to do so?
And would sacrificial love mandate that each twin do so

every time? Each trying for the sake of love to give
the other cookies might itself make for conflict and a
fight that mother would have to settle. Surely the higher ideal is an equal sharing of the common goodies in a
community of mutual enjoyment.

For the second case consider a husband and wife who
own a factory in a small town who pay better than average wages for the area. The pay rates are fair in terms
of the skills required, labor availability, the market
for the product and so on. Let us say that the wages
are "just" by community standards. Suppose the owners
determine that they could raise wages by an average of
50¢ per hour and still make a profit twice as large as
the highest paid worker. For the moment leave aside
such questions as to whether they might on the present
wage standards take the larger profits and invest them
in ways that would bring even greater prosperity to the
town. There are, of course, many other questions as well
that would have to enter into the determination of what
justice requires. For example, do the owners deserve
their higher return due to their initiative and creativity? After all, the plant is the main source of the
community's prosperity. Without it poverty and hard-
ship would increase. Leaving aside all of these issues
and simply taking the issue abstractly, the question is
whether justice would do less for the workers than love.
Here it would appear that whatever justice would require the owners to do for the workers, love could
(would?) always do more, at least up to the point of the
owners giving everything to the employees. In this example the issues get complicated, as we shall see.

Emil Brunner offers still another example of the
interplay between love and justice. The contrast he
makes is between the roles we play in official or

institutional life and the personal relations we have
with individuals. The locus of justice is in the ration-
ally-known and humanly-created orders and roles which
form the "skeleton of civilized historical humanity."[1]
Love operates in the interstices of these social networks as persons confront each other one to one. Justice is found in the rational order of systems, organizations, institutions. In the roles we play in these
orders, love can only express itself as justice. The
believer changes love "into the current coin of justice,
since that alone is legal tender in the world of systems."[2] But beyond and apart from official roles, in
our personal relations with others, love can properly
do its work. Brunner's familiar example is the judge
who must condemn the accused in strict accordance with
the law. The judge as person must somehow express a
personal solidarity with the criminal. Love will convey
a sharing of guilt, a continuing bond with and concern
for the prisoner who, as a person, has a divine destiny.
Within this framework love is not only different from
but does more than justice. While Brunner's thought as
a whole may be too sin-oriented, too pessimistic, too
dualistic, he has pointed to a dimension of the relationship between love and justice which must be taken into
account.

A fourth example may be instructive of still another dimension of the relationship between love and
justice. Currently there is a debate between advocates
of "affirmative action" and those who fear "reverse discrimination." Is it just to give preferential treatment to individuals who belong to groups that have suffered discrimination in the past in order to allow
those groups to catch up? In a familiar case recently
before the Supreme Court, Mr. Allen Bakke argued that

he was denied admission to medical school because blacks
were given preference, although he had higher scores.
If individuals are to be considered as such apart from
the total societal and historical context in which they
live, then his charge of reverse discrimination has
merit. If individuals are seen as members of groups
organically related to the history and structure of the
total society, then arguments for preferential treatment for previously excluded groups can be supported.
While there may be many creative solutions to these
issues which try to take both sides into account, there
is a real difference between looking at a person as a
discrete and separate individual as such and viewing
that person as a member of a group. In situations
where certain groups have been discriminated against in
the past, which principle does justice require in the
present? Here we have values in tension with each
other. Justice requires principles to adjudicate such
conflicts. The point is that when justice has done its
work, love can do no more. There are structural limits
which cannot be transcended. Love can only insure that
the principles of justice which are employed are the
highest, best, and most discriminating given the facts
of the case. Love cannot transcend the structural
limits and the inevitable trade-offs themselves.

Examples might be multiplied, but this is enough to
illustrate the point that sometimes love can do more or
something different from justice, and sometimes it cannot. In the first case love and justice come to the
same point -- equal division of cookies between two
children with equal needs. The other three cases are
more complex and require extended comment and the addition of some distinctions. In the instance of the married owners of the factory, it is certainly possible for

them to become sacrificial even to the point of accepting
a subsistence wage and dividing the profits entirely with
other employees (leaving aside what might be saved for
future or diversified investment for the further benefit
of the community). However, if we turn from what they
may voluntarily sacrifice for the benefit of others to
the task of setting wages and/or dividing profits among
the employees, the situation is different. Here justice
can be nothing other than "love distributed"(Joseph
Fletcher) in accordance with some principle. While the
owners can give all they have to the employees, they
cannot give all to each employee. Some principle of distribution must be used which will put limits on what
each worker will receive. One might debate whether justice requires distribution on the basis of equality,
need, merit, contribution to the company, or some combination thereof of these and other factors. But some
principle is required and inevitable. In any case, justice can only do so much, love can do no more. Neither
love nor justice can go beyond the built in limits of
the situation. With respect to themselves, the owners
have three basic options. 1. They can pay only what
the law or labor market facts require and keep the rest
for themselves (after future investment needs have been
justly taken care of). 2. They can include themselves
among the recipients of the total profits and reward
themselves in accordance with whatever principles of
just distribution apply to others. 3. They can sacrifice
their interests and retain only a subsistence wage for
themselves, dividing the rest with others. Love at its
ecstatic heights might willingly and joyfully choose
the third option. In this expression love (agape) transcends ethics. Love as ethical principle, i.e., as united
with justice, would choose option two in accordance with

the ideal of self-realization in community or mutual
love. (Here we leave aside the larger question as to
whether in the best society that communal love could en-
vision, such powerful choices about investment, wage
determination, and profit sharing would remain in private hands.)

The example of the believer who confronts a con-
demned criminal in the role of judge and as a person in
one to one relationships involves still another distinction. In this case the distinction is between office in
an organization and personal functioning within the
interstitial spaces of social networks. Here again love
can do more than justice, since there is an area of
decision above and beyond social structures. Hence,
love may express itself in a two-fold way: within the
order of justice prevailing in a social system and
beyond that in personal relationships in which mercy
and compassion can be expended. It is true that some
orders are better than others, more just, more humane,
more expressive of communal love. It is a duty to improve and transform organizations, institutions, and
laws wherever possible. Brunner himself urges this,
although he is cautious less efforts at improvement result in greater disorder and less justice. However,
even when the most just order possible has been achieved,
there are structures, limits, and laws to be observed
and roles to be played within these ordering principles.
Brunner is certainly right in imagining situations in
which love and justice require us to do what is in itself a _prima_ _facie_ evil, though right in certain contexts. The soldier who kills in wartime in the service
of a just war may be acting rightly. The general who
puts down a destructive insurrection which would cause
untold chaos and misery may be doing love's work. A

member of a SWAT team who kills a crazed gunman who has
begun to murder periodically one after another the hos-
tages whom he has cornered in a bank is preventing greater injustice and suffering. A peasant in a revolutionary army who participates in the violent overthrow of a
cruel and tyrannical regime when all non-violent means
have failed may be serving justice in the only way possible (assuming that a better order is the aim and a
reasonable prospect). Apart for "our 'office' these
things would be absolutely wrong."[3] Love's "strange
work" in preserving order and furthering justice can be
supplemented by the "more" of love's "proper work" of
healing and mercy. Love's positive work is two-fold:
(1) seeking to transform the existing orders into more
humane instruments of human fulfillment and (2) doing
works of individual charity above and beyond institutional structures.

    The fourth example involves a conflict between
values. A list of "right versus right" issues could be
extended indefinitely. Such problems will make up a
good part of the social agenda in coming decades:
economic growth versus ecological caution, equality
of opportunity versus equality of result, the right of
Nazis to march and demonstrate in a town with a large
number of Holocaust survivors, freedom to sell pornography or see X-rated movies versus the right of a community to enforce majority standards -- to name just
four more. The quest for an appropriate policy on abortion involves a nest of conflicting rights and values.
Where does a woman's freedom of choice end and the right
of the state to protect nascent personhood begin? In
conflicts between right and right, trade-offs and compromises are inevitable. Ambiguity is unavoidable. No
perfect solution is possible. Limits are built into the

structure of reality and value. Principles of justice must be elaborated which wisely and appropriately adjudicate conflicting claims and values. Once the best principles relevant to the actualities are devised under love's guidance, love can do no more.

Here is where Reinhold Niebuhr's view of the relation of love and justice is most relevant. Love, which seeks the perfect unity and harmony of life with life, transcends all social situations and all principles of approximate justice. Every institution, law, and social structure both embodies and contradicts justice. Love both judges and negates every imperfect level of achievement as falling short of love's ideal aim and points the direction toward higher and better embodiments of justice. But when justice has arrived at the highest and best principles that are relevant and applicable for the given facts, love can do no more, except stand in transcendent purity above history as an absolute ideal -- the "impossible possibility." While I would not want to conceptualize love and justice the way he does, preferring instead to see them as polar elements in tension within a unified moral norm, Niebuhr's idea that love always transforms love upward until the limits of the possible are reached is compelling.

The relations between love and justice are complex. Love both transcends justice and is fully expressed in just structures, principles, and institutions. Hence, there are times when love can do more than justice and situations in which it cannot. Justice involves allocating, distributing, balancing, measuring, and judging to determine what is due to all parties. It does so in accordance with principles which guide calculations and judgments to conclusions within the limits of the possible. When the "best justice" has been achieved

either in principle or in fact, love can do no more, for
it can only be expressed in social and structured situations as justice. Love does lure, judge, and transform
actual and proposed structures of justice toward the
highest level that is possible measured by the intent
fully to honor intrinsic human value and to promote the
widest range and depth of enjoyment. But as embodied in
accordance with its demands, love is or becomes nothing
other than justice.

     Love may do more than justice when there is an area
of action or resources over which we have control apart
from or beyond the allocative functions of love expressed in just structures. In situations where many legitimate claims are being pressed, love expresses itself
fully in the most just arrangements or distributions or
adjudications of whatever sort that are possible for
that configuration of valid interests. As a general
principle it has been suggested that love may do more
than justice in self-other situations but cannot do more
in other-other relations. This is a helpful distinction
and corresponds to the point I have made here. However,
I have argued that love has a justice element that applies even in self-other (or self-others) situations.
Justice requires impartiality and equality of treatment
among all claimants, including the self. Self-sacrifice
is called for ethically only when the neighbor's need
exceeds my own or the requirements of the ideal community
mandate it. However, beyond that love in its ecstatic
and transethical expressions may voluntarily give without limit, without counting the costs. In such total
abandon the lover is unmindful of relative claims and
interests so that joyful surrender to the loved one is
not experienced as a sacrifice but as the expression and
fulfillment of self. As achieving what the self most

truly desires, one loses life and self only to find it
in a more profound self-realization. Agape in its highest expressions always stands ready and willing to give
all for the other and will gladly do so if, when, and
where it is best to do so, all things considered.

The foregoing may have resemblances to a doctrine
of supererogation. However if that concept means that
we may voluntarily do more than God requires and hence
earn extra merit, then nothing of that sort is being
suggested. That sort of rationalistic legalism is far
removed from the personal-experiential-relational view
of morality being espoused here. Right action expressed as love toward neighbor arises spontaneously out of
gratitude to the creating-sustaining-forgiving love of
God. One loves others and seeks justice as a natural
expression of a transformed personality, as a good tree
brings forth sound fruit. Legalism is transcended in
this personal reality. Loving the neighbor is no more
an expression of what one _ought_ to do than it is a manifestation of what one _will_ do who has been reborn by
the forgiving grace of God and who lives in grateful
joy before God and neighbor. One loves because one is
or has become a loving person. Christian ethics is in
part critical reflection on what one will do when rightly related in faith to God. Nevertheless, there are
standards, principles, and norms of Christian ethics
which define what is right and, hence, what one ought
to do. Hence, ethics is both imperative (what one ought
to do) and indicative (what one will do.) Moreover,
when questions of justice arise, deliberate calculations
must be made by reason to give everyone what is due
under love's bidding. Finally, love in its ecstatic
heights naturally and spontaneously transcends rational
calculations where the self is free to give beyond the

limits of justice for self. It is within this context
that the rational-ethical requirements of justice are
transcended by the ecstatic-transethical dimensions of
agape which freely gives without limit, heedless of self.

The tension between particularity and universality
is undoubtedly the most ambiguous and problematic of
the distinctions made between love and justice. The
universalism of agape, patterned after God's love for
all persons and all creation, is well established both
in theory and in the New Testament witness on which the
theory is based. Nevertheless, there is a particularism
and partiality that appears to be present in love that
needs balancing by the corrective and guard which justice supplies. For example, the very notion of God's
election of Israel implies some special favor and regard, even if this be only the purely instrumental role
of bringing all nations to righteousness. The tension
between the scandal of particularity and the universalism of God's concern is well known in the Bible. The
same tension arises from the eschatological vantage point.
It is primarily Israel to whom the New Age of perfected
righteousness, peace, and prosperity is promised, however much others may share. It is the righteous, the
faithful, the just, the doers of good, the church, the
saints who in the New Testament witness inherit the Society of God -- the two-fold destiny that is so prominent.
Granted that the punishment of the wicked may be an act
of God's justice against the voluntary rebellion and
self-exclusion of persons from the bliss of the coming
age, nevertheless the particularism of love in the notion of election of some to inherit eternal life is also
present in the New Testament and in much orthodox theology.

While the election of some to damnation and some to

salvation may be an act of arbitrary sovereign will which
is contrary to both love and justice, love may have its
own particularism. The parable of the laborers in the
vineyard (Matthew 20:1-16) illustrates the partiality of
love poured out on those chosen by the employer. If
agape is not dependent on the worth of those to whom it
is shown, as Nygren maintains, then the particularism of
love is less vulnerable to the criticism of justice.
Since no one deserves God's love, anyone who receives it
should be grateful, while those who do not have no
grounds for complaint. While this parable may illustrate the reality of grace and the right of a sovereign
God to have mercy on whoever is chosen, the equalitarian,
universal, and impartial mandates of justice are required to complete the moral norm. While love in the
purest New Testament sense includes the universal element, later New Testament writings tend to narrow the
focus of love in its full expression to the Christian
community itself. Outka points out that a similar re-
striction hovers around the edges of Barth's view of
agape.[4]

The indiscriminate generosity of love tends to be
particular in its objects but unbounded in its outpouring
to those chosen, at least in some circumstances. For
example, if in going the second mile with one person,
one neglects duties to others who have a claim on one's
generosity, one might be accused of not proportioning
love's ministrations in accordance with the requirements
of impartial and universal justice. Love has a tendency,
then, toward expending itself without limit to those who
are loved. Unless corrected by the impartiality of
justice, it may limit the community of those to whom it
is particularly directed.

To summarize a complicated relationship, it may be

said that love patterned after God's own benevolence
toward the whole creation has its own intrinsic universalism. Nevertheless, justice is the reinforcer and
independent guarantor of impartiality and equality. As
such it provides any needed corrective to love's tendency to elect some for special and unbounded generosity
that is latent in love's uncalculated and spontaneous
ecstatic outpouring which does not count the cost to
self or observe any limits beyond what the loved one immediately present needs or can be given. Love in its
distinctive agape dimension is an act of grace. The
recipients have no claim on the supramoral beneficence
of love. Agape is a free gift. Hence, it may be poured
out on those who are elected to receive it in ways that
violate the strict requirements of impartiality and universalism.

In short, love-justice is a single but bipolar norm
whether in relation to one neighbor or many. Love requires that all be done and given that can be done and
given. Justice mandates that all be done for all, including the self. Love in the heights of its self-
abandon leads us to give up voluntarily our own claims
for the sake of others. Love goes the second mile. This
is its transforming power. Justice, with its equalitarian bent, permits us to defend our rightful claims and
to resist their being denied or infringed upon. These
two tendencies exist in dynamic balance and tension,
each drawing the other back toward the other. At the
center is the ideal of reciprocal giving and receiving
in a community of mutual self-realization. Love transforms the rational concept of calculating justice into
communal love which seeks to honor human worth to the
fullest and promote the richest and most intense enjoyments for all persons. Justice gives structure,

integrity, and proportion to love as it seeks to distribute its ministrations rightly amidst the complexities,
conflicts, trade-offs, and ambiguities of actual life.
In dynamic balance and dialectical tension, they unite
to define the whole of obligation in all human relationships.

Justice consists in giving each person or party
what is due in situations in which many or different
legitimate interests and claims are involved such that
everybody cannot have everything. If the foregoing discussion is correct, love, which seeks to meet needs and
promote enjoyment to the maximum possible, is the measure of what is due. This is a more Biblical way of
thinking than the merely formal and rational definition
of justice as impartiality between/among persons. The
righteousness of God in the Old Testament is divine
good will at work liberating the oppressed, showing compassion to the poor and needy, and bringing God's people
into a good future of peace, harmony, and prosperity.
Righteousness is God's love in action to save and to
fulfill humankind. Righteousness (tsedeq) as the pattern of divine activity establishes the norm of justice
(mishpat) for human behavior, requiring mercy for the
weak and equity for all.[5] The supreme act of righteousness is setting humankind free from the bondage of the
law in a free offer of forgiveness and reconciliation
for sinners (Romans 3:21-26). The right-making acts of
God by which we are made just by grace through faith express the character of God as both righteous and loving.
The pattern of God's activity as the norm for human
righteousness makes justice a summary term for the whole
of right living. Justice stands for "the sum total of
all goodness, of all virtue" (Emil Brunner). In the
Bible, then, human justice patterned after divine

righteousness exists in the closest organic unity with
love.

At this point the New Testament conception of the
Society of God is the realm in which God's ruling activity is liberating and fulfilling human life. This rule
will be made perfect and complete at the Endtime. History moves towards a good future of absolute blessedness
which God will inaugurate. A way in which this apocal-
yptically oriented conception can be made relevant for
use in the modern world has been discussed in a previous chapter. Here it only needs to be added that the
Society of God refers to both a present and future reality. Moreover, it is both a gift/promise and a demand.
The activity of God whose aim is the coming of the Society requires an appropriate response from those who
hear and heed its message. The fitting response is to
receive the gift/promise of liberation and fulfillment
(self-realization) with joy and gratitude and to meet
its demand by attuning our actions to God's actions in
ways that allow and promote the coming of the Society
in its fullness.

In the next section I shall argue that this relig-
iously-based conception of moral responsibility correlates positively with a philosophy of the just and
good society whose supreme norm is self-realization in
community. This social ideal is the counterpart and
complement of the definition of justice as communal
love. Love and the Society of God -- the twin foci of
Christian ethics -- will be shown to coincide with a
philosophical theory of the just and good society whose
foundations and themes will be elaborated in the pages
to follow.

B

Biblical religion leads to a concept of justice
as communal love which seeks the highest possible individual self-actualization in community with others. The
same conclusion can be reached by the methods of Christian natural ethics. To this task we now turn.

Two devices have been used in recent moral philosophy to clarify the basic principles of ethics and justice. One is the"ideal observer"(IO). The other is the
"original position" (OP). The former is associated with
Roderick Firth and others.[6] The latter has been brought
into prominence by John Rawls.[7] Inevitably the choice
of a mechanism of this type embodies certain presuppositions which affect the outcome. Each abstracts from
actual life decisions in given circumstances. This
serves a useful purpose in laying bare the fundamental
considerations of justice without the distorting effects
of self-interest and non-essential details. But each
of these imaginary instruments abstracts in different
ways. By so doing each tends to put in the background
what the other considers central. However, both together can provide a start toward the fullest and most
adequate definition of those elemental considerations
which satisfy the whole range of our moral intuitions.

THE IDEAL OBSERVER. Imagine an impartial, relevantly informed, rational, benevolent being who sets out
to construct the framework of an ideal society composed
of human beings just like us. By impartial is meant
that the IO regards all individuals alike with no preferences or prejudices toward any. The IO has at hand
all the facts about human nature, social relationships,
and facts in general which are required to make moral
judgments. By rational is meant that the IO can

construct a systematic set of theories and moral principles relevant to justice in accordance with evidence.
Rationality also includes the ability to relate means to
ends in the most efficient way. The IO is benevolent in
wanting to order society in accordance with justice and
goodness.

An IO will design a society, we may suppose, in
order to maximize the welfare and happiness of individuals. To be more specific, the aim is to enlarge to
the fullest degree possible the range and depth of satisfying experiences. Possible social orderings are
graded according to their potential for fulfilling this
end. Increasing the enjoyment which accompanies the
actualizing of human potential has two interrelated facets: publically distributable useful goods and privately enjoyed activities. The first has to do with efficiently providing for all a sufficiency of material goods
and human services necessary for a satisfying life.
No limit need be put on the quantity and variety of
goods and services produced and distributed as long as
basic needs and harmless desires are being met in ways
that do not jeopardize the claims of future generations
on available resources. The second has to do with en-
larging the opportunities for individuals to fulfill
their creative potential in contributing to the production of distributable goods and services (social
usefulness), participating as a free citizen in govern-
ance and guidance of society (political responsibility),
and in pursuing their own individual interests (personal self-expression). The latter includes religious,
recreational, aesthetic, and other activities which are
important and rewarding to individuals.

An IO will not prefer the good of one person to
that of another. Hence, the full satisfaction of each

individual is valued and desired equally. If some individuals or groups are experiencing a lower level of
enjoyment than is possible for them, an effective way
to transform the situation within the constraints of
other aims will be sought. The greatest total good for
a society is not an end as such but only as it is a
consequence of maximizing the intensity of the enjoyment of individuals.

An IO will recognize that each individual has inherent value as a creative, self-determining person
that must be protected. Also, each one requires the
freedom to pursue the common interest as a citizen and
producer of goods and services. Freedom is also required to realize self-chosen ends sought for private
enjoyment. Hence, there must be a system of rights to
secure the dignity of each person and a system of opportunities to pursue valid aims. Essentially, these
rights and liberties are those necessary for individuals
to be what they are -- creative, self-determining,
value-seeking beings who are themselves inherently valuable. Freedom will be used as a comprehensive term
to refer to these rights and liberties. First, there
is freedom from the unnecessary and damaging encroachment of others. Secondly, there is the freedom to pursue legitimate aims in the enhancement of the common
good and of private enjoyment. This includes the standard rights of democratic citizenship -- freedom to vote
and hold political office, freedom of conscience and
worship, freedom to make contracts, etc. Since an IO
will have no preferences among individuals, all rights
and liberties will be held equally. Moreover, in order
to maximize the opportunities for self-fulfillment, the
system of rights and liberties will be as extensive as
possible consistent with the equal freedom of others.

Hence, the pursuit of social and individual good must be constrained by the equal rights and equal claims of every individual.

It is obvious that I have poured content from my own mind into the formal structure provided by an IO. Such a device is inevitably circular and partially relative. It is not a fail-safe mechanism for straining out all of the subjective presuppositions which a given interpreter will bring to the situation. The IO method will not produce an absolute, pure, and universally valid set of norms persuasive to all who use it. However, it does have the merit of lifting up formal standards important to methodological procedure. Just principles are the outcome of deliberations based on rationality, impartiality, competence, relevant information, universal perspective, and benevolence. But the conclusions of those who honor these formal virtues will be a mirror image of their own subjective value commitments and ideological presuppositions. Given the recognition of the inevitable circularity and relativity that accompanies the use of this device, it can nevertheless provide a valuable starting point of ethical reflection.

THE ORIGINAL POSITION. Imagine a group of representative individuals gathered to formulate the basic principles of social interaction that would be acceptable to rational persons pursuing their own self interest, but disinterested in the welfare of their neighbors. The contract is drawn up behind a "veil of ignorance." The parties have the necessary general information about people and society needed for their work. They do not know particular facts about themselves -- their position in society, their native talents, their psychological propensities, their conception of the good life, or even to what generation they will belong.

Neither do they know the specifics of their own society, its level of economic and cultural advance, etc., although a condition of moderate scarcity is postulated. The aim is to decide what would be fair rules of procedure in a society designed to secure the cooperation of all.

These are the basic considerations laid down by John Rawls in his seminal and influential A THEORY OF JUSTICE. I will first set forth the principles of justice at which he arrives using this procedure. A criticism of his views will show the virtues and the limits both of the device itself and of Rawls' own conclusions.[8]

Certainly one principle that all would insist on is equal liberty for all. Everyone will be guaranteed the basic rights of citizenship, freedom of assembly, eligibility for office, of speech, of vote, and in general full participation in the affairs of society and state. Moreover, it is to everyone's advantage that the range of personal freedoms be as extensive as possible given an equal set of liberties for everybody else.

A second principle that will win consent is that all social goods such as liberty, opportunity, income, wealth, the basis for self-respect, authority and so on are to be shared equally, except where inequalities will benefit everyone, especially the least well off. The opportunity to have a larger share of any social good must be open to all on an equal basis.

The first principle of equal liberty takes precedence over the second principle of equal distribution. Moreover, justice has priority over efficiency and maximizing welfare.

Rawls's work has provoked an extensive literature full of praise and criticism. These evaluations cannot be catalogued here. However, it will be useful to recall

some of them to further the development of the theory of
justice that is unfolding on these pages. One question
has to do with the "maximin" principle that Rawls thinks
would be adopted. This means that persons interested in
their own welfare but disinterested in the welfare of
others will choose in the OP principles which will insure them the best of the worst possible outcomes --
the maximum minimum. Under conditions of uncertainty
when possible outcomes are unknown, one will choose principles, Rawls thinks, as if an enemy is to assign one's
social place. The two principles of justice are designed to guarantee that no matter what happens, each
person will have the best of the worst possible situations that could ever arise.

A number of critics believe that Rawls has made a
factual misjudgment about human nature and propensities.
It may well be that some people at least have a more adventurous, if not gambling, streak and would prefer to
take greater risks of loss if that opens up the possibility of larger gains. A maximax strategy may be equally
as rational as the maximin principle. I conclude that
Rawls' position is defensible but not firmly established.

More important is a criticism made in different
ways by J.R. Lucas and Robert Nozick. Even if the max-
imim strategy would be chosen, it is a counsel not of
justice but of prudence, says Lucas. It is "concerned
with my own advantage, not others' rights."[9] The force
of this objection is partially mitigated by the recognition that everyone in the OP has opportunity to establish principles that guarantee his or her own interests
and rights, so that everybody has such protection. Whatever rules guarantee my rights protect the rights of
others. However, Robert Nozick's case against the OP is
more telling. He contends that if there are rights or

benefits to which people are justly entitled and not
subject to the calculations of the OP, then Rawls' position cannot be correct. "If any...fundamental histor-
ical-entitlement view is correct, then Rawls' theory is
not."[10] Should one not be allowed to keep and control
what one justly inherits or receives as a gift from
another? In particular, any entitlements based on individual merit simply have no place in the argumenta-
tion that would take place in the OP, since no one,
strictly looking out after his/her own interests, could
be sure of having any such merit by which benefits
would be distributed and would not take that principle
into account. However, it would not seem to be such a
great violation of self-interest after all. Individuals
might reason that if they were especially meritorious,
selfishness would dictate that they insist on the reward.
One would only have to allow others the privilege of
benefitting from their merit. Only a hard-hearted ego-
tist, it would appear, would deny ones neighbors that
mild concession! Defensively, Rawls' view would protect
the person who might end up without such merit because
of laziness, lack of talent, or whatever. But, again,
as Lucas argues, that is a counsel of prudence. But is
it a principle of justice?

My own way of putting it is that there is a dilemma
between what can be called a "sense of justice" present
in our moral intuitions and the principle of self-interest at work in the OP. The common "sense of justice" present in ordinary reasoning about right and
wrong makes a place for unequal reward based on merit.
Unless inequalities based on merit (or other entitlements) are permitted, Rawls is open to the charge of
Nozick that no "entitlement theory" could ever gain acceptance in the OP. To put it otherwise, with a "sense

of justice" that grants us what we are entitled to, one
cannot get into Rawls' system. That would destroy the
rational and procedural features of the OP. But without a "sense of justice" one cannot be assured of getting justice out of Rawls' system.

The point here is that no purely procedural mechanism, whether that of the IO, the OP, or whatever,
can guarantee that just principles will emerge. The IO
and the OP have the merit of neutralizing the effects
of particular self-interests, so that impartial, rational principles can be discerned. By so doing, they
guarantee that some features essential to justice are
included, but no formal procedure alone can necessarily
guarantee all that is essential to justice. The IO at
best combines universal insights with parochial visions
of rightness and goodness. The OP guards against the
worst outcomes for everybody and provides a defense of
self-interest limited by the equality given to everybody else's self-interest, but it cannot for sure guarantee a scheme in which merit or other entitlement has
a substantial place, as required by the "sense of justice" present in our common, ordinary intuition about
what is fair.

Richard Brandt adds another way in which the conditions prescribed for the OP determine the outcome.[11]
The rule-makers in Rawls' mind think of themselves as
existing human beings. But suppose they thought of themselves as a possible human being. Would this affect
their outlook on the rightness of abortion? Or suppose
they only knew that they were to be sentient beings.
Would this influence the conception of animal rights in
relation to human rights? This only suggests again
that principles of justice that emerge from the OP
depend on the conditions that are set up. It is

questionable whether any possible set of prescriptions
for conducting the deliberations that take place in the
OP can be devised which escape this circularity. My
conclusion is that only if one prescribes the conditions
on the basis of justice (a "sense of justice") can one
guarantee that justice will emerge from the contracting
parties in the OP. But since there is no universal
agreement about justice, we are doomed to continue argument. One cannot transcend the relativity and subjectivity which characterize our different "senses of justice" by some procedural magic which will eliminate
parochial views and produce a self-evident or convincing
universalism. The criticism that has greeted Rawl's
impressive attempt illustrates the point.

   With a "sense of justice" which obviously has subjective features but without which justice cannot be
discovered, one might return to the OP. With this mod-
ification universal agreement about justice will not
likely arise, and we will be right back where we started
before the OP was invented. There is no way out of this
dilemma. Granting a "sense of justice" to the representatives in the OP readmits all those subjective, parochial, intuitive, conflicting insights about justice which
Rawls designed the OP to eliminate. The very intent of
the OP is to allow disinterested rationality to flourish procedurally to produce principles that admit self-
interest but neutralize its dangers. But that procedure generates rules that violate a widespread moral intuition about what is fair. Granted this insoluble
dilemma and using my "sense of justice" as the norm for
everyone in the OP, the principles of justice would be
rewritten as follows:

   The first principle would stand as is. The principle of equal liberty for all is sound.

A second principle that would gain acceptance is an
equal sharing of social goods, income, authority, status,
etc. except where unavoidable and necessary inequalities
benefit everyone, especially the least well off, or are
based on reasonable inheritance and gifts, or are earned.
Some inequalities may be necessary and unavoidable in
order to attract persons to essential or needed posts in
society requiring special skill, discipline, risk, ard-
uous training, efforts, etc.[12]

A policy relating to inheritances and gifts will
recognize both the legitimacy and limits of these entitlements. Contextual policies will have to be developed
to set these boundaries. The contracting parties might
well find it acceptable to allow inequality of reward
based on merit. Unfortunately, there is no simple formula for deciding when and what inequalities are justified, necessary, unavoidable, reasonable, or merited in
accordance with these basic principles. That inequalities based on unequal merit are just seems well founded.
But how merit is defined and evaluated and how much inequality merit deserves require social judgments about
which people disagree and must seek consensus and functional compromise. Unfortunately for justice the realities of political power will, in fact, be such that
self-interest may predominate over ideals agreed upon
in advance in the OP.

However, lest unfortunate circumstances, bad luck
and inferior natural assets result in a condition in
which some persons fall below tolerable levels of welfare, a minimum floor of income and other benefits
necessary to guarantee a level of decency for all should
be provided. While superior genetic endowment, fortunate family circumstances, good luck, and the like
are not deserved, persons are entitled to the benefits

that flow from them. Such unequal rewards are necessary
to satisfy the sense of aspiration and entitlement, while
a minimum set of social benefits is necessary to preserve the sense of decency and to prevent suffering.

My thesis is that by examining the results gained
from these two imaginary devices, a first approximation
of the basic principles of the just and good society can
be obtained. Each moves toward the conclusions of the
other, but both are needed to get the most complete
picture. The OP has the advantage of engaging the persons who will be citizens in a search for principles
that they would be willing to live by with their own
good in mind (but, in my revision, also with a "sense of
justice"). The emphasis here will be on formal arrangements and procedural rules which govern social interaction. The result will facilitate the discovery of minimal and irreducible principles of fairness. What it
provides primarily is a framework within which individuals could contentedly seek their own good on the basis
of their religious, philosophical, and political preferences whatever they happened to be. Moreover, agreeing
that the rules of the game were fair, they would (in
principle) freely cooperate with others for mutual advantage regardless of what their particular social position, talents, generation, and societal setting turned
out to be. The OP device results in a deontological
ethic. It produces an ordering based on principles
which are authoritative. The validity of these principles does not depend on whether they result in producing the greatest good. The concept of the good enters
primarily as individuals pursue their own ends in accordance with the basic rules of fairness. The provisions that unequal gains for some be merited, harmless
to others, or mutually beneficial is not chosen because

it maximizes the good but because it is right to do so,
i.e., the provisions were chosen in the OP.

The IO has the advantage of seeing society as a
whole from an impartial view. Given the fact that the
IO is rational and benevolent, the resulting principles
will have undeniable merit. Such an approach naturally
looks toward social arrangements which will promote the
highest good of the society or of the members who com-
pose it. The initial result is a teleological ethic.
The IO will proceed by asking how the range and depth
of experienced satisfactions can be maximized. All subsequent principles are evaluated in the light of that
ultimate purpose. It defines moral obligations in terms
of what achieves the greatest good or the highest net
balance of good over evil. However, since all individuals are valued as such, the pursuit of the good of all
or of other individuals must not infringe upon the
claims of any. Hence, the good must be sought in ways
which do not violate the rights of individuals to an
equal claim to fulfillment. The effect of this qualifi-
cation is to introduce a deontological principle within
an initial teleological orientation. In short, while
the OP focuses on the freedom and equality of individuals in pursuit of their private good, the IO focuses
on the maximizing of the good of all within the constraints of the freedom and equality of each.

Self-realization in community provides the underlying content which I pour into the structural framework provided by the OP and the IO. It is because these
devices are useful in generating and corroborating the
implications of this norm that I have found it valuable
to start with them and not because they provide by and
in themselves a complete or adequate source and test of
moral theory. Self-realization in community requires a

further and independent justification in the metaphysical
system which provides the warrant for this norm. Beyond
that, one effective and necessary test of any ethical
system is its power to elucidate and provide a grounding
for the commonly held moral intuitions of ordinary citizens. But these intuitions themselves need to be examined and criticized in the light of what is finally the
case regarding reality and value. But this brings us
back to the point of view of some interpreter of reality
and value whose claims must be tested by the whole community of those who seek to know the truth and to do
what is right and good. In short, all attempts to validate ethical reasoning are circular and finally end in
a transrational grasp of reality and value in some moment
of revelatory intuition. Out of this experience are born
foundational truths and norms for a given individual or
community from which ethical theory springs and upon
which it ultimately depends for its validation.

Using these two imaginary constructs leads to a
first approximation of the basic principles of a just
and good society. A complete theory requires an adap-
tation to particular circumstances and a filling in with
many levels of qualifying principles and relevant facts
in order even to begin to deal with the complexity of
specific ethical decisions. But at the highest level
of generality the following can be said. Abstracting
from the considerations introduced by the use of IO and
the OP, it becomes clear that there are three basic principles. Perhaps it would be more accurate to say that
initially ethical theory is subject to pulls from three
directions, each calling for unqualified adoption.
They are: maximize the good, maximize the equality of
all, maximize the liberty (freedom) of each. These three
obligations are relatively autonomous and irreducible.

Each mutually constrains and limits the other. We may
speak of the coinherence of the apposites. The just and
good society will be one in which these three principles
exist in a dynamic balance created by the pull of each
on the others. Further principles related to given
facts are needed to complete the system of justice.
Different social circumstances will require a different
ordering of priorities.

Obviously, three principles cannot be maximized.
Hence, total good, equality, and freedom cannot function
simultaneously as the first priority. But the principles
are stated this way to emphasize the fact that each is
to be sought to the fullest degree possible consistent
with the appropriate constraint of the others. How much
enjoyment or welfare is to be sought? As much as possible consistent with the equality of all and the freedom of each. How much equality is to be aimed at? As
much as possible consistent with the freedom of each
and the achievement of maximum good for all. How much
freedom should each person have? As much as possible
consistent with the well being, equality, and liberty of
others. The point is that each exerts a pull on the
other two toward a higher level of achievement. More
extensive freedom, greater equality, and an increase in
the achievement of the good are always desirable where
possible. The norms of the just and good society call
for increasing one or the other or all three when
changes for the better can be made. Equality is the
most complex of these principles and requires the greatest elaboration. In particular, the distinction between equality of opportunity and equality of result
needs to be developed and the relevance of each spelled
out. This will be done later, but for the moment the
unqualified principle must suffice in order to preserve

the simplicity of the argument.

The following simple illustrations will show both the necessity of including all three of these orders of obligation in a complete ethical theory of the just and good society.

Imagine an agrarian society that is very wealthy and in which all goods and services are divided equally among all citizens, but half the people are slaves.

Imagine a prosperous society in which equality of opportunity has been attained to such a high degree that a few hard working, ambitious people with superior genetic endowments have extremely high incomes while large numbers of people are very poor and some are starving. Consider that 80% of the income is being earned by 20% of the population, while 80% make out with the remaining 20% of the total income.

Imagine a society in which most everyone exists near the edge of starvation and that every year things get worse but that the free citizens vote to share all goods equally.

The improbability of any or all of these societies should not deter us from seeing that an indefinite number of configurations are possible in which total good, equality, and freedom can be variously related to each other. Likewise, a number of tradeoffs would appear eminently rational to our moral sensibility.

In the first case surely it would be better to have the same prosperity shared equally by free citizens. In the second case surely it would be better for all to have enough than for some to have so much and most very little. In the third case surely a hierarchical society which could overcome dire poverty and become wealthy would be an improvement over the prospect of free and equal citizens starving to death. Would the

democratic third society vote to trade places with the
slaves of the first society? Would the slaves agree to
the swap? Even if we agree that the second society is
the best of the three, do we not feel a tug in the direction of egalitarianism and sense that the great disparities of income are hard to justify? The point is
that any society that has less well-being, less equality, and less freedom than it could have is morally and
humanly defective compared to another that has more of
all three. Any gain in one or the other without a
corresponding loss of any of the others is desirable.
Any loss in one or more without a compensating gain in
one or both of the others is deplorable. Any gain in
one or two at the expense of a loss in one or both of
the others has to be weighed in the light of the totality of moral and factual considerations and interpretations of fact that intervene between this high level
of abstract generality and a specific moral choice.
But these simple illustrations do serve to establish
the fact that happiness (the experienced good that
matters in human life) equality, and freedom are the
basic moral principles of the just and good society.
At the highest level of abstract generality, the three
may be regarded as equal. However, particular weight-
ings will arise under given factual circumstances. Attention must be given later to the principles which
govern relative priority to be assigned to each factor
under a variety of dynamic configurations.

    It might be argued that actually there are two
basic principles -- maximizing total welfare and maximizing individual freedom. Equality is a regulative
principle that must be attached to each of the others.
The initial principle is that common social good is to
be shared equally among all (where no qualifying

considerations obtain). Moreover, all liberties are to
be distributed equally. Everyone will have as much
liberty as is consistent with an equal liberty for all
others. It cannot be gainsaid that there is a point
here. However, the practical result is the same. Efficiency of discussion is served if equality is added
as a third and independent principle. Also, it should
be noted that freedom and equality constitute a part
but not, by any means, all of the good or welfare that
citizens enjoy.

     The result is an intuitionistic scheme in Rawls'
definition. [13] This is the view that ethical theory
requires an irreducible family of first principles. At
this level there are no priority rules to establish
the relative weights to be assigned to each norm. We
can only judge in particular instances that this or
that combination is best. No higher order principle or
formula exists for determining that one balancing is
more just than another. One just knows intuitively
that ordering A is preferable or at least equal to B as
compared to C, which is inferior to both. I have set
forth three principles that are abstractly equal, with
weighing and balancing determined contextually by reasoning and intuition. Rawls' strictures against intuitionism so conceived are cogent. A plurality of principles
with no priority rules opens the possibility of stalemate without any recourse to rational solution. If
everyone's intuition agreed, this would pose no problem.
But sometimes intuitions conflict and may simply cancel
each other out.

     One needs either a single supreme principle, such
as utility, or a set of priority rules. Rawls takes
the second option. He solves the priority problem with
a method of lexical ordering whereby equal liberty takes

precedence over the second principle. This means that
in the OP persons would not agree to exchange a lesser
liberty for an improvement in economic conditions. Moreover, justice takes precedence over efficiency and
utility. However, Rawls acknowledges that it is impossible to eliminate an appeal to intuition entirely. We
should try to order principles where possible to avoid
a stalemate of contrary intuitions. Moreover, Rawls
himself compromises his own priority rules under conditions of poverty in which one might indeed sacrifice
equal liberty for an increase in economic welfare. The
lexical ordering is the long run tendency of a society
under conditions of moderate scarcity. But he does not
tell us how to judge when the level of welfare has been
reached that warrant his stated priority rules.[14]

Hence, the difference between my intuitionism and
his view is a relative one. I can only claim that my
way is required by the totality of factors which determine moral reality and that, on the whole, it is to be
preferred to alternatives. In one sense I do have a
single referent in addition to the three principles of
social good, freedom, and equality. Self-realization
in community has been given as the operating norm of
the theory of justice. However, that single standard
is not a superior ideal which takes precedence over the
other three. Rather the three simply spell out or
unpack what is contained in the single norm. The three
are derived analytically from the one. They are the
ways by which self-realization in community is judged.
Self-realization in community is the same norm stated
under one heading as the norm stated under three principles dynamically balanced and ordered contextually.
They are alternative statements of one and the same
supreme norm of justice. These in turn are identical

with the definition of justice as communal love.

The proposal defended here is also in Rawls' terms a mixed theory.[15] I accept his first principle of equal liberty for all. However, for the second principle of Rawls I substitute a concern for maximizing utility subject to the constraint, as will become evident, that a social minimum be maintained for all. This mixed conception combines the teleological orientation of utilitarianism with the deontological principles of equality and liberty. The difficulties of measuring utility and making interpersonal comparisons of utility are notorious and need not be rehearsed. Those difficulties will be dealt with by attempting a general definition of the good in objective terms but then urging that social policy should focus on meeting the basic needs of persons for primary goods such as food, clothing, housing, medical care, and so on. The result is not far from Rawls's alternative which would arrange society so as to maximize the welfare of the least advantaged. Both views end up practically by urging a social minimum plus special payments for sickness, unemployment, and other exceptional needs using transfer payments to the poor as a means. Beyond that the market system is allowed to create inequalities, assuming equal opportunity and fair competition. The high progressive income tax needed to support the social minimum will otherwise moderate extreme inequalities. But abstracting from the mechanism of the IO in harmony with the norm of self-realization in community, the concern to maximize the good is essential to ethical theory, despite the complications it adds to the task of measurement and comparison. In passing, it may be remarked that my conception of maximizing utility is closer to the average principle (per capita) than to the classical principle of total utility.[15]

A first approximation of the principles of the
just and good society has now been made. Beginning with
a Biblically based notion of justice as communal love,
I have tried to show how an identical norm can be arrived
at philosophically by the methods of Christian natural
ethics. This philosophical norm is centered around the
ideal of self-realization in community. To develop
this norm is the task of the following chapter. At the
moment let it be said that whatever else self-realization
in community means, it includes the goal stated by
William Frankena: "It seems to me that everyone who
takes the moral point of view can agree that the ideal
state of affairs is one in which everyone has the best
life he or she is capable of."[16] Nothing other than
this ideal is the implication of the ethics of the
Society of God.

CHAPTER VI

THE JUST AND GOOD SOCIETY:
A Second Approximation

A first approximation of the principles of the
just and good society involves three imperatives: increase happiness, enlarge the realm of individual freedom, and achieve universal equality within the constraints each places on the others. A second approximation must now be attempted in which these abstract
ideals are given more concreteness. This involves working out the meaning and logic of the three principles
themselves as well as their implications. It also requires a specification of the order of priorities that
emerges under a variety of situations. Some of the
principles and interactions that need to be spelled out
have already been touched upon or implied in the initial
inquiry using the devices of the IO and the OP.

A

THE GOOD. The good has already been defined as the
subjective enjoyment that accompanies the objective fact
of healthy functioning and fulfillment in a person.
Whatever contributes to this experience of satisfaction
can also be called good. In this section several related
dimensions of this concept require further exploration.
First of all, what is meant by the good life, the good
person, and the good society?

The Good Life
Life becomes better as the range and depth (intensity) of satisfying experiences increase. The good life
is made up of a rich texture of complex and intense enjoyments which combine contrasting elements into a

larger harmony of interests. Happiness is the accompaniment of healthy functioning in which the needs of the
objective organic structures of the body/spirit are being
met. Food, love, and meaningfulness suggest but do not
exhaust the list of requirements of the self. Happiness
is enhanced when the satisfaction of needs is comple-
mented by an appropriate and balanced network of satisfied desires. Those moral philosophers are surely partially right who maintain that something is good because
it is wanted. Part of healthy functioning and fulfillment consists in the satisfaction of those tastes, talents, and interests which are both freely chosen and expressive of what an individual peculiarly is.

The good life, then, is made up of a combination of
the desired (subjectively wanted) and the desirable
(objectively needed), the satisfying and the satisfactory. Of course, not all desires are healthy or harmless. Some wants are destructive to self and others,
sometimes by being pursued to excess and at other times
because they have become the servants of egocentrism.
Pride, arrogance, and selfishness can turn what is whole-
some when moderately pursued into something enormously
destructive to the extent that the self is falsely made
the center of all value. Hence, in the truly good life
desire must finally conform to the desirable, and wants
must be tailored to the constraints of justice. The
underlying assumption here is that at the ultimate level
the best life is that enjoyed by the good person, but
in much of actual life the two are ambiguously related
and frequently disjointed. The fact that the righteous sometimes suffer while the wicked prosper is a tale
often told. The good life is the healthy life. Just as
some foods that taste good are not healthful, particularly when consumed in excess, so the immoral may be

immediately pleasant (desired) but not ultimately whole-
some (desirable). Fact and value are another pair of
apposites which finally coinhere.

A continuum may be imagined between the minimal
organic needs of the healthy body, which are subject to
rather precise determination, and the ultimate quest of
the spirit, which is open to a wide variety of interpretations. Questions about the former can be most
relevantly dealt with by the methods of empirical
science and generally settled on the basis of accumulating evidence, while the latter are issues which philosophy and theology debate endlessly. The poles run between objectivity and subjectivity, but not in any
simple way. There is a truth about God and ultimate
values. Objective data and rational reflection are as
relevant in the realm of religion as in the field of
nutrition. Yet the range of data and the complexity of
the issues allow a wide spectrum of subjective descriptions and prescriptions, of theologies and ethical systems, which are not subject to universally convincing
proofs. Theology, then, stands at the opposite end of
the scale in this sense from physics and chemistry. The
main point here is that when it comes to matters that
arise at the pinnacle of the spirit, Buddha, Socrates,
and Jesus must all be heard, although their prescriptions for life may not be compatible in some major respects.

There is, however, a dimension of life in which
choices, preferences, and tastes may be freely expressed
in complete harmlessness. One might argue that those
serious activities and more trivial diversions which are
most complex and require the most skill ultimately are
(for a given person) more pleasurable. Certainly once

one discovers that tic tack toe can be played so that it
is impossible to lose, it is divested of its appeal,
while chess is endlessly fascinating for even the sharp-
est minds. Nevertheless, if one enjoys checkers and
prefers for whatever reasons to forego chess, who can
judge fairly between the quantitative and qualitative
pleasure each provides to its enthusiasts? Surely there
are qualitative and objective standards in art and music,
but the attempt to state and evaluate them generates
much controversy. At some point one must simply say
there is no disputing about tastes and consent to
Jeremy Bentham's dictum that "pushpin is as good as poetry" and let those who prefer each enjoy them without
pestering them with philosophical subtleties. At any
rate, justice has little stake in the questions of
whether audiences at the Grand Opera or the Grand Ol'
Opry have more enjoyment. On the other hand, John
Stuart Mill's observation that it is better to be an
unsatisfied Socrates than a satisfied pig has enormous
implications for thought and life.

What this adds up to is that the good life is that
state of excellence and healthy functioning in which
the major potentials for enjoyment are being actualized.
There are three major elements which make up the life
of dynamic organic wholeness which is experienced as
happiness. First, there are the foundational values
associated with essential needs of the body for survival, health, and security. Next are the important
psychic values associated with emotional and spiritual
well being. This includes the need to love and be loved,
to have a sense that life is meaningful and purposeful,
to belong, to have a rightful and fulfilling place in
family and society, to be just and to experience justice. In general, what is involved here is a sense of

harmony between oneself and society, the world, and
the ultimate powers and purposes that govern the cosmos (God). Finally, there are elective values which
are a matter of taste, interest, and preference. Included are what we do as fun and games, recreational
pursuits, aesthetic enjoyments, and whatever we want
to do for our own enrichment and pleasure. Individuality reigns supreme here. Recreation may be for health
as well as for fun. Aesthetic standards have objective
status. But there are few rules and not many requirements beyond what we like and want. We can, of course,
change our interests and develop more complex and hence
more enjoyable activities through learning and discipline. But this is a morally free and neutral option.
We don't have to if we don't want to.

The good life is not identical with pleasure, although it will include pleasures of various sorts,
quantitatively and qualitatively evaluated and ordered
in accordance with some rational plan. Sometimes what
is satisfying in the larger sense may be unpleasant or
painful. Moral duty, for example, may demand the
sacrifice of one's own preferences. But doing the
right is an essential ingredient in the good life of the
good person. It is the total ensemble of essential
biological needs, important psychic values, and elective choices together in a rich and vivid harmony of
contrasts which makes up that intensity of experience
which is the enjoyment of life. Finally, it is life as
a whole and the whole of life which is enjoyed. Happiness is the accompaniment of the health of the unity
of body and spirit, fully alive and functioning in fulfilling ways. We may speak of an ontological hedonism.
It is good to be. It is one's being, one's existence,
one's actuality, one's becoming as a whole person that

is enjoyed. Self-realization is another way of sugges-
ting that wholeness of life in which potentials of a
given self are being fulfilled in healthy and harmonious ways.

The good life of the good person in the good society
is the total ideal which morality is designed to serve.
Short of this final harmony are many disconnections and
much disjointedness among these three goals. In particular, individuals may experience various dimensions
of the good life but may not be good persons in the
sense of contributing to the good society or to the good
of others. The good life most often has to be sought
in a society in which justice and misery are present
in varying magnitudes.

Sometimes the very best persons cannot even be tol-
erated by society as the examples of Jesus, Socrates,
Gandhi, and King appear to show. Nevertheless, the lure
of the ultimate ideal of the universal harmony of good
persons living the good life in the good society constantly directs and draws us into those creative actions which will lessen the present ambiguity in pursuit of that supreme goal.

One caution is needed, lest the emphasis on maximizing the good be misleading. What is to be maximized
is the fulfillment of persons in community. This does
not mean a fanatical or relentless effort to enlarge
everything related to human life in quantitative terms.
"More" with respect to some things does not necessarily mean "better." The principle involved certainly
does not mean the mindless quest for unbounded production of material goods. The good life does not
mean unlimited consumption. It actually may mean moderation or even reduction in emphasis on material
things both for the sake of justice for others and for

the sake of true happiness as well. Moderation may
frequently be the path to the maximization in question
here. The good life is the happy life, the fulfilled
life, the full actualization of the genetic potential
of a given person. The ideal is that everyone should
have the best possible life of which one is capable.
Maximization refers only to the effort to increase the
goodness of life for all in a just society. While
quantitative elements may be involved, the directive
to maximize goodness is fundamentally a qualitative
measurement. Balance, proportion, and harmony may be
more important clues in this regard than simply more
of everything.

                                B

The Good Person. Another dimension of meaning is introduced by the idea of the good person. Experiencing
the good life and being a good person are related but
not identical except at the ultimate level of utopian
harmony suggested by the Biblical hope of the Society
of God. Moral excellence may be associated with personal suffering or even partly produced by it. Being
good may involve taking the suffering of others upon
oneself in order to relieve it, necessitating a sacrifice of the personal enjoyment that might have otherwise been possible. A good person is one who seeks
his/her own good in accordance with the dictates of
justice. The good of the other is counted as equal to
that of the self. Morality moves in the direction of
generality and universality. The self is not made the
center of value because it in truth is not the center.
The generality and universality sought by persons whose
aim is moral excellence include both a temporal and a

spatial reference. The relevant future is taken into
account as well as the moment. The good person seeks
his/her good as a part of the common good and the good
of all. It is an inclusive and not an exclusive search.
In the largest sense the good person seeks a harmony
between his or her individual quest for wholeness and
those purposive tendencies in the cosmos which promote
the universal good of the whole. Somewhere between complete absorption in the immediate enjoyment of the self
and total devotion to the well being of all sentient
creatures a hundred years from now lies the path of the
good person in search of the good life.

In seeking to work out the relationship between the
individual quest for fulfillment and the enjoyment of
others, no simple distinction should be made between
self-realization and self-sacrifice. Nor is it correct to posit a premature harmony of interests between
the self and other. The truth is both somewhere between and also beyond both of these alternatives. Part
of an individual's good is the sharing in the common
purposes and achievements of the society as a whole.
Self-realization takes place in community and requires
community. We are members one of another. Participation in a community in a mutually supportive relationship of giving and receiving is integral to the good
life. Ultimately and ideally, there is a harmony between individual ends and social ends but conflict as
well as coincidence of interests abound in actual life.
Moreover, some groups gain by changes which put other
groups at a disadvantage. The complex interactions in
society mean that ambiguity can never be overcome. An
approximation of justice is the best that can be hoped
for.

A more precise definition of the life of the good

person can be arrived at by looking at the demands of
the need of others upon the actions of the self. The
specifications previously laid down imply rather stren-
uous requirements. There it was argued that every potential has a claim to fulfillment equal to that of
every other equal potential and that in principle the
potential of the self has no priority on the actions
of the self over the same potential of another person.
It would follow that one should consider another's good
equal to one's own as expressed in the imperative of
Jesus that we should love our neighbors as we love ourselves. But even more demanding is the implication
that moral action should be directed toward the filling
of the largest unrealized potential. Hence, it follows
that each person should be devoted to meeting the greatest need, whether that need be in ourselves or in
others.

Is it morally imperative, then, that every person
be oriented all the time toward honoring the worth and
serving the good of the worst of individuals or groups
in the society? The answer has to be a qualified no
for several reasons. In the first place, it would be
very difficult or impossible to do. Strictly speaking,
the consequence would be that only the interests of the
most deprived could ever be legitimately served. But
one cannot feed the hungry unless one is fed, and in
today's world where agriculture is based on technology,
the hungry cannot be fed unless there are highly edu-
cated as well as well-fed researchers and supporting
personnel. The worst off can never be easily identified or located. One faces the tension between meeting
a less severe need next door that can be met and serving
the neediest who are unidentified and far away. There
are always more hurts than one person or group or

society can ever heal, providing moral reason for the
Christian teaching of salvation of grace and prompting
Immanuel Kant to postulate immortality as the precondi-
tion for completely fulfilling one's duty.

The consequence of a policy of strictly serving the
worthiest recipients would be a rigid egalitarianism,
since moral actions, like flowing water, would level
off at the lowest point. This would mean focusing on
immediate needs only and neglecting the fact that the
greater good of all, including the worst off, requires
attention to the future and more distant goals. The
long range pursuit of excellence requires some sacrifice
of present satisfactions in the interests of superior
gains in the future. Hence, there is tension between
the immediate more severe need of some and the distant advanced good of all. Here are incommensurable
values that baffle even the most refined utilitarian
calculus. Countervailing claims arise in the less
needy in that every potential for enjoyment has some
right to the means to fulfillment. Supporting a symphony
orchestra or taking art lessons is less essential to
sheer survival but very important to some if life is to
be meaningful and satisfying.

Finally, there are the countervailing entitlements
that arise out of merit. In part what we should get is
determined by what we deserve, what we have earned.
To what extent are those who are worst off in that
position as a result of laziness, foolishness, culpable
ignorance, etc. -- factors relating to choice and effort
for which individuals themselves bear responsibility?
Blaming the victim is a favorite refuge of the irresponsible among the advantaged, but arguments are to be
settled by facts and reasoning, not by motives.

The foregoing points need to be put within the

framework of more fundamental structural considerations. It may be instructive in this connection to
compare two divergent statements. Leo Tolstoy said,
"Future love does not exist. Love is a present activity only."[1] Alfred North Whitehead argued the opposite:
"The greater part of morality hinges on the determination of relevance for the future."[2] Without claiming that these two thinkers had what follows in mind,
these two statements can be used as starting points to
distinguish two extreme polar orientations. The first
might be called nominalistic immediacy. Tolstoy held
to what Paul Ramsey called an "unenlightened unselfishness" which determined right action by blind chance.
Whoever happens to be before me at the moment with a
need that I can meet demands my whole attention. I
cannot refuse to help a freezing child here and now
because some day my children or even future children
of mine yet to be born may need the clothes I have to
give. This indiscriminate and unbounded generosity
takes the immediacy of this particular moment as the
only point of moral reference. The contrary point of
view may be called extensive universalism. Every moral
action must be examined in wider frames of reference
including both spatial and temporal extensiveness. The
ultimate context would be the effect and meaning of
this particular action for all experiencing subjects for
all time. Somewhere between the immediacy of dealing
with the one neighbor before me in the present moment
and devotion to universal good at the level of cosmic
generality lies the relevant frame of reference for
the determination of the mandates of love and justice.
     This abstract generalization can be made more con-
crete and practical by examining the biological and
social givens which provide the setting and the initial-

ly prescribed roles of moral action. To put it differently, Christian natural ethics needs some sort of
functionally equivalent notion of the created orders as
elaborated by a theologian such as Emil Brunner. The
family, the state, and the economy are the given framework within which the vocation of seeking justice and
living in accordance with love is to be carried out.
We are first to accept and adjust to these orders --
to take them as they are. Secondly, we are to work
within them to inaugurate a new line of transforming
action in accordance with the higher mandates of the
Gospel.

Put into a philosophical framework, this means the
recognition of the given organic structures of natural
and historical life into which we are born. Brunner
views the orders first of all as dykes to restrain the
chaotic disorder springing from fallen humanity's
radical sinfulness. Moreover, he so stresses the goodness of any order in so far as it is order that he
urges its maintenance as best unless the better order
can be "immediately realized without any break in continuity."[3] This latter view has prompted Reinhold
Niebuhr to urge that Brunner is more strongly motivated
by the fear of disorder than the love of justice. Nevertheless, without necessarily approving his conservative
bent, what is valid in Brunner's realism about society
can be incorporated in a more positive view of the
given orders of biological and social life into which
we are born. These circumstances define the roles or
at least provide the initial setting within which our
vocation of seeking justice and expressing love can
most properly be lived out.

Brunner's view is too pessimistic, too "sin" oriented. The orders arise, he thinks, as means of

preservation, as dykes against the sinful tendencies
of humanity. They are ways that God mercifully governs
a fallen world. While they may and do serve that purpose, it is more accurate and useful to describe these
orderings as arising naturally out of the structures of
human existence in order to meet the needs of human beings. The family arises as a means of providing a framework for the procreation and rearing of children. The
roles of parent, child, and sibling arise naturally and
inevitably out of the sexual differentiation of human
beings into male and female and out of the biological
facts of reproduction. Human cultures elaborate an as-
tonishing variety of family patterns, but the fact of
family is biologically based. The same holds true of the
economic, political, and cultural realms. Economies
arise out of a division of labor to produce necessary
goods and services for survival and enrichment. Govern-
ments arise to regulate the relationships among people,
to keep the peace, to provide law and order, to promote
justice. Both the economic and political orders emerge
out of the cooperative efforts of people to do together
what they cannot do very well or at all as separate
individuals. The cultural sphere provides a social
framework of historically-developed forms for expressing
the moral, aesthetic, religious, and truth-seeking impulses of humanity. Science, ethics, religion, philosophy, ethics, art, athletics, music, etc. develop through
socially-created forms of expression in institutions and
through creative individuals.

The created orders or social structures are not to
be thought of as rigid, static, once and for all givens.
They are dynamic, flexible, changing, and open. History
reveals an impressive variety of socially-created arrangements and institutions for the development and expression

of these human needs, drives, aims, and wants. Yet they
all are based naturally, that is, on biological structures, social needs, and spiritual aims -- all of which
are present in human nature and potential as given and
evolved in nature and history. The socially-created
forms rest on natural givens. At base they arise out
of the human self as both autonomous and related, a discrete individual and a thoroughly social being organically related to others. The resulting social orders
which are generated by human creativity out of this
natural base are channels for the fullest development of
human potential and for the achievement of the widest and
deepest range of satisfaction. More immediately, they
provide the roles and functions by which our daily life
is organized. As rooted in the nature of things, the
social orders or orderings may be appropriately thought
of as ordained by God, though not as directly willed in
any of their particular forms.

        Certain roles are determined for us biologically.
We are the children of given parents. We choose marriage
partners (if we marry) in the context of a given system
of family institutions with distinctive customs of court-
ship, sexual mores, and so on. We become the parents of
given children. All of this adds up to definite spheres
of responsibility and expectation as children, siblings,
spouses, parents, with all the connections which these
relationships entail. The time and place of our birth
gives further and wider contexts of initial placement
and opportunity within defined spheres. We are born into
some particular political, economic, cultural, moral,
and religious setting in which certain institutions and
ideologies prevail. Within these initial placements
determined for us by the accidents of birth and modified
by our emerging choices, we must find the most appropriate

role as a seeker of justice. These given and created
orderings with their relative and always imperfect embodiments of justice provide the setting and the opportunities for the contextual determination of the extent
to which we will combine accommodating and transforming
stances to the givens into which we are biologically
and socially born. We may become conservatives, liber-
als, or revolutionaries. Or we may attempt some type
of near total withdrawal into some smaller communities
in which the just and good life can only be found. All
of these are choices with respect to givens. The import
of this is to provide a structural basis for locating
and defining social roles for persons which channel
their justice-seeking impulses.

The work of the world is increasingly done by a
complicated interlocking network of interdependent organizations -- schools, hospitals, corporations, agri-
businesses, labor unions, small businesses, voluntary
agencies of every description, and government. Most
people will make their primary contribution to the order
and justice of society by finding and responsibly fulfilling a variety of roles in this network of organizations. Kenneth Boulding has pointed out that the
criticism of organizations has two dimensions -- the technical and the moral. The technical evaluation examines
how well present functions and goals are being achieved.
The moral evaluation examines the goals and functions
themselves. Technical criticism calls for "scientists."
Moral criticism calls for "saints."[4] Doing justice in
part is enabling people in organizations to be more
scientific and saintly in fulfilling their roles. This
is not far from Brunner's suggestion that within the
created orders we need first to accept, adjust, and ac-
commodate and then to change, redirect, and transform

organizations and institutions in the light of love's
imperative. In extreme instances this may require the
responsible citizen to become a revolutionary in order
to turn the world upside down, risking disorder for the
sake of achieving a more just and satisfying society.
Generally, more moderate reforms using the mechanisms
of the existing social systems will be wiser and more
effective. And a conservative role in preserving
achieved order and values also has its place. The imperatives of love-justice are mainly carried out, then, in
a two-fold way: (1) being as scientific and saintly as
possible in fulfilling our given and chosen roles in the
created orders in their multiple organizational expressions, including being to the appropriate degree a revolutionary transformist; and (2) individual acts of
charity within the more private sphere that arises within the interstices of the organizational network which
shapes our vocation.

In summary, taking the radical imperatives of
love-justice seriously, making every potential for satisfaction equal to every other as deserving actualization, counting the neighbor's need equal to our own, and
viewing the total good of the community as requiring self-
giving and sometimes self-sacrifice -- all this does not
necessarily mean adopting the indiscriminate generosity
of Tolstoy's "unenlightened unselfishness." Nominalistic immediacy may have been more relevant for the
early Christian community due to the expectation that
the present social order would end soon, although I have
indicated the limits of this claim. Perhaps more important is the fact that the early Christians were by
and large of peasant stock who simply by social lot had
no responsibility for the preservation of the social
order, although they were enjoined to be obedient

citizens of the state (Romans 13:1-7; I Peter 2:13-17).
The result of this, according to Whitehead, was that
"with passionate earnestness they gave free reign to
their absolute ethical intuitions respecting ideal possibilities without a thought of the preservation of society."[5]   The Roman Empire could not have functioned on
the basis of the injunction to forgive seventy times
seven. These impractical absolutes, most relevant
where nominalistic immediacy is appropriate, were no
basis then or now for the running of a complex society.
Whitehead further maintains that it was in the very
perfection of these impractical ideals that the power
of Christianity lay. They provided a transcendent
gauge by which the defects of society could be measured
and thus "spread the infection of an uneasy spirit."[6]
As such these ideals were instruments of the progress of
civilization contributing to the victory of persuasion
over force.

One may argue the question as to whether the absolutism of love expressed as a philosophy of nominalistic
immediacy was ever intended to be a literally mandated
code, even for Galilean peasants in the grip of apocalyptic fervor. It certainly is not to be taken as such
today. That is, the "unenlightened unselfishness" of
Tolstoy is not literally mandated now if the created
orders of society are to be preserved and if they are
the most relevant and effective channels of moral expression, as I claim them to be. Observation of the
evolutionary process itself would seem to offer support
to this conclusion of social philosophy. The cosmic
past reveals an increasingly complex series of interdependent forms of life which suggests an intentionality
in nature that aims at complex harmonies and satisfactions.
Apart from a civilized social order with a division of

labor which facilitates human creativity, the deeper,
richer, and more intense human satisfactions are impossible. "Unenlightened unselfishness" will not generate
these finer harmonies in so far as they are dependent on
a complex social order and its organizational structure.
To sum up aphoristically, two things may be said: (1) It
appears that we cannot have the promise of Beethoven and
modern hospitals without the possibility of Hitler and
nuclear holocaust; (2) while it may properly be enjoined
on some to sell all they have and give it to the poor,
most citizens will fulfill the obligation of love-
justice by being responsible workers and voters who are
continually being transformed by "the infection of an
uneasy spirit" contracted by contact with the moral absolutes of impractical ideals. This latter inspiration
will lead them constantly to question the status quo
and to seek ways of reforming social structures in light
of moral absolutes, not eliminating the possibility of
violent overthrow of existing regimes in extreme circumstances. My own opinion is that the United States is
in need of reform not revolution.

     In short, it cannot be laid down as a strict rule
that moral action is only and always to be directed to
serving the needs of the worst off. Especially it does
not mean the adoption of a philosophy of nominalistic
immediacy. However, what does result from the principles
being advocated is a bias toward the neediest. This
bias is the moral implication of the "uneasy spirit" of
which Whitehead spoke. This stance will be at the center of individual morality and social policy. A bias
toward the neediest is the outcome both of Biblical
religion and of a Christian natural ethics centering on
the honoring of intrinsic worth and promoting enjoyment
leading to the imperative of communal love which seeks

self-realization in community.

The morally developed person will be pulled in the
direction of action for the sake of the poor, the outcasts, the deprived, the helpless, the victims of accident, disease, and social oppression, the unloved, and
the unlovely. No formula can be written with exact prescriptions for deciding between actions which promote
the higher interests of self and family and nation as
over against the more basic needs of neighbors more
distant from us. How can I decide between using my resources for giving music lessons to my children and feeding children who lack food, for buying a color TV set
and giving to the International Rescue Committee to re-
settle helpless refugees? Tensions between values that
finally become incommensurable are inevitable, even if
I have the moral good will to do what is right when I
know what morality requires. Growth toward moral excellence requires a continuing transformation of values in
which the dynamic elements are shaped into more intelligent and sensitive configurations of value priorities
tilted and pulled away from selfish rationalizations
toward more generous commitments toward the hurting and
the helpless. Beyond all human limitations or analysis
and action is the final appeal to the religious resources of grace, of divine forgiveness and shared suffering amidst the tragic conflicts of existence. An autonomous ethics divorced from the ultimate situation of
human beings involved in both finitude and sin knows
neither the heights nor the depths of existence and experience. Such an ethics finally fails both philosophically and morally.

On both pragmatic and theoretical grounds one can
argue for a vocational ethic involving a division of

labor. Our first responsibility is to care for ourselves
and for those nearest to us by blood and covenant (family) by geographical proximity (neighbors), and associa-
tional proximity (church, job, nation, etc.). It is my
duty to others more distant to meet the needs of those
nearer to me. This is no simple equation for serving all
the requirements of those nearest before providing anything for those more distant but a start in the right
direction with limited but useful practical implications.

One further point is relevant here. The ideal is
the good person living the good life in the good society.
The good person can contribute to the good life and to
the good society by maximizing enjoyments.
That course of action is best which actualizes those
possibilities which have the most potential for opening
up the widest possible range of intense satisfactions
for the largest number of people in a continuing and
expanding process. The aim is to create a network of
mutually-supportive activities with the richest combination of connected meanings and purposes possible for a
given society. The norm is dynamic organic wholeness.
Morality calls for creative, adventurous, imaginative
vision-making. That ideal is best which enables novelty
to be harmonized with established order to create a rich
texture of organic connections and mutual support. The
good person seeks to live in accordance with that
vision which continually creates new possibilities which
preserve the best of the past and which open up the most
extensive possibilities for future growth.

Creative advance does not mean primarily quantitative increase but rather enlargement and deepening of
qualitative meanings organically united into a system
of mutually sustaining activities and goals.[7] Maximizing satisfactions means to increase the range and

intensity of vivid contrasts into larger patterns of
harmony. This aesthetic model suggests a dynamic context of creative forward advance in which growth takes
place in a way that makes possible the greatest further
growth on and on. A marriage is enriched to the extent
that the couple can increase the range and depth of
meanings and aims uniting the two and then connect them
into a rich-textured harmonic intensity. This does not
mean that differences are to be submerged. Indeed
differences can add the zest and vividness of needed
contrast, as long as they are incorporated into a larger
harmony of mutually-appreciated experiences.[8] The more
organic growth occurs, the more can occur. Racial discrimination should be overcome not only because it is
just to do so but also because in the long run the larger interests of both whites and blacks are served by
mutual harmony. The family of nations can all benefit
by an international network of interdependent activities
mutually advantageous to all. However, between the ultimate harmony envisioned in utopian expectations and the
actualities of concrete life lie many intervening levels
in which individual selfishness and group self-interests
have many apparent advantages. The preference of selves
and societies for their narrowly conceived good over the
larger harmonies will always frustrate the realization
of the highest ideals. But the lure is there, and its
persuasive power is the foundation of hope for those
progressive advances toward the larger good for all.

If there is a summary statement about the good person, it is that responsible morality pulls one away
from making the self the center of value. The lure is
in the direction of universality, generality, and inclusiveness and finally toward God and the divine aims, intentions, and willing as the center of value. In more

immediate terms it means taking into account other beings
(persons first but all sentient beings ultimately). It
also means giving a place to the relevant future as a
factor in present decisions.[9] Adjudicating the demands
of self and other, present good and future potential,
involves a weighing of complex factors in accordance with
principles that have been set forth but which still
leaves gaps to be bridged by sheer intuition and partly
arbitrary choice. But any morality is insufficient
which does not constantly feel the lure of the wider context, of the larger good of the community of beings as
a whole incorporated finally in the divine struggle for
self-realization which is also world-realization.

The good person, then, is one whose actions are
tilted in the direction of the worst off, while balancing
a different ordering of obligations to those who are
closer or less needy. There will always be baffling
tensions between the claims of the neediest and the nearest, but again no morality is adequate which is not constantly transformed by a bias for the least advantaged.
Complications of fact (incommensurability among competing values) and weakness or corruption of will (egoism
overvaluing the self) require a final transmoral resolution in religious resources of grace and forgiveness. Throughout the good person is lured forward and
upward toward those ideals and actions which maximize
the maximizing possibilities for continual organic
growth in self and society which enlarge the range and
depth of intense enjoyments.

C

The Good Society.
Turning now from the good person and the good life,

it must be said that the good society is not measured by
the happiness of the total number of individuals added
up. Nor is it some measure of the well being of the
society taken as a single unit. The truth lies between
and beyond either of these extremes but is inclusive of
both. The individual is, of course, the only experiencing subject. There is no finite social organism or
communal self that experiences either pleasure or pain.
Yet there is a definable meaning of the common good which
is a part of the total good which the single self enjoys. It is the social ordering which is of primary importance here, that is, the way in which the relationships among individuals and groups are structured and
the dynamics which operate to give direction to the society as a whole. Social orders can be graded in terms
of their effectiveness in promoting the widest possible
range and depth of satisfying experiences for individuals.[10] Satisfaction includes the variety and intensity
as well as the importance of the enjoyments produced by
the optimum combination of objective needs and subjective wants.

No a priori blue print can be drawn up which details the path every society must follow. There are
many goals, many forms of beauty, many goods, and
numerous configurations of values that are productive
of satisfaction. The norms of justice and goodness are
universally applicable and relevant, but they are applicable and relevant to the particulars of a given
society in the form it has assumed out of its own distinctive past. Morality is defined contextually out
of the confrontations of universal norms and particular
situations. What is ideal depends on what is possible
for a given actuality. What is best means what is best
for this society here and now. Process is always

patterned and can be reformed under the lure of relevant
ideals, but ideals become concrete and specific for the
Gestalt that is and can be. We must look for the special
excellence possible for ancient Greece and for contemporary China, for medieval Europe and for the United
States today. Justice and goodness lure a society toward the evolution of its own peculiar perfection. Hence,
there is a relativity of morals, but a relativity that
is molded by the universal relevance of absolute ideals
dynamically arranged and ordered to fit the given.[11]

More must now be said about the location of the
good. In particular, how are we to distinguish between
the common good and individual good? Without attempting to make a complete catalogue of all elements that
make up the good society, it is possible to see a continuum which gradually moves from consideration of the society as a unit to the individual as the unit. This way
of looking at it avoids two extremes. In the one the
rights and interests of individuals are sacrificed as
needed in the service of the society as a whole. In the
other the common good is seen as merely the sum total
of individual satisfactions. The more correct view sees
the organic connection between the part and the whole.

The clearest example of the good of the whole is
perhaps seen in the provision of defense from outside
enemies. Here, in a world of nation states, the whole
society is seen as a unit. In those cases where a war
is just or relatively just, it may be possible to justify asking citizens to give their lives for the good
of the whole. Next are a range of services which
everybody wants and needs which require a universal network of facilities, such as transportation and communi-
cations systems. On a more regional level are utilities, garbage collections, police, fire protection,

schools, local roads, etc. Another grouping consists
of the more spectacular or unique natural wonders which
should be sufficiently available for everyone's enjoyment under public control, such as mountain scenery, the
great canyons, waterfalls, desert wilderness, beaches,
etc. Increasingly, we are aware of the need for con-
certed common efforts to guarantee pure air and water
as a part of the preservation of the natural environment and resources upon which survival and prosperity
depend. By and large we are talking so far about goods
and services that are either indivisible and non-
distributable or require an extensive network used in
common.

Another facet of the common good requires an economy capable of providing a sufficient quantity, quality, and variety of needed and wanted goods and services
that are divisible and distributable to individuals and
families -- food, housing, clothes, medical services,
and so on. Another element in the common good is a
political order which provides for democratic decision-
making in the determination of social priorities and
the ordering of the common life in ways that promote
life, liberty, and the pursuit of happiness.

Finally, the heritage from the past is a constituent
of the common good. In the largest sense this includes
the developed structures of the political and economic
orders as well as the sum total of all other social
inventions and physical technologies. No person living
today can take credit for this heritage, but all benefit
from it. Especially worth mentioning here are cultural
gifts from the past as distinguished from the political
and economic realms. I refer to the accumulated products of humankind's creative effort to discover,

appreciate, and express the true, the good, and the
beautiful. Reason and imagination have created realms
of meaning, morality, and religion articulated in myths,
symbols, and images of all sorts as well as in formal
structures of abstract thought. Included in the cultural heritage are the science, philosophy, theology, art,
music, literature, law, ethics, and so forth in which
the aspirations of the human spirit have been expressed.
All these dimensions of the common good require educational institutions and procedures to transmit this
treasure so that each new generation may know, enjoy, and
appreciate it as well as contribute to its enrichment.

All of the above in some sense are part of the common good in that they involve the whole. With respect
to these matters all to some extent suffer or prosper
together. The other side of the matter, however, is making these common goods available to individuals. There
is no question in the case of military defense, which is
by definition provided either to all or to none. Parks
and natural preserves owned by the society as a whole
are there for everybody, but only those who can afford
to go where they are can actually enjoy them. Whatever
is commonly held or controlled must be universally
available in fact for the picture to be complete. At
the other extreme are all those privately produced goods
and services which are exchanged in the market place for
money. While the level of prosperity and welfare in a
society as a whole may be very high, some individuals
may suffer deprivation. Hence, adequate social production must be accompanied by equitable distribution. We
have arrived now at the other end of the spectrum from
the good of the whole society considered as a unit to
focus on those areas of life in which the individual
(or the household) is the unit.

In between the society as a whole and the individual
are many intermediate levels in which what benefits some
groups may penalize others. A familiar example is in the
trade-off between inflation and unemployment. In a time
when both are threats -- stagflation -- the Phillips
curve, which correlates the ways in which one rises as
the other falls, may have limits. Doubtless there are
stubborn structural factors in the economic system which
may generate both at the same time. Nevertheless, within certain parameters it appears that measures which are
effective against inflation may increase unemployment
and vice versa. The nation's "inflation fighters" --
as Heilbroner and Thurow call them -- are drawn especially from the ranks of the poor, minorities, women, and
others.[12] Since the effects of inflation are felt (whether real or imagined) universally, sometimes there is more
pressure to reduce inflation, since only some are unem-
ployed. However, at some point the threat of unemployment becomes a political threat to incumbent politicians
as well as a national disgrace. The point is that policies designed to fight one or the other affect different
groups differently. The ideal of full employment in a
non-inflationary economy would be a common good indeed,
but that goal seems nearly impossible to achieve at the
moment.

Likewise, "affirmative action" to benefit individuals
who are members of groups who have been discriminated
against may function as "reverse discrimination" against
individuals who belong to groups especially privileged in
the past. However, these persons may not as individuals
have been responsible for the past injustices, nor may
they as individuals particularly benefit in the present
from these historical wrongs once equal opportunity for
all has been achieved. Let me illustrate. I have a son

and two daughters, all of whom in some near future may
be applying for teaching jobs. Selfishly, I would hope
that when Paul applies for a job, he will be treated as
an individual and not discriminated against because he
is a white male. I would hope that Nancy and Melissa
might be treated as members of previously disadvantaged
groups and given special preference because they are
women. However, as an impartial parent who loves all
his children equally and as a philosopher of justice, I
cannot find a clear basis for preferring one or the
other practice. I know of no way to assist disadvantaged groups in catching up quickly without hurting individuals of the current generation who belong to groups
who were oppressive in the past. We have a tragic and
unavoidable conflict of mutually-exclusive values. To
argue that one or the other policy is plainly right and
the other plainly wrong reflects a blindness to the
complexity of moral reality. Again, the point here is
that in this case there is no common good that helps
everybody. What helps some, hurts others.

The same point may be made by illustrating the
issue as a short-range/long-range problem. For example,
in some divinity schools the number of women students
is approaching 50%. Let us agree that for a variety of
educational reasons it would be desirable to have a
relatively equal number of men and women teachers. Suppose that on a given seminary faculty there are presently nine males and one female. The quickest way to get
equality would be to fire four men and hire four more
women. Many faculties today are overloaded with mid-
dle-aged white men. The way to get the best balance of
age, race, and sex would be to fire four older white
faculty. However, this would discriminate against men
who have devoted many years of faithful service to an

institution, frequently at very low salaries in the
early days. Now that they have achieved some status
and income, they are eliminated. The long-term solution would be to hire an equal number of males and
females as positions open up when faculty die, resign,
or retire. Over a period of years the faculty would
come to have an equal number of both sexes. However,
this discriminates against present women (and male)
students who may benefit from having a balanced faculty in terms of gender. The medium range solution
would be to hire only women as new positions open up
until there are five men and five women. This discriminates against young males just out of graduate
schools who, as individuals, deserve an equal chance
with the women. Is there a policy that will help
everybody without hurting anybody? I don't think so.
Aiding some discriminates against others.

Two grounds for "affirmative action" can be
specified, once true equality of opportunity has been
established. 1. If individual members of previously
advantaged groups have themselves benefited from this
historical imbalance, it is not unjust for them to take
second place now to the newly enfranchised. Converse-
ly, if members of previously disadvantaged groups have
themselves suffered in some way from these past injustices, then preferential treatment in education, employment, etc. is legitimate, even mandated. In short,
those individuals who have been helped or hurt in the
past or present by being members of certain groups may
be discriminated against or given preferential treatment in the present in order to rectify past injustice.
But once this transition has passed and everybody from
birth has equal opportunity, then preferential treatment ceases to be an instrument of justice. People who

have been hurt by being members of groups may legitimately be helped by treating them as members of groups.

2. The second legitimate reason for preferential treatment has to do with the needs of institutions
or groups. If a theological school for educational
reasons finds it important to hire women faculty, then
it may be unfortunate for qualified males to be passed
over, but it is not unjust. The same holds for other
areas of education, employment, etc. If the nation or
a region or a business needs women lawyers, in contrast
to lawyers of either sex, then preferential treatment
of women is justified. Males, who have not themselves
benefited from past discrimination against women, may
be hurt in the process. But no injustice is necessarily done anymore than occurs when a brick layer cannot
find employment because his skill is in oversupply while
other categories are undersupplied. Corrective action
is needed, but unless some injustice has been done
somewhere to cause the situation, we deal with the
tragic rather than the immoral.

The previous discussion has centered on the location of the good with respect to the distinction between individual and common good. A second consideration with respect to location has to do with the hierarchical structure of the self and the stratification
of society. Certain needs of the self are more essential to fulfillment and enjoyment than others. The
organic structures and processes of the body which
support life and health take first place, along with
enough security to insure a continuing confidence in
survival and safety. Beyond that those potentials for
the higher satisfaction which depend on the fundamental
organic health of the body and spirit can come into
play. The human quest for fulfillment inevitably turns

first to food, clothes, medical services, security, and
safety. While these do not guarantee that life will
make sense unless accompanied by a confidence in justice and purposiveness in existence, the human venture
can hardly be meaningful without them. Obviously, one
must survive before one can flourish. Yet those who
are well fed and have all the advantages that money can
buy and that society can provide in the way of material
benefits and social advantages may live miserable lives.
Boredom, despair about the meaning of life, and starvation of the spirit may be worse than physical hunger.
More people commit suicide presumably for lack of meaning than for lack of bread. Without food one cannot
live, but without love life is not worth living. The
means to exist are most essential, but the courage to
be is most important.

The relationship between what is essential for
physical survival and what is most important for the
good life is a well known contrast in moral philosophy.
The essential (the lower but foundational needs of the
body) is the basis on which what is important (the higher values of the spirit) can be actualized. The point
here is that ethical action in the just and good society will make the meeting of the most essential needs
prior to providing opportunities for the actualization
of the most important pursuits. Feed the hungry before preaching the Gospel to them -- that is the basic
rule. Food before piano lessons, but rational choices
may be made in order to reduce the cost of meeting nutritional needs in order to afford musical training.

The same problem arises in society between the af-
fluent and the poor. The former can afford the essen-
tials and still devote resources to pursuing their elective values. The latter have no such choice. Hence,

class stratification necessitates a principle of social
policy which will favor the least advantaged in society.
In practice this means identifying the worst off group
in terms of an index of primary goods and designing
policies to improve their status relative to other
groups. As the essential needs of all are met, other
options emerge within the framework of justice that may
extend opportunities for the pursuit of chosen values.

It is assumed here that the full flowering of the
human spirit in the actualization of its rich, diverse
potential rests on the essential health and security of
the body in association with what in religious terms is
called faith and hope. Faith and hope for our purposes
may be defined as a firm confidence in the basic order
and harmony of life and in the nature of things which
undergirds and generates a sense of meaning and purposiveness in human existence. Those persons who live in
faith and hope are most likely to be able to love other
people and all living beings. Love of all beings is the
cardinal ethical virtue required in citizens in a just
and good society. These three virtues arise at the apex
of human life.

However, ethics based on religious or philosophical
commitments takes as its first priority the meeting of
the essential needs of the body and of the least favored groups in society. Moral action cannot, in this
sense, create either faith or hope or love. In fact,
moral action presupposes them. But justice in society
can provide the framework in which persons can resolve
the ultimate questions of religion, morality, and meaning for themselves out of their own free search in
association with their fellows. Resolution, of course,
includes both theoretical and existential dimensions.

In summary, the meeting of essential needs is a

necessary but not sufficient condition for the fulfilling of life. Social policy and individual ethical
action should make primary the providing of the necessary in order that the sufficient may be freely sought.
Yet while feeding the hungry takes priority over preaching the Gospel to them, it may also be true that unless
some "Gospel" has been successful in inculcating the
beliefs and values which create a compassion for the
needy, the starving may go unfed. Hence, the relationship between different ordering of needs and values is
reciprocal and complex.

D

LIBERTY: Liberty is rooted in the nature of selfhood. A person should have social liberty because a
person is a metaphysically-free, that is, self-determining, being of inherent worth with a potential for enjoyment. Exercising liberty is expressing what one is.
One has and needs freedom commensurate with the worth
and potential one has. The right to life, liberty, and
the pursuit of happiness is rightly said to be inalien-
able because of an endowment by the Creator embodied in
the very structure of human nature. Human beings have
a right to exercise their freedom to protect, honor,
and enhance their worth and to actualize their potential
for enjoyment. Freedom is for the purpose of self-realization. The just and good society provides the fullest possible opportunities for the social expression
of this metaphysical freedom.

In societal relations the freedom of one can be
limited only by the just claims arising from the freedom, equality, and welfare of others. Within that
framework each person has a right equal to that of any

other person to take advantage of available resources
and opportunities for the double purpose of contributing
to the welfare of the whole and to fulfill interests
and aims peculiar to that person. In the economic
order this means freedom to pursue careers appropriate
to one's talents on the basis of equal opportunity. In
the other extreme where the common good of the whole is
involved, liberty is most legitimately restricted to
the greatest degree. The ultimate extreme would be
those severe limits placed on individual action which
truly affected the very survival of the group as a whole.
We define illegal acts that harm others as crime and
those gross betrayals of the society as a whole as
treason (e.g., committing acts of war against the U.S.
or giving aid and comfort to the enemy: U. S. Constitu-
tion). In addition, there are harmful acts of one person against another in private relationships that may
not be illegal but are immoral. People may infringe
on each other's rights and offend each other's worth in
a variety of ways that should not be an object of legislation. Some sexual interactions, for example, between consenting equals may be exploitative and wrong
but are not properly a part of the legal code.

To require motorcyclists to wear helmets is legitimate only if the welfare of persons other than the
cyclists is significantly affected. If injuries or
deaths of non-helmeted riders cause an increase in insurance rates, medical costs, or taxes for everybody,
then these factors have to be weighed against the
freedom of the motorcyclists. The case is more difficult when the effects on others are indirect. The
case is clear, of course, in prohibiting people from
driving drunk or running red lights. Here direct harm
to others is the issue.

Should the state prohibit snake-handling rituals
which sometimes might result in death to the victims of
a poisonous bite? Should the state prohibit polygamy?
May the state force parents to provide needed blood
tranfusions to their children in violation of their religious conviction? These are difficult issues because
conflicting perspectives come into play. A good case
can be made for permitting adults voluntarily to participate in religious rituals that may by their own
actions bring harm to them. Polygamy has more social
implications and involves the moral consensus of over-
whelming majorities over against the views of minorities. But why should it not be permitted, if marriages
are entered voluntarily and all spouses and children
are adequately protected. In the last case society's
right and obligation to protect children is a strong
argument in favor of providing blood transfusions to
children who would otherwise die or suffer irreparable
medical treatment. The rights of parents are extensive
but not absolute with respect to their children. Here
social judgment about the child's rights must take
precedence. Individuals may believe anything they
choose in the privacy of their own hearts. Their actions respecting others are subject at a reasonable
point to social evaluation and legislation.

The fact that cyclamates are currently kept from
the market but cigarette packages only contain a warn-
ing can be given a political explanation but not a moral
justification. Surely cigarettes can be shown to be a
more potent and inexcusable danger than cyclamates,
which have a dietary value for the obese. The line between providing information on possible harm that could
come from use of products and prohibiting their sale or
use is a difficult one. Automobiles kill thousands

each year, but society has judged that the compensating
gains outweigh the risks. Should not use of cyclamates,
as well as cigarettes, be a matter of individual, but
informed, judgment? Can anyone give a reason based on
morality and justice why alcoholic beverages can be sold
legally while marijuana cannot? Counting the deaths
caused by drunk drivers and the destructive effects of
alcoholism, which causes the greater social harm?

The consensus of social judgment regarding the
balance between individual liberty and social good is
legitimately the final appeal in many such cases. Individuals are free to campaign democratically for
change in opinion or legislation or where the issues
are judged to be of such overriding importance to engage in responsible civil disobedience. The individual
must decide when to disobey. Society must decide with
what tolerance individual deviance is to be permitted.
The result is fraught with many perils for both individual and society. Pragmatic considerations and experience, as well as the _Gestalt_ of particular circumstance, have to be taken into account in finding a way
through the thorny forest of complexities and ambiguities that arise.

Some of the most difficult issues facing American
society today have to do with social decisions regarding which areas are to be left to individual or group
freedom of choice and which are to be subjected to the
constraints of societal consensus and the coercive
power of the state.[13] In addition to the examples already commented on, a few others may be cited. If I own
a business and want to hire people to work for me,
should I have freedom of choice to employ whomever I
want. Suppose I am prejudiced against Jews, blacks,
women, and Southerners. Do I have a right to hire only

Gentile, white, male Northerners? The present legislative consensus is that I do not.

Some bioethical issues are quite thorny. We have
recently been reading of the case of Chad Green. The
courts ordered chemotherapy for two-year old Chad to
treat leukemia. The parents objected. Finally, they
fled to Mexico to have the child treated with laetrile.
Chad subsequently died. Does the state have the right
to force medical treatment on children against their
parents' will? This depends in part on the strength of
the societal consensus and of medical science regarding
the consequences of providing or withholding various
kinds of controversial treatment. Mary Northern was
taken from her house in Tennessee by the police. Her
feet had been frostbitten and then burned while she was
trying to thaw them out by an open fire. Gangrene set
in. The doctors tried to convince her to have her feet
amputated to save her life. She refused, the courts
ordered the operation anyway. Should Mary Northern have
the right of freedom of choice with respect to her own
feet and her own life? Here we would probably judge
that one consideration has to do with the mental competence of the person. But assuming sound mind and
judgmental competence, what is our verdict? In Pitts-
burgh a judge ordered a man to explain why he should
not be forced to give twenty-one ounces of bone marrow
to save the life of his 39 year old cousin. The doctor
testified that removing the marrow presented minimal
risk to the donor and offered the recipient a 50%
chance to live. Because they were cousins, the trans-
plant was likely to be successful. Should the state
force one person to give up a part of his or her own
body to save the life of another? In my view the case
would have to be a powerful one to justify this practice.

I mean that minimal risk for some relevant person and
maximal consequences for the patient where no voluntary
alternatives were available would be criteria. Even
then such a forced invasion of the body of a person is
questionable, but there are circumstances in which the
case could probably be made.

It may be useful to examine two further issues
much in dispute at the present time. To do this, I
wish to propose some mid-range principles that can assist in mediating between high abstractions and particular cases dealing with the tension between individual freedom and social constraint.

1.   The state should limit freedom of choice when
     actions resulting therefrom
     a.   will cause significant, irreparable, or
          unneccessary harm to another person or
          persons and/or
     b.   have extensive social consequences in
          violation of widely or universally held
          beliefs and values.
2.   The state should guarantee freedom of choice
     when the consequences of that choice
     a.   are limited to those making the choice
          or have trivial, beneficial, or non-objec-
          tionable effects on others and/or
     b.   involve matters on which a plurality of
          views are held based on well articulated
          principles rooted in cultural traditions
          or widely recognized moral, philosophical,
          or religious beliefs.

Under 1b, for example, Mormons have been forbidden to
practice polygamy. Under 2b freedom from combat is
permitted to conscientious objectors to war.

In the light of these principles, let us examine

the question of social policy regarding abortion and
tax exemption for schools which practice discrimination
against blacks. Consider the relationship of a mother
to a child or foetus. We would all agree that the state
should permit freedom of choice with respect to whether
a child is to be breast-fed or bottle-fed. Likewise,
we would agree that a mother should be prohibited from
killing a five year-old child because of persistent
disobedience or because he/she was an unwanted inconvenience or financial burden. The principles stated
above guide us very well in both cases toward what is
a universal consensus. But should the state prohibit
a woman from terminating an unwanted pregnancy in the
early stages, say the first trimester? Or should freedom of choice be permitted?

How shall we decide? The question comes down to
two points related to the guidelines I have elaborated.
1. How do we regard the status of the foetus? It
should be noted that the question is not primarily
when human life begins. It seems apparent that human
life begins at conception. Certainly life processes
start then. And it is human life and not cat life or
worm life that we are talking about. The precise question is when does the fertilized egg or embryo or
foetus or developing infant acquire the full status and
rights of personhood? Let it be further noted that this
is a philosophical question and not a scientific one.
Those who believe that the full status and rights of
personhood are acquired at conception rightly conclude
that the state should forbid freedom of choice with
respect to abortion. For them abortion is murder. It
is comparable in essential respects with taking the life
of a five year-old child. Those who believe that conception is the point at which a process begins which

actualizes personhood, which emerges at some later time
in pregnancy, can agree that abortion in the early
stages may, for good reason, be morally permissible.
It may serve certain legitimate rights and purposes of
the mother or parents without unduly infringing on the
rights of the foetus.   Therefore, the woman should have
the freedom to choose an abortion.

    2.   The second issue involves a tension between
two of the principles elaborated.   The anti-freedom of
choice advocates hold to one of them.   Freedom of choice
proponents lift up the other.   Anti-abortionists argue
that abortion has extensive social consequences in violation of widely-held beliefs and values.   Pro-choice
advocates argue that freedom of choice should be permitted since a plurality of views are held on this subject which have sufficient warrant in tradition, morality, or religion to give them credence.   Moreover, forbidding abortions would have extensive negative social
consequences.

    My own conclusion is that a case can be made for
permitting legal abortions by free choice in the early
stages of pregnancy.   But I believe that the case has
to be made on both grounds.   Abortion does not violate
the rights of a person with full status.   A foetus has
much actual value and even greater potential value and
should be aborted only for good and sufficient cause
and not for trivial reasons or mere inconvenience.
Moreover, the further the pregnancy proceeds the greater must be the grounds for terminating it.   Full personhood emerges over a period of time.   It is not present at the moment of conception.   The second ground
is that divergent views are held by responsible people
arguing from well articulated moral points of view
rooted in cultural traditions recognized by society.

The argument from freedom of choice alone is weak.
Those who advocate legal abortions on this ground frequently are in the forefront of those calling for coercive state action to prohibit freedom of choice to those
who would discriminate against women or blacks or homosexuals. In so doing they are in danger of being inconsistent and arbitrarily selective in choosing where
the state should or should not permit freedom of choice.
Those who argue that from the moment of conception the
full rights of personhood are present are consistent in
arguing that the state should prohibit abortion. If
the embryo or foetus is indeed an "unborn child,"
freedom of choice is not a moral option with respect to
abortion, for abortion is murder. Only if the full
personhood can be denied on responsible moral and philosophical grounds is legal abortion a permissible social policy. Some pro-choice advocates tend to ignore
or avoid this question because it is so controversial.
Abortion as a private matter of conscience and of public policy, indeed, presents us with painful dilemmas.
There is no solution that does not have unwanted but
unavoidable consequences.

Consider three people. The first believes strongly that abortion is the unwarranted termination of innocent life. The second believes that human life is a
process that begins at conception but that full personhood with all the associated rights emerges some-
time late in pregnancy. The third really doesn't know
what to believe. The second and third individuals may
consistently advocate legal abortions and freedom of
choice for individuals. But is it not inconsistent for
the first person to take the freedom of choice option?
Yet many who write freedom of choice resolutions for
churches and other groups do just this. Some of them

say, "I personally believe that abortion is wrong, but
I don't want to force my beliefs on those who disagree
with me." Would the same person also say, "I personally believe it is wrong to discriminate against women,
blacks, and homosexuals in matters of employment, but
I don't want to force my beliefs on those who disagree
with me"? Is there a relevant distinction between a
willingness to grant freedom of choice in the abortion
issue but not in matters of discriminatory hiring? If
there is, the inconsistency may only be apparent. A
person who believes both are wrong might argue like
this: "I am convinced that the defense of racial or
sexual discrimination in hiring is based on inferior
grounds, on prejudice that is without moral warrant.
However, while I finally reject it, I have respect for
the view that the foetus is not a fully actual person
and thus for the position that abortions are permissible
in the early stages of pregnancy for good reason.
Hence, I am willing to grant freedom of choice in the
case of abortion and not in the case of discrimination
in employment."

     It is superficial to see the issue simply as a
matter of some people trying to use the coercive power
of the state to force their own views on others.
That is the argument that segregationists in the
South used when federal troops forced integration of
schools. The question is whether there is a sufficiently strong social consensus on the matter or abortion
to justify enforcing majority views on dissenting minorities. Such consensus does not guarantee the rightness
of the policy, but there is no other way for a democratic
society to function. Decisions always have to be made
by societies about practices which are thought to cause
intolerable harm to non-consenting persons. The issue

today is whether there is strong enough agreement
to establish a community standard to be enforced by
the power of the state. We can only hope that the
prevailing cultural conscience is wise, sensitive, and
just in its attempt both to protect innocent life and
to protect freedom of choice by individuals. My point
is simply that the moral status of the foetus cannot
be ignored in sole preoccuption with the freedom of
choice argument. Genuine uncertainty about this issue on the part of a person or dispute within a group
can be a basis of advocating universal freedom of
choice. Certainty about its immorality (because it
harms an actual or potential person intolerably) on the
part of a person or group is inconsistent with an ad-
vocacy of universal freedom of choice. If a person or
group is deeply convinced that abortion and legal seg-
regation of the races in schools both do intolerable
involuntary harm to persons, how can that person or
group agree to permit freedom of choice in the first
case but not in the second? It cannot be done consistently unless there is a relevant distinction between the two issues that justifies a different outcome.

     If the group in question is the society as a whole
functioning as the state, the same principle holds.
The difference is only that the government holds a
monopoly on coercive power and can enforce its decisions. If the nation through its democratic processes determines that conflicting but morally defensible positions are held on the abortion issue, then
freedom of choice may be legitimately granted. However, if the moral consensus of the country, strongly
felt, is that racial discrimination is not based on
morally sound arguments, even if many people hold

them, then it is legitimate to enforce majority views
on dissenting minorities. The assumption here is that
contrary conclusions may rest on plausible and defensible grounds rooted perhaps in differing philosophical,
religious, or cultural traditions. Let us be clear,
nonetheless, that national moral consensus does not
guarantee moral rightness. Moreover, a consensus may
change. That is just the risk democracy takes in let-
ting the people rule. Neither does permitting freedom
of choice to individuals guarantee that all women who
choose abortions will do so on morally sound grounds
even as defined by national moral consensus, much less
by moral truth as such -- which nobody infallibly possesses.

Should tax exemption be denied to schools that
practice racial discrimination? The Supreme Court recently considered the issue. In particular the court
case involved Bob Jones University of South Carolina
and a private Christian school in North Carolina. The
IRS began denying tax exemption during the Nixon administration on the basis of the Civil Rights Act of 1964.
The University contested the action, and the suit made
its way to the Supreme Court. The University maintains
that its policies are based on religious grounds and
therefore should have the Constitutional protections
guaranteed under the freedom of worship.

A distinction is needed between spiritual acts of
worshiping God and inner acts of belief, thought, and
feeling, on the one hand, and social practices and be-
haviorial expressions of such spiritual and inner
states of mind and conscience, on the other hand. I
have argued that in the former absolute liberty prevails. However, when it comes to outward expressions
and acts which harm people, especially people outside

the worshiping group, that is another matter. Here
decisions must be made by the society as to how far a
group is to be allowed to express its religious convictions in outward acts contrary to social consensus.
A line must be drawn between the permissible and the
forbidden. Obviously, acts of charity to feed the
hungry or to shelter the homeless are above that line
and are to be commended. Likewise, child sacrifice as
a part of worship is below that line.

Where do racially discriminatory practices fall
on this continuum? In listening to the pros and cons,
one notes that the defenders of Bob Jones argue from
the freedom of religion side. "While we abhor what
they stand for, nevertheless spiritual freedom is so
precious that we defend it even when we are offended at
the outcome. Moreover, tomorrow society may decide it
cannot tolerate dissident groups whose values are as
far above the social consensus as racial bigots are
below that line." The President of Bob Jones argues,
"What we do is out of religious conviction, and it
harms no one." The critics argue from the social practices point of view. "This society cannot condone and
underwrite racial discrimination." Society is put in
the difficult position of balancing permitted freedom
of speech, religion, and inner liberty to worship God
according to the dictates of individual conscience, on
the one hand, and prohibited social practices that flow
from such inner beliefs and values. A democratic society has to reach legislative consensus regarding what
is a permitted social practice, even if it is based on
religious conviction. Obviously the social consensus
has changed, and that line is drawn at a different
point now than it was in 1896 when the Supreme Court
ruled on Plessy versus Ferguson.

The issue is a difficult one. It is no wonder that
church and civic groups lined up on both sides, depending on whether religious freedom and liberty of conscience are to be made primary or whether the reprehensible social practice appeal is made. The President
of Bob Jones University asks whether Jewish synagogues
that segregate men and women are to be put under the
ban or whether Catholic schools and churches that refuse to train and ordain women for the priesthood are
to be denied tax exemption. After all, he argues, we
do not exclude blacks from the college but only forbid
interracial dating and marriage, and that applies to
both races. He is right in asking where and how we
draw the line. Clearly, some social practices are so
public, reprehensible, and harmful to people that the
society must prohibit and/or penalize them. However,
in a pluralistic society where many options are open to
people, private schools, churches, and organizations
where membership is purely voluntary should be given
wide latitude within and among themselves to think and
do as they please. Beliefs and practices that are voluntarily chosen by adults for themselves alone should
be permitted. Involuntary harm to others is another
matter altogether, whether done to members inside or
outside the group. The strongest case for Bob Jones
University and Catholic Churches is that the practices
in question are both intragroup and voluntary. Whether
serious violations of the social consensus should be
penalized (e.g., by denial of tax exemption) or prohibited altogether is a matter of social wisdom to be
worked out contextually and politically.

The principles I have stated are in tension with
each other. Is the result a stand-off with no guides
to social policy? A good society will cultivate and

express sensitivity to the distinction between groups
which violate its consensus from above and those which
violate its consensus from below. Peace groups which
absolutely refuse to take life or do violence or harm
to others exemplify the former. Conscientious objection to participating in all wars is a witness to perfectionist values which society should honor by providing special exemptions. Nazi organizations and the
Ku Klux Klan which advocate racial and religious hatred
violate consensus from below. They must be allowed
freedom of speech and assembly but prevented from harm-
ing those whom they hate. Harm is exceedingly difficult
to define, especially when mental and emotional damage
is included along with physical or bodily damage. This
latter point is illustrated by the desire of Nazis
recently to march in Skokie, Illinois -- a town with a
large Jewish population, some of whom had survived the
Holocaust in Germany. Extremes above and below the
social value consensus are easy to define. The anguishing issues arise when the midpoints are reached in which
freedom of thought and worship are in balance with questionable social practices. Some arbitrariness and muddling through from issue to issue are inevitable. The
hope is that sensitivity to the subtleties of relevant
differences between cases can lead to an approximate
justice in balancing conflicting values.

The degrees and kinds of restrictions upon liberty
vary with the degrees and kinds of harm done to other
individuals or to the society as a whole. For all
practical purposes of legislation the person who murders
one other person must be treated in the same way as
far as restraint of liberty is concerned as the person
who makes war against his/her society. But treason is
a more heinous act than murder because it threatenes

the common good of all and not the life of one individual alone. Equality is a regulative principle that
applies at every point on the continuum. Whatever liberties are granted and whatever restrictions are imposed must apply equally to all persons under the same
circumstances.

E

    EQUALITY: Equality, like liberty, is rooted in
reality. It springs from and is commensurate with the
intrinsic worth and potential of persons. Every being
has a claim on other beings equal to its worth. Every
potential for enjoyment has a prima facie right to be
actualized, and every such potential has a right equal
to that of every other equal potential. Persons as
persons thus have rights equal to that of others who as
persons have no more and no less intrinsic worth and
potential for enjoyment. Persons have superior claims
to those of other beings known to us on earth because
their worth and potential are greater but no living being is without some rights and some claim to fulfillment. These statements would seem to be no more than
a spelling out of the view of reality and values previously expressed. They add up to no more than a tauto-
logy: Equals are equal. But it is not a trivial taut-
ology, nor is it the full story.
    Equality has to be considered in two different
ways. Persons as persons are equal, but in every function in which persons engage inequalities abound. Those
who have superior potential in any particular area would
seem to have superior claims on the means to fulfillment.
This follows from the fact that every potential has a
right to fulfillment equal to that potential. Every

person has a claim to seek fulfillment of his/her own
specific potential which may be more or less than other
persons have in any given dimension of human functioning. Hence, for every person to have an equal claim to
fulfillment means that individuals must be treated unequally. How is it possible to combine the generic
equality of persons as persons with the specific inequalities of individuals with different capabilities?
With respect to the generic equalities the rule is:
treat equals equally. With respect to specific inequalities the rule is: treat unequals unequally.

Imagine a circle, a center with a surrounding cir-
cumference. All individuals located within this circle are members of the class of persons and as generic
persons equally so. Some may be much nearer the center than others, and the line that divides the threshhold between persons and sub-persons is hard to define.
Yet despite the indefinite location of the circumfer-
ence surrounding the center which defines personhood,
for ordinary purposes we can identify the class of individuals who are within the circle. Within the circle
differences abound -- wide ranges of ability, interest,
talents, intelligence, aptitudes and all that makes up
the whole spectrum of human potential in all its diverse modes. The just and good society must take into
account both the generic equality of persons as persons
and the specific inequalities of persons as individuals.

Several considerations suggest themselves at once.
In the first place, not every potential or interest in
every individual can be actualized. All realization
is finite, and each choice eliminates others. The
person who is both gifted musically and athletically
obviously cannot perfect each talent to the same degree.
Every hour spent at the piano is sixty minutes that

cannot be used on the tennis court. Each person must
select a configuration of compatible aims which optimize
the fullest range and depth of satisfactions.

In the second place, many of the potential problems that might arise are resolved merely by providing
equal opportunities to persons at the generic level.
Within that framework individuals can develop whatever
potential they may have. The initial successes of
genetically gifted, highly motivated people frequently
open up further opportunities for them so that each
person can find a path that is appropriate and satisfying.

In the third place, the most difficult issues arise
around the problem of incommensurate values. Another
way to put it is in terms of the tensions between excellence for some and equality for all. Suppose (all
other factors eliminated for the moment) one has a
choice between two public policy proposals of equal ex-
penditure. One package includes increased support for
the arts and an educational bill that would substantial-
ly support special programs to locate and develop the
specially gifted talents of children in a variety of
artistic, professional, and academic fields.
The other package contains a rural redevelopment program which would eliminate pockets of severe poverty in
the country. Obviously in making a decision of this
sort, all other considerations cannot be eliminated.
The rule, however, is: meet basic survival and security needs of all before providing for the elective potentials for enjoyment and fulfillment of any. Society
should follow the principles observed in families:
food for all before piano lessons for any. Yet qualifications and exceptions resulting in a variety of configurations may be legitimate for sufficient reason.

For example, support of exceptional musical genius
that will benefit all generations to come may justify
mild relative deprivation for some in the immediate
situation. But the rule is as stated and exceptions
require a reason. One advantage of a prosperous society is that it has more choices and can provide greater opportunities for all to find the kinds and levels
of fulfillment appropriate for each person. The ideal
situation is to provide a basic range of equal opportunities in the economic, political, and cultural
realms and beyond that to provide a range of freedom
for all to have an equal opportunity to pursue to the
fullest the unequal gifts, talents, and interests that
pertain to each.

In areas where rights, privileges, obligations,
and opportunities are legally distributed to citizens
as such, the rule of generic equality prevails. Each
person counts for one, no more and no less. Voting
rights are an example. One person, one vote -- this is
the basic principle. A saint who is also the best informed and wisest genius in matters of government and
justice gets no more than one vote. Legal rights and
obligations ranging from the rights of free speech,
guarantee of a fair trial, and punishment for crime
all the way to eligibility for passports fall under
this rubric. Circumstances may alter rights of persons
but not distinctions among persons as such. In all
other areas of life the way is open to honor the
specific equality of persons to seek unequal goals
suitable to their own potentialities, needs, and desires.
The rule here is that the greater the extent to which
the good sought is commonly produced, the more relevant
is equality of distribution without regard either to
merit or potential for enjoyment. The defense of the

country is the most obvious example of a particular
good shared equally by all. All publically owned or
sponsored facilities, services, and projects are rightfully distributed to all citizens as such or equally
to all qualified for particular benefits. In the economy and society where resources and opportunities are
concerned, the rule still is that generic equality is
a relevant consideration to the extent that the social
benefits in question are dependent upon the structure
of the system commonly created and supported and upon
which individuals depend.

The minimal effect of this principle is that no
one should be allowed to fall below a certain level of
decency with respect to basic needs.[14] Inequalities
should never be permitted which push any person or
group under the level of income and welfare necessary
to meet essential requirements of health and security.
I am assuming a certain level of prosperity in society
which makes this precept of justice possible. One way
to provide this social minimum would be in terms of a
Guaranteed Annual Wage or a Negative Income Tax, plus
allowances for sickness and other special needs. But
how is the level of the social minimum to be set?
Milton Friedman, who endorses the Negative Income Tax,
says simply that it would depend on what taxpayers are
willing to pay. Since for him the idea is a matter of
charity and not of justice, no further appeal can be
made. One might propose an intuitive norm, for example, taking one half the median family income as a
formal rule of thumb to identify the least advantaged.
The problem here is that intuitions differ, and there
is no way to justify this one in preference to others.
One might try to derive some standard of basic needs
for food, shelter, medical care, etc. plus allowances

for special circumstances. This is promising as long
as estimates of needs were generous and well intention-
ed.

John Rawls has offered a more technical solution.[15]
He proposes that after a just savings principle has been
determined (he does not know how to determine this),
then the social minimum should be raised until it begins to interfere with economic efficiency. At that
point further increases would be counter-productive.
At the level beyond which the poorest would be worse
off with higher transfer payments but up to which they
would be benefited, the social minimum is set. In principle, this suggestion is cogent, and it does serve to
implement the bias of a theory of justice in favor of
the least advantaged. Knowing when higher tax rates
become detrimental to universal well being is not easy.
The subject would obviously be the occasion of much
acrimonious debate in which ideological self-interest
and economic theory would be inextricably mixed. But
such is the case with every complex policy matter involving an attempt to combine justice with sound technical judgments. The more important issue at the moment is the political one of getting the proposal to the
center of the societal agenda. Then the problem of
providing a basic income for all in ways that preserve
incentives (maximize efficiency) can be tackled.

Once an appropriate social minimum is provided for
all and the special needs of the helpless are met, the
theory of justice has lessened interest in insisting
that all inequalities of income be shown to benefit
all. The vagaries and complexities of the market system which distributes income are such that precise application of just principles is impossible. How will
one judge whether athletes who make a million dollars

or more a year merit such fabulous earnings? The most
difficult issue is not the justification of inequalities
as such but the degree of inequality in various contexts that are permissible in the just and good society.[16] A certain arbitrariness is inevitable, but wide
differentials produced in a market system under conditions of equal opportunity can be allowed as long as
a progressive income tax and reasonable inheritance taxes imposed on the wealthy and a social minimum for the
poor modify the extreme results of the system. The
rate of the income and inheritance taxes and the level
of the social minimum will always be partly arbitrary.
In the last analysis they will be determined as much
by pragmatic considerations and political realities as
by principles of justice.

It follows from what has been said that the claim
of equality in the sharing of social benefits is related
to what is common. This can be spelled out in several
ways. (1) At the highest level of abstract generality
a common claim is held on the basic natural resources
of the earth that come as a part of the given for human
action and which no human being was responsible for
creating. Of course, respect has to be paid to those
historically-established claims and rights which locate
the control of the earth's bounty and potential in the
hands of particular nations, groups, and individuals.
Yet no conception of justice and goodness holds its
ideals high enough which does not recognize the ultimate
lure of the equal claim of all persons upon the natural
riches of this planet. Special reward is due to those
who invent the technologies and do the work which makes
the potential resources available for human use. The
principle that those who mix their labor with the earth
establish a claim to private property (John Locke) has

some validity. Pragmatic considerations and political
realities as well as the legitimate claims of those
who now own and control the land where treasure lies
limit the realization of the equal sharing of all in
all that nature provides. Nevertheless, the final truth
and value is the "The earth is the Lord's and the fullness thereof, the world and those who dwell therein"
(Psalm 24:1). That Biblical statement would appear to
be a truth of reason as well as a teaching of a particular religious group. In the last analysis such an
ideal cannot fail to have real effect on policy where
justice and goodness prevail. Its most relevant policy
directive would again point to the desirability of actions by persons and societies which would favor those
least advantaged by the present arrangements which deprive them of their just share of the world's given
potential.

     (2) A pull in the direction of equal sharing is
also established by the fact of the historical accumulation of wealth, knowledge, technology, social wisdom, and so on bequeathed to the present generation from
the past. Gears and wheels are essential to modern civilization, but no living person can claim special credit for the benefits they make possible. Again, those
persons and groups which invent new technologies or
make important discoveries which benefit all should
profit temporarily for their contributions. Patents and
copyrights recognize that a just reward should be guaranteed. But in time and as the innovative technique
is discovered by others and becomes part of the common
social treasury, this claim to special benefits is di-
luted.   There is no absolute claim to permanent prerogatives, exclusive possession, or special privilege
based on some past achievement. The present wealth of

material and social goods and the productive capacity
of a modern industrial economy have been created over
such a long period of time by so many people of every
race, class, region, and religion that a substantial
common treasury has been established on which every person born today has a claim. While this treasury cannot
be precisely defined, it is real in fact and relevant
as a principle of distributive justice. Merit on the
part of persons now living may create differential
claims to reward, but as persons (and apart from other
relevant historical particulars and pertinent facts),
each has a claim upon this common treasury of social
goods equal to that of every other person. This historical accumulation of wealth for which no living person
can take credit establishes a lure in the direction of
equality which cannot be ignored.

     (3) A third factor is the structural interdepend-
ence of individuals in a modern economy. The production of goods and the creation of wealth and income are
social processes which have organic dimensions transcending the interactions of individuals making voluntary contracts. Yet this framework, which is not
created by particular individuals as such, is a common
good essential to contractual relationships among individuals and results in their mutual benefit. More
will be said about this in dealing with the tension
between individual liberty and equality. Here it must
be said that the organic character of society creates
a pull in the direction of the equal sharing of socially produced goods and benefits.

     The practical implication of these three princi-
ples creates a leaning toward actions which favor those
individuals and groups that are presently worst off.
It also gives further credence and weight to the

desirability of a social minimum which would establish
a floor of income and benefits sufficient to meet basic
needs (or one that is appropriate for the wealth or
poverty of a given society).

(4) A fourth factor creating a common good is more
ambiguous. The gifts and talents with which individuals
are born are capacities for which they cannot take credit. On this basis it is reasonable to argue that
genetic endowments are a social asset from which all
should benefit. Nevertheless, the counterclaim that
while we may not deserve our natural gifts, we are entitled to the rewards that flow from them also has merit. The degree to which we are our bodies and own our
bodies establishes a peculiar intimacy that does not obtain between individuals and the natural resources and
social wealth they control. Perhaps the relevant distinction here is between our genetic endowment from the
past (which we do not deserve and did nothing to create)
and our actions in the present (for which we are responsible and which create merit). Our bodies are given
but their use in constructive tasks is our own act.
There is a peculiar identity between the self as objectively created subject and the self as subjectively
directed agent. Since it is the actions of individuals
and not their genetic endowment as such that enters into the social stream of events, they deserve a reward
for their contributions in accordance with merit.[17]

Against this background we can examine the problem of the concentration of wealth in the hands of a
few and its inheritance by subsequent generations. One
study showed that 1.6% of the adult population holds at
least 30% of the wealth, i.e., all things having value
in money, exchange, or use.[18] Whether this figure is
exactly right or not, the fact of great concentration

at the top is beyond dispute. Is this just? Andrew
Carnegie, that well-known non-socialist, thought that
all inheritance should be outlawed in the interest of
providing equal opportunity for each new generation.
One need not go that far, but surely some limitation on
the power associated with the possession of wealth is
called for. The reasons for supporting a reasonable
inheritance policy are to be found, in part, in the
first three points enumerated above. The creation of
wealth is a social process which involves many interdependent factors. The workings of the market system
may create rewards out of proportion to the contributions made by individuals. There is no necessary connection between the returns to individuals and groups
based solely on market factors, on the one hand, and
on considerations of justice, on the other hand. Henry
Ford was surely due a significant gain for the genius
and imagination which made the Model T available to
masses of people. It is not at all self-evident that
he was due a billion dollars for his efforts! His success was due in part to factors which he had no role in
creating -- all the associated inventions and technologies essential to the automobile, for example, including the availability of refined petroleum. More important were the workers who mass produced the cars and
the millions of consumers who purchased them in the context of a society ready in all sorts of ways for the
introduction of this technology.

     Economists are needed to work out the implications
of various schemes for taxing inheritances in ways
that both preserve fairness and maximize incentives.
One proposal involves taxing the transfer of wealth from
parent to child at a lower rate than the second transfer to the grandchild, and so on. Presumably this

encourages incentive in the first generation to acquire a large increase in wealth, as well as in the
children and grandchildren, etc. who are the benefic-
iaries of a decreasing legacy. Some combination of a
tax-free minimum plus a rate that becomes increasingly
higher as the transfer becomes more distant from the
original accumulator -- or some other system -- would
need to be worked out on the basis of principle, experience, and pragmatic considerations.

Relevant at this point is the consideration of
envy as the basis for the demand for equality. This
charge is a favorite theme of conservatives.[19] The
have-nots look at the haves and are jealous of their
more fortunate status. Equality is associated with
the vulgarity of mass tastes and mediocrity in every
area of life. In short, equality is the enemy of excellence. It is the refuge of the weak and inferior,
who, lacking the competence of their superiors, raise
the cry of equality out of envy. A first reply to this
conservative attack is that the pride, arrogance, self-
righteousness, and anxiety of the favored few is as
likely a reason for the opposition to equality as envy
is a source of the support for it. Doubtless both the
smugness of the haves and the jealousy of the have-nots
are present in any dispute of the place of equality in
the canons of justice. But the moral principles still
have to be debated on their own merits apart from the
motives of those who contend for opposing views.

What requires attention here is the extent to
which the subjective sense of relative deprivation is
a valid element in the demand for greater equality.
Recent decades have witnessed a rising standard of living for nearly everybody in the industrial countries.
The worst disparities between persons have been

significantly overcome. Yet despite the decrease in
real inequalities the demand for equality grows, rooted
in the sense of relative deprivation and rising expectations.[20] Here again the social question of how to
deal with resentment is not identical with the moral
issue of justice, although it may be the more difficult
to resolve at least in the minds of contending parties.
The relevant question is: Is the sense of relative deprivation rooted in the actual fact of injustice, or
is it rooted in envy? If it is rooted in denial or just
claims, then remedial action is called for. If it is
rooted in envy, then other resources of culture must be
called upon to create a more balanced sense of value.

                              F

    The second approximation to the principles of jus-
tice can be further developed by looking at the specific interrelationships that arise among the good, freedom, and equality. The three basic motifs both enhance
and constrain each other. The extension of equality
tends toward the increase of social good and of individual freedom. The extension of freedom tends toward
the increase of individual good and toward equal rights
for all. The increase of social good enhances the possibility of extending freedom and equality to individuals. The constraints of each on the other can be set
forth in a double dialectic.
SOCIAL GOOD IN TENSION WITH FREEDOM AND EQUALITY. The
presupposition of basic freedoms and equality of rights
depends on a minimal level of security and prosperity.
Their extension to the fullest expression requires a
certain general harmony as well. A society that is
being threatened with extinction by an outside enemy

or by internal poverty and starvation can scarcely
afford the luxury of democracy if a society governed
by a hierarchical and beneficent dictatorship can
guarantee survival in the absence of more desirable
alternatives. If justice and good will prevail, freedom and equality will begin to appear as emergency conditions subside. However, if the society is divided into warring factions, an emerging strong party may find
it necessary to repress rebellious groups until sufficient health is attained to allow democratic institutions to grow. Equal freedom for all may await the
achievement of a certain level of prosperity. The extension of individual freedom may be denied within limits for the sake of greater equality of participation in
economic reward or for the purpose of increasing the
supply of goods and services. This holds especially
when poverty conditions prevail. Granted that the realities of power do not always coincide or have any necessary connection with the requirements of justice,
nevertheless a variety of dynamic configurations can
develop in which social good, equality, and freedom arrange themselves. They may exert differing degrees of
pull on each other as circumstances change.

Barring cruel and inhumane policies, the "dictatorship of the proletariat" may have a measure of justification in emergent socialist societies, if indeed
it is necessary to effect a transition to a better
order. Premier Fidel Castro's insistence that denial
of full civil and human rights in Cuba is a necessity
for the present if the social order designed for the
well being of all is to come into being may not entirely offend justice, if indeed his claim is factually
true. The same holds for Gen. Carlos Romulo's contention that democracy is not possible in the Philippines

because the social substructure and value system necessary to sustain it are absent. Whether this to any
extent justifies his defense of the denial of equal
political rights to opponents of the current regime
is doubtful, but he may not be entirely wrong in saying that no fully democratic society can flourish there
at the present. Surely his contention that in developing countries "freedom from want" takes priority over
"freedom of expression" has some limited truth, assuming that one cannot have them both at the same time or
at least not yet. Lee Jun Yew, prime minister of Singapore, in 1978, defended the lack of political freedom
in his country by pointing to the fact that he presided
over probably the highest urban standard of living in
the world. Singapore has devoted itself to the production of wealth through economic freedom rather than to
the distribution of its products. Yew maintained that
he only puts his enemies in prison and feeds them well,
while his Communist foes would both destroy the free
economy and rule by absolute terror and painful exe-
cution.[21] The world is indeed ambiguous and complex.
Some facets of justice can in some circumstances shine
only by turning others away from the light.

In the final analysis the _Gestalt_ of a particular
society in its historical and current manifestations
plays a large part in determining both what is possible and what is best for that given situation. No
set of completely _a priori_ requirements can be imposed
from without in abstraction from particular circumstances, although there is a logic within the basic
principles which, at the highest level of generality,
defines the structure of a just and good society, no
matter what its form. Furthermore, the dynamic interplay between these principles specifies the directions

which any society must take if it is to move toward
the ideal for it. The immediate possibilities for a
given society depend on the total actuality of the present as it has emerged from the past. Sometimes even
the best that is possible may not be very good from
the standpoint of an increase in justice.

One additional factor important here is the relationship between efficiency and justice/goodness.
Taken abstractly, efficiency is a friend. To be able
to do or achieve more with fewer resources is a gain.
A motor that uses less fuel and reduces pollution while
giving the same results as its competitors is pure benefit, except as research and production costs need to
be deducted. Its development could increase employment
as well. However, when the use of certain technologies
gain efficiency at the expense of putting people out of
jobs, a more complex situation arises. In such cases
the utilitarian principle modified by deontological
concern for fairness works well. What trade-offs result in the greatest net good for all? Justice also
requires, however, that those who are hurt by innova-
tions be compensated out of the gains achieved for others
or by society as a whole. A social minimum could be
the appropriate means for this. The utilitarian principles also hold when efficiency must be weighted
against other values -- improved work conditions, worker participation in decision-making, product safety,
etc. Somebody has to pay the costs of decreased efficiency. Workers may take less pay, or consumers may pay
more. In general the rule is that those who receive
the benefits pay the cost.

It may sometimes be difficult to incorporate considerations of efficiency into a theory of justice.
Several years ago on the CBS Evening News, one story

dealt with a poor family from Tennessee. The father
complained that the welfare money ran out before the
month was up. They had to go with little or no
food for a while until the next check came. The next
day an official from the local welfare office appeared
on the show to argue that the amount of money provided was sufficient. The problem was that the family
was so ignorant in matters of budgeting and nutrition
that they could not make proper use of what they had.
Suppose this explanation to be at least partly true,
what does justice require? If meeting of human need
is the criterian, should this family be given more
money so that they can be nourished equally with
other welfare families who would then receive less
money? But this would reward the inefficient at the
expense of the efficient. Is this fair? Obviously,
efforts to improve efficiency on everybody's part
is a strategy mandated by the imperatives of the
just and good society. In this case the first step
might be to institute efforts to increase the
efficiency of the family. Assistance with preparing
and living by a budget could be provided. Some
training in nutrition might help. Perhaps they
could learn how to buy low-cost foods that provided
a healthful diet. Only when education and persuasion
fail should efficiency be enforced on the family
by insuring that the money be spent wisely.

Efficiency is a relevant consideration, but it
is not a fundamental moral principle. It comes into
play as a factor when the goals, requirements, and
constraints involved in the technical and moral dimensions

of a situation have been defined. Getting the most
for the least is not an independent norm of morality as
such. However, it becomes relevant in so far as it
affects the freedom, equality, and welfare of people.
In those cases it has to be factored in so that the
most appropriate balance of freedom, equality, and welfare is enhanced and not hindered by lack of efficiency
or immoral means of achieving it.

G

FREEDOM IN TENSION WITH EQUALITY. Freedom and
equality exist in a peculiar dialectic which needs to
be spelled out. Equality is a regulative principle in
a way that freedom and social good are not. It requires
that common social good be shared equally (assuming for
the moment equal need and/or desert and no other qualifying contingencies). It also requires that liberty
be shared equally (assuming no relevant qualifications
which contingently emerge). As first presumptions both
principles follow rationally (tautologically but non-
trivially). Beings with freedom and potential for enjoyment have an equal claim with other equal beings to
exercise their freedom and to actualize their potential.
As attention shifts from society as a whole to individuals, the focus moves from an equal sharing of common
good to an equal freedom to seek private good. Socialist ideologies emphasize the first pole, while capitalist perspectives stress the second. In this sense it
can be said that socialism makes equality prior while
capitalism gives first place to freedom. Each, of
course, likes to claim that it can appropriately balance both values. The principles of a just and good

society require that the dialectical tension between
them be recognized and that they be appropriately
blended under changing circumstances.

Pure libertarianism will invariably lead to an
indeterminate range of inequalities of wealth, power,
and status. The result may be great differentials
between those at the top and those at the bottom.
Superior native gifts combined with motivation, effort,
fortunate circumstances, luck, and other enabling factors create wide divergences of social outcome. Once
attained inequalities tend to be self-perpetuating
through institutionalization and heredity. Contingencies of circumstance and the structure of the social
order may either tend to exacerbate or to mollify inequalities once established. Parents pass their advantage on to their children, giving them a head start on
equally talented children from less fortunate homes.
Success breeds success. The almost certain result of
a social order slanted toward freedom of the individual
is that inequalities are perpetuated out of proportion
to the native gifts, motivation, effort, and merit of
individuals. Equality of opportunity is very difficult
to achieve and maintain. If it were perfectly attained,
presumably the resulting meritocracy would produce new
inequalities based now on IQ, native talent, and effort
instead of on unfair social advantage. Whether based
on biological or sociological factors, the inequalities
that result from a onesided individualism may reach
proportions offensive to justice and become the occasion
of considerable suffering and deprivation.

A rigid egalitarianism also has undesirable consequences. Individual excellence tends to be inhibited.
Talented and deserving persons are prevented from realizing their full potantial. They are denied a fair

reward for their efforts in making superior contributions. Equality can be made and kept operational
only by constant interference in the natural outcomes
of free exchange and interaction or by coercion and
regimentation. Hence, whether in a market economy or
in a planned society, a strict egalitarianism is
either unfair or inefficient or both.

Robert Nozick poses the question sharply as a
challenge to all egalitarian views.[22] Imagine a just
distribution of holdings, judged by any criteria you
desire. Let us call this D_1. Now suppose that Wilt
Chamberlain (the illustration is a bit dated) should
work out a contract whereby he receives 25¢ from every
ticket sold to basketball games in which he plays.
Fans are perfectly willing to pay this for the privilege. The effect of this arrangement is that D_1 has
been altered. We now have situation D_2. By what principles of justice, Nozick asks, would any third party
have any claim on what was paid to Chamberlain by the
free acts of the first two parties -- the fans and himself? For the government to intervene in this situation
to restore D_1 would have the effect of invalidating
"capitalist acts between consenting adults."[23]

Given his own principles of justice, Nozick's challenge is unanswerable. He offers what he calls a historical entitlement view. A just account of holdings
has three parts: original acquisition by just means,
transfer by just principles, and rectifications of
violations of the previous two standards. In other
words, if you receive a gift or a legitimate inheritance
or acquire holdings by voluntary exchange or arrangement, it is yours to keep. No one can justly take it
from you to distribute to others according to some
"patterned principle." A "patterned principle" requires

distribution according to need, merit, I.Q. or some combination of these or other factors. No matter how much
people acquire by gifts, inheritance, or voluntary contract, it is just for them to keep it. Hence, regardless of how great the inequalities in a society are,
they cannot be justly rectified if they result from
free exchanges among consenting adults.

Is there any just basis, then, for redistributing
income and other benefits in the interests of equality
among all members of a society? Let it be noted that
Nozick does not object to individuals giving to the
poor and needy, as long as they do it voluntarily. He
only objects to forcible redistribution according to
some "patterned principle" of justice. Moreover, he
makes provisions for rectification for past injustices
by governmental action. A great and unsolved problem
for his view is how to ascertain whether present holdings have been justly inherited from persons back over
the generations. What American land, for example, was
unjustly appropriated from the Indians and invalidly
transferred by inheritance to the present generation?
Nozick even admits that patterned theories may be a
rough rule of thumb to rectify past injustices.
Hence, the principle that society should be organized
so as to maximize the least well-off in society cannot be condemmed unless it can be shown that no principles of rectification apply. Derek Phillips argues
that Nozick actually offers more and better grounds for
social policies that have egalitarian consequences than
does Rawls.[24]

In addition to these considerations, can more be
said? I believe so. Nozick assumes a high doctrine
of individualism. Individuals are the primary or sole
unit. Social arrangements and institutions arise by

voluntary contract. This point of view ignores the
interdependence of individuals in a complex society such
as ours. Society has organic features. We are members
one of another. The production of goods and services
and the resulting distribution of income involve a
social process which cannot be fully accounted for merely by reference to "capitalist acts between consenting
adults." Wilt Chamberlain did not invent the game of
basketball. He probably played in arenas financed by
public money. Neither Chamberlain nor other sports
stars who make a million dollars a year had anything to
do with creating television, which is broadcast over
public airwaves. In short, some of the ingredients necessary to Chamberlain's good deal with the fans involve organic realities, systems, structures, relationships which are not accounted for by individual trans-
actions. Nozick neglects the social framework -- the
organic and systemic elements -- essential to the
creation of wealth and income. This structural interdependence is not created by individuals taken as isolated units. Social process and reality constitute an
organic whole which is greater than the sum of its parts.
This fact makes it just for society to tax those who
especially benefit from this system and to use the
revenues for purposes of distributive justice. In
short, Nozick's view of society as a collection of autonomous individuals making voluntary contracts ignores
the organic structure essential to individual achievement.

The problem of the just and good society is to find
that dynamic balance which results in the most extensive
range of individual freedom, the most equal access to
means of fulfillment, and the greatest social good possible under a particular set of given circumstances.

Freedom and equality in particular will take on different meanings depending on the factual situation relating to the interdependence of individuals in a specific
society.   The more it is the case that a theory of
social nominalism is actually descriptive of the prevailing facts, the more equality of individual opportunity is an appropriate ideal to be sought. Social nominalism is the view that only individuals are real. Society is a name for the sum total of the individuals
composing it. Equality of opportunity maximizes the
possibility of individuals using their freedom to earn
unequal results. The more a theory of social realism
is factually true of a given society the more equality
of opportunity must be supplemented with equality of
result. Social realism is the view that society is an
organic whole made up of individual members. To put it
differently, the more the production of goods and services depends on the structure of the system itself and
a high degree of interdependence, the more relevant
becomes the principle of equal distribution of its products.

     It can be argued that the United States is now
undergoing transition in this direction with the consequence that a new paradigm for relating freedom and
equality is both needed and emerging. Among many ana-
lysts who might be chosen, I will make brief reference
to the work of George Cabot Lodge and Daniel Bell. In
a recent book Lodge refers to "the new American ideology."[25] His thesis is that the ideology that has dom-
inated American thinking since the 18th century is
breaking down. It is being replaced by another configuration of ideas that takes into account the structural
changes that are taking place in society. Each ideology is made up of five key ideas.

Old Ideology	New Ideology
1. Individualism	1. Communitarianism
2. Property Rights	2. Rights of Membership
3. Competition Based on Consumer Desire	3. Community Need Taking Precedence Over Individual Preference
4. Limited State	4. State as Planner
5. Scientific Specialization	5. Holism

Old Ideology

1. <u>Individualism</u>. The individual is the basic unit. Society is the sum total of individuals and arises by a social contract. Equality refers to equal liberty and the equal right of all to enter freely into contracts with others. Fulfillment achieved by individual effort is a basic dogma.

2. <u>Property Rights</u>. The best guarantee of individual rights is the ownership of property. This provides a bulwark against government tyranny and against the encroachment of others.

3. <u>Competition</u>. Each seeks his/her own private good by individual effort. When individuals freely and fairly compete, the "invisible hand" (Adam Smith) will guarantee the wealth of the nation. The mechanism of the market will insure economic efficiency and provide a just allocation of goods and services based on individual merit.

4. <u>Limited State</u>. The State should do only what individuals cannot do for themselves. Its main functions are to provide for the common defense, protect individual and property rights, and guarantee the freedom on contract against force and fraud.

5. <u>Scientific Specialization</u>. Attention is paid to

the parts as analyzed into their ultimate constituents.
The whole is the sum total of the parts.

New Ideology

1. <u>Communitarianism.</u> Society is an organic whole made
up of groups and sub-groups. Community is a reality in
itself, more than the sum of its parts. Society is an
interdependent system constituted by individuals and
groups. Fulfillment of the individual comes by meaningful participation in a community to which one contributes and from which one gains benefits.

2. <u>Rights of Membership</u>. Membership in the community
conveys rights and justifies claims upon the total resources of the community. The number of socially con-
ferred rights increases -- the right to a job, to a
minimum wage, to health care, to securty in old age.
The number of groups claiming protection grows -- blacks,
women, the handicapped, homosexuals, the elderly, ath-
eists. When a person goes to work for General Motors,
he or she immediately becomes a member of two giant
bureaucracies -- the labor union and the corporation.
Contracts are negotiated for individual shareholders and
workers by representatives. Ownership of property as a
source of rights and protection decreases while benefits
or losses associated with group participation increases.

3. <u>Community Need Taking Precedence Over Individual</u>
<u>Preference</u>. The mechanisms of the market place leave
some social needs unmet, requiring political action to
achieve them. Car manufacturers sold cars during the
last decades by stressing style, luxury, size, and
power. The community, prompted by Ralph Nader and
others, decided that safe, non-polluting cars are essential whether or nor consumer preferences expressed in
the market place produces this result or not. Hence,

political measures were taken to force manufacturers
to produce safer and now more efficient cars. In an
antitrust suit the government tried to force International Telephone and Telegraph to divest itself of
the Hartford Fire Insurance Company. The corporation
lawyers argued that the United States needed ITT to be
big and strong in order to compete with other countries
and to assist in achieving a favorable balance of payments in world trade. Community need thus takes priority over the principle of maximizing competition.

4. The State as Planner. Since the time of Franklin
Roosevelt the state has taken an increasingly important
role in regulating the economy and guaranteeing the
social welfare of citizens. Increasingly the federal
government sets goals and orders priorities. Energy
policy based on long-range assessments of needs and
resources is a particularly contemporary example of the
role of the state as planner.

5. Holism. Nature tends to be made up of systems.
Reality is organic. Every thing is connected to everything else. Hence, knowledge must take account of
wholes or organized unities as well as parts.

The interdependence of individual and society,
the stress upon the reality of community, the stress
on holism in the pursuit of truth about realities that
hang together in interconnected systems all point to a
new way of perceiving, believing, and valuing that
stands in contrast to a previous era and ideology.

This analysis is confirmed by that of Daniel Bell
in his description of the emerging post-industrial
society.[26] The modern liberal state was based on the
ideas of Adam Smith, Jeremy Bentham, and John Locke.
In their view individuals were the focus of the freedom and reward system. Individuals were to be set free

to pursue their interests and enjoy the fruits of their
labor achieved through the market mechanism of the economy and through democratic political practices. A new
moral basis is now being sought, geared not to the realization of individual ends but of group and communal
needs. In this emerging setting equality takes on a
different meaning. The old ideology generated the demand for equality of opportunity so that all could compete fairly for the rewards provided through individual
efforts. The new ideology generates a demand that equality of opportunity be supplemented by some degree of
equality of result. The reasoning is that in an interdependent society viewed as an organic system, all
people have a limited claim on the sum total of available natural and human resources. Hence, inequalities
produced by the unpredictable tides of fate, fortune,
accident, luck and the vagaries of the market system,
as well as by entrenched advantages of the privileged,
suggest that outcomes as well as opportunities be taken
into account. Bell maintains that the central value
question of post-industrial society will be the debate
over equality of opportunity versus equality of result.

        The "new ideology" fits well with the organic-re-
lational view of society advocated on these pages. My
criticism of Nozick's nominalism rests on a "communitarian" understanding of society. The Bakke case referred to earlier is illuminated by the paradigm shift
noted by Lodge. The older ideology looks at discrete
individuals and supports a norm of equal opportunity
for all. On this basis Allan Bakke should have been admitted to medical school since he had higher scores than
some blacks who were accepted. The new vision sees individuals as members of groups and in relation to the
total historical and social context that has shaped

their lives. This "communitarian" view has implications
which justify attention to equality of result.

     Beneath all the specific arguments pro and con in
the "affirmative action" versus "reverse discrimination"
debate lies a fundamental difference in paradigm reference which is determinative. At this level ethical
perceptions have a <u>Gestalt</u> quality. You are for or
against Bakke depending on whether the old paradigm or
the new is in the foreground. Finally, one accepts one
ideology or the other, depending on which intuition prevails with the ultimate clarity of self-evidence. Arguments may be offered for or against one paradigm or the
other, but in the last analysis it is the intuited
<u>Gestalt</u> which determines which type of evidence is com-
pelling. The relationship here between intuition of
paradigm and arguments for or against a given paradigm
parallel exactly the relations between faith and reason
discussed in a previous chapter.

                              H

     A summary of the main principles that have been
set forth may be useful at this point to focus upon
the central tendencies of the system. A number of the
themes, principles, and rules have been elaborated.
It remains to be seen whether they constitute an integrated whole with inner coherence and practical appli-
cability. The basic motif is that social welfare,
freedom and equality are the three values that constitute the heart of justice, each to be maximized to
the extent allowed by the pull of the other two. Further principles emerge when the inner logic and the
relationship of each of these is considered in relation
to the others. The imperative to maximize the good may

be limited by the concern to provide the most extensive
liberty possible to each and to insure greater equality
to all. This dynamic may emerge especially under conditions of relative prosperity and stability. But
liberty and equality may be curtailed in order to increase the availability of essential goods and services,
especially under conditions of extreme poverty or emergency.

Difficult and complex issues arise in working out
the dialectic of freedom and equality. Individual liberty should be as extensive as possible. The most obvious limitations on liberty flow from the necessity of
granting an equal liberty to all other persons. This
is a structural and permanent given. But liberty may
under certain configurations be limited by the overriding urgency of insuring the survival and security
of the community as a whole and to guarantee the claims
of individuals to an equal sharing of the common good.

Equality is in a peculiar way a regulative principle to insure that no unwarranted discrimination occurs where human worth and potential establish claims.
It functions along the continuum between individual
liberty and the common social good. At the first pole
it requires that no more and no less liberty be granted
to one person than to another. At the other pole it
demands that persons as persons share equally in social
good in so far as it is common. Good that is common to all is established on three firm bases. The
first is the given natural resources of the earth.
The second is the historically accumulated social treasury of wealth, practical knowledge, technology, productive capacity, and the cultural inheritance of truth,
goodness, and beauty -- the whole of the gift from the
human past. The third is the interdependence of

individuals created by the organic structure of social
systems which produce goods and services.

In all three of these instances, goods or the capacity for producing goods (economic and non-economic
values) are givens which are not the product of the efforts of any particular persons here and now. Neither
fact by itself or in combination with the others produces the grounds for a strict egalitarianism. Historically established entitlements to natural resources,
current contributions of individuals to the still accumulating social treasury, and the merit of specific individuals within an interdependent system all create
differential claims which have to be honored. It is in
working out the relationship between the generic rights
to equal sharing of social goods and the specific merit arising out of individual freedom that some of the
most perplexing issues of justice arise. Factual judgments related to a complex of historically arising contingencies make discriminating judgments between equal
and unequal claims in varying circumstances extremely
baffling.

Generic equality is the rule where politically
defined rights, obligations, and privileges are
involved. Every person is equal to every other person
before the law. Generic equality is also called for to
the extent that a truly common good is at stake. In
all other areas the dialectic between freedom and equality must be worked out, allowing differential claims to
be established by the merit of individual actions.

A central feature of the outlook that is being
developed is that it leads repeatedly to the call for
actions that will benefit those who are worst-off. It
is in this connection that need becomes a relevant
principle of distributive justice. This is so for two

converging reasons. The first is the rational assertion that every potential has a right to fulfillment
equal to that of any other equal potential. The second is the hierarchical structure of the self which entails the principle that those basic organic requirements of the body take priority over the higher impulses of the spirit, for which the former are foundational. One must survive before one can worship, eat before one can think. It follows that those persons and
groups at the lower end of the socio-economic scale
have the greater need. More potentials and more basic
potentials lacking resources and opportunities for
actualization are to be found there. This is not to
deny that some wealthy persons may actually be more un-
happy, more miserable, and experience more physical and
mental pain than some poor people.

I have distinguished between the more essential
and the more important values. However, social policy
aimed at the achievement of a greater degree of distributive justice must follow the priority of essential
before important needs. This is true both for the
theoretical reason that the essential is foundational
for the important and the practical consideration that
policies can be more effective in this area. The anguish of the spirit calls for loving care by concerned
individuals and appropriate professionals, but in the
innermost recesses of the heart the individual is finally alone in her/his solitariness before the ultimate
questions of meaning and fulfillment. The point here
is that as one moves from the foundational essential
needs of the body to the apex of the spirit's quest
for wholeness and joy, purely ethical action and just
social policies as such become relatively less effective. Assuming the availability of material resources,

it is easier to feed the hungry than to comfort the
despairing, although it may be more important for the
whole self in its unity to overcome meaninglessness
than to have a balanced diet. For all of these reasons,
then, meeting the foundational needs of those persons
and groups with fewer material resources and social opportunities will be a central obligation in any society
intending to be just and good.

Need refers to the absence of the means to achieve
fulfillment of a potential for enjoyment. It is met
when the means are provided. As such it is a principle
of distributive justice that stands between generic
equality and individual merit as a basis of claims upon
social resources and benefits. Generic equality applies where persons are appropriately treated as persons
with a right to no more and no less than other persons.
Need varies with the kind and degree of unfulfilled potential. In this dimension persons with unequal needs
and potentials have unequal claims. Merit creates unequal claims that vary with the efforts, achievements,
and contributions of individuals exercising their own
freedom. A good part of justice is to find the appropriate weighting to be given to generic equality, need,
and merit within a variety of changing social configurations. The lure of the good adds the other dynamic that
has to be considered if the most desirable policies are
to be developed. The aim in every case is to move toward that social harmony which maximizes the intensity
of enjoyment of individuals within a given society and
to do so in accordance with justice.

All of these principles finally spring from a
double base -- the deontological imperative to honor
the intrinsic worth of persons and the teleological imperative to maximize well-being. Both of these

injunctions arise as a fitting response of attunement
to the Creative Purpose of an Ultimate Power and Goodness which lures the whole cosmos and every experiencing subject within it toward the richest, fullest
heights of enjoyment. The cosmic and historical process is driven and drawn in the direction of an all-
inclusive harmony of self-realization in a community
embracing all beings in mutual support. This Final
Goal is world self-realization which is at the same
time divine self-realization. To reproduce in our actions toward other beings the quality and the aim incarnate in the actions of a Supreme Love in quest of
this Universal Society -- that is the clue to responsible living and to fullness of life.

CONCLUSION

A

The quest to understand morality and justice can never reach finality. This particular essay, however, has to be brought to a conclusion. Two issues require brief comment. The first is that the analysis of justice presented here has centered on theory and the elucidation of principles. Little has been said, except in passing or by implication, about the institutional framework in which these principles are to function as guides toward just practices. In particular, are some economic and political systems more expressive of the principles of justice than others? Is some form of socialism mandated by the norms of the just and good society? Or can a type of modified capitalism serve better as the socio-economic framework of the quest for justice? Was Winston Churchill right in saying that democracy is the worst form of government, except in comparison to the alternatives? Complete answers to these questions would require a discussion at least as extensive as the present analysis of the principles of justice themselves. This is not the place to undertake that project, but the issues are so important that they cannot be entirely ignored.

Society can appropriately be divided into three relatively autonomous but interdependent spheres: the socio-economic, the political, and the cultural realms. Put forward in the form of bare assertions, my own conclusions regarding the institutional forms most appropriate for the expression and achievement of the good life in the good society are as follows:

Realm	Preferable Institutional Form
Socio-economic	A mixed system using the mechanism of the market but with considerable governmental direction to achieve the common

Realm	Preferable Institutional Form
	good and to protect and promote the interests of the least well off.
Political	Constitutional democracy combining majority rule with protection of minority rights and with a wide range of civil liberties for all.
Cultural	A value system based on the norm and goal of self-realization in community nourished in appropriate institutions and expressed in fitting symbols commonly affirmed but with subgroup pluralism and individual freedom in the realm of ideas and ideals.

Obviously such a bare skeleton only suggests a general direction leaving much undefined. The cultural norm of self-realization in community has been the subject of the last two chapters. The political norm of constitutional democracy is widely accepted in the modern West and need not be argued for here. The economic debate, however, is far from settled. In the absence of a full-scale treatment, I have included a paper in an appendix which will at least outline the views I would be prepared to defend.

B

The second issue also has to do with theory and principles, but in relation to their use in determining moral choice and social policy. The way the two chapters on justice and the good society were developed may have left the impression that the proper procedure is

to develop principles and then to apply them to situations. Care must be taken to correct any misunder-
standings that may have been created by the form of the
argument. It is necessary to have guiding principles,
norms, and ideals. But in keeping with the importance
given to the nature of morality as responsive, the
empirical and contextual elements need to be put once
more in the center of attention. One does not begin
with principles and then apply them. Rather, the
starting point is some individual or some group in the
context of a particular set of circumstances as they
have developed out of the past. In the present moment
of decision certain options and possibilities arise for
shaping the future. In this context one asks what
response is fitting, what creative intervention will
most effectively promote individual self-realization and
social justice? Given what has happened in the past and
what is going on right now, what is the most appropriate line of action that can be taken with the aim of
knitting together as many of the potentials for justice
and enjoyment into the best possible harmony of interests and goals, taking into account the needs, claims,
and aims of all relevant persons? In some circumstances
even the best response may not be very good or productive of much good at the moment. Compromises, ambiguities, and trade-offs in complex matters are to be
regularly expected. Often we have to be satisfied with
only a rough approximation of justice with a balancing
of needs and goals and potentials for enjoyment among
the parties involved.

    Given this contextual framework, ideals, norms,
and principles serve as guides, lures, directives, and
sources of illumination in the light of which some con-

crete imperatives, some "ought" may arise. But in trying to unite general principles with specific contexts,
one begins with persons and groups in the immediacy of
particular situations shaped by a set of constraining
circumstances which define both the limits and the possibilities of moral action. In this context one asks,
"What is the most fitting, effective, creative response
that can be made for the sake of achieving self-realization in community?" It is people and their fulfillment that matter. To paraphrase what Jesus said about
the Sabbath, principles and norms are for the sake of
humanity. Humanity was not made for the purpose of
living by precepts. Or, to paraphrase what Whitehead
said about experience, the sole justification of any
moral principles whatsoever is the illumination of immediate choice.

     All this is said to reinforce the central claim
that morality is to be seen in terms of fitting response
to a Creative Intentionality at the base of all things
whose will and purpose define the ultimate context of
responsible action. In Christian terms this means
reproducing in our intentions and acts toward others
the quality (love) and the aim (the Society of God) of
the Creator-Redeemer revealed in the person and work of
Jesus known to be the Christ through the witness of the
New Testament. In philosophical categories this means
responding to the divine aims exhibited in the evolutionary processes of nature and history by honoring the
intrinsic worth and by promoting enjoyment (self-realization) in all sentient beings, especially persons.
Related to the quest for a just and good society, responsible human action seeks the increase of freedom,
equality, and well-being (good) of all in a society
dedicated to self-realization in community. Given this

framework of understanding, decisions about what ought
to be done arises contextually in ways that have been
specified. This means that morality has to do mainly with discernment -- that sensitivity to facts and
possibilities which provides the clue to patterns of
life that attune our actions to those of an ultimate
Creative Purpose whose aim is to persuade the world into ever higher harmonies which increase the enjoyment
of life.

APPENDIX

Economic Justice in a Capitalist Society

(This paper was prepared for a conference of clergy
sponsored by Economic Education for Clergy and de-
livered in New York City on October 26, 1982).

My task as a theologian on this occasion bears
some resemblance to that faced by economists: how to
make the most efficient use of relatively scarce resources to accomplish a relatively inexhaustible task.
Time and competence on my part are limited, while the
subject is vast and complex. For the sake of effi-
cency, I would like to propose two hypotheses. The
first thesis has to do with the relation of capitalism and justice. The second proposes a model to guide
us toward a greater achievement of justice in the midst
of our own capitalist economy.

I

My thesis is that a progressively evolving capitalism in a democratic society directed by a quest for
increasing the freedom and equality of individuals
while maximizing the welfare of all is not necessarily inimical to justice. Put more simply, a capitalist
economic order is not in principle contrary to justice.
Given appropriate governmental intervention and direction, an economy organized basically on a capitalist
model has as much potential for justice on the American
scene as any other fundamentally different system. To
get more specific, the presently functioning system is
far from perfect, but it can be reformed in ways that
would lead to an approximate justice without abandoning
major reliance on a competitive market mechanism,

individual freedom, and the private ownership of the
means of production. My own preferences lean toward a
mixed system that would incorporate more features generally regarded as socialist than the present American
economy embodies, but it is not my purpose to develop
specific policy recommendations. I just want to identify my bias.

A whole set of assumptions surrounds the foregoing
statements, only some of which can be articulated here.
But one which is essential is that we cannot isolate
the socio-economic order and ask the question of justice in that context alone. There are two other elements in the total picture that must be taken into account. It is useful to view the complex reality of
society under three headings.[1] First, there is the
socio-economic order, by which is meant the basic way
people are organized to produce and distribute the
goods and services they need. At the moment we are
talking about a mixed system whose basic form is advanced capitalism. In the second place, we must speak of
the political order by which power is distributed and
decisions are made regarding the common life. Here we
assume a democratic polity with majority rule, minor-
ity rights, and free and equal citizens who are governed by their consent. Finally, there is the cultural
order, by which I mean all those systems, symbols, and
creative expressions by which truth, meanings, and
values are generated, disseminated, and transformed.
Here we refer to science, morality, religion, education,
art, and so on. A primary cultural value in America
has been individual self-realization. My point is that
capitalism as an economic system functions within the
larger context of a political order and a cultural
realm. Hence, the question of justice must be asked

about the way in which all of these systems function
together in all of their complexity and interaction.
My own assumption is that these orders are relatively
autonomous but interdependent. Change can be initiated
in either sector with consequences for the other two.
Moral advance in a society depends on whether sufficient
political power can be mobilized to incarnate justice
in functioning institutions.

    A second assumption or sub-thesis is that capital-
ism is a distinctive way of organizing the socio-economic order which has peculiar strengths and weaknesses.
Hence, capitalism poses a particular set of problems
for the political order and the quest for justice.
Here is not the place to get into a lengthy discussion
about the definition of capitalism. Perhaps for our
purposes we can agree that among its chief features are
that capital for producing goods and services is accumulated in private hands; use is made of a competitive
market to make dominant economic choices; and individuals are free in principle to enter the system in any
ways they choose as owners, producers, workers, consumers, etc. Capitalism thus conceived in its various
stages of development has been enormously successful in
producing wealth and distributing it fairly widely,
at least in countries with a democratic political order.
Its virtues are well known: its stress on individual
freedom, its efficiency and capacity to promote growth,
its decentralization of power into a plurality of competing enterprises -- to mention a few. The flaws of
capitalism are, generally speaking, the opposite side
of its positive attributes. Many of these faults and
insufficiencies spring from the centrality of individual freedom employed in the pursuit of self-interest.
I list here merely for illustrative purposes some of

the standard objections raised by critics.

1. Capitalism by sanctioning and magnifying the pursuit of self-interest tends to generate great economic inequalities. Some succeed and some don't, for a variety of reasons.

2. Capitalism in practice leads to a concentration of economic power and corresponding political power. Capitalists may profess the virtues of competition but tend to seek monopoly. Disproportionate power in the hands of some leads to injustice as a rule.

3. The market system is incapable of doing certain essential things. One problem is that of maintaining equilibrium and steady growth. I refer to the familiar cycle of "boom and bust." Beyond that are needs for national defense, systems of roads, schools, post office, and for certain services which tend toward natural monopolies such as utilities, and on and on. Finally, there are questions related to the support and direction of scientific research and technological development, the need for an energy policy, space exploration, preservation of the environment, and so on through a long list.

For at least these three reasons the last half century has witnessed an ever increasing role of the government. As we all well know the question of the proper function of the government in reducing inequalities, in curbing excessive economic power in private hands, and in promoting the general welfare in the interests both of prosperity and justice has been central to political debate for decades. The present (Reagan) administration came to power promising among other things to get the government off our backs.

To sum up, capitalism does some things very well

but in the process creates other problems. Beyond that
there are functions and needs that private enterprise
and the market cannot serve at all or do so poorly.   In
both cases the intervention of the people through the
instrumentality of government in pursuit of both social
welfare and justice is essential. By implication I
have rejected the severest criticisms of the far left.
I do not believe that capitalism is intrinsically exploitative or that the government in a capitalist society will inevitably be merely the political arm of
the entrepreneurs who control the means of production.
Nor do I agree with some cultural critics that capitalism simply legitimizes selfishness into a system, that
it is incurably materialistic, or unavoidably leads to
a crass and vulgar mass culture, consumerism and hedonism. That all these evils are possible and historically present in varying degrees in capitalist economies I do not doubt. Moreover, there are structural
tendencies in capitalism that lead in all the directions enumerated. However, the full truth is generally
more complicated than the simplistic and extreme criticisms acknowledge. Again, I insist that economic arrangements, political realities, and cultural values
interact in complex ways to produce the actual situation we live in with all its ambiguities and numerous
contradictions.[2]

    This is not the place to engage in an analysis
of comparative economic systems. Were I to do so, I
would describe socialism as having a different set of
strengths and weaknesses, which in some ways are the
reverse of the virtues and vices of capitalism. Hence,
I find each in its pure form severely lacking.[3] To
oversimplify, capitalism has the technical merit of
efficiency and the moral merit of stressing individual

freedom. Socialism has the rational merit of planning
production for use rather than profit and the moral
merit of seeking the common good of all. Both systems
have a place for equality as a moral value. In capitalism the stress is on the equality of individuals in
competing for economic rewards. In socialism it is on
equality in sharing socially-produced benefits. Ideally,
capitalism leads toward equality of opportunity, while
socialism yearns for having the needs of all equally
met. However, the belief that unregulated pursuit of
self-interest will through the guidance of "the invisible hand" guarantee the general welfare and without
creating morally intolerable inequalities is a capitalist myth. Likewise, the belief that a command economy
can efficiently maximize the common good to be more or
less equally shared and do so through centralized planning without running the risk of tyranny in the restraint of individual freedom is a socialist myth.

However simplistic I may be in this scandalously
oversimplified analysis, my main point is that neither
system justifies the absolute moral claims which have
been made for each. Some in my own faith have argued
that capitalism is based on the Bible and that it goes
hand in glove with Christianity. Prominent Protestant
theologians have claimed that socialism is the only
Christian alternative. I deny both as unwarranted dog-
matisms, while affirming that in some contexts and
countries one as the dominant mode of economic organization may be preferable on both technical and moral
grounds.[4] To be appropriate an economic system must
fit the total set of social, political, and cultural
facts and potentials that are present in a given country
at a specific time.

To complete this analysis, it must be added that

there are determinative factors in a society relative
to the concern for justice that are independent of particular economic systems as such.   Let me mention three.
1.   In modern industrial and post-industrial societies
one of the engines running the system is science-based
technology.   The problems raised for human welfare in
this context are transideological in that they rise in
both capitalist and socialist countries.   I refer not
only to political questions such as the threat of nu-
nuclear war but to more economic questions such as the
impact of automation on employment.   2.   A second set
of problems is suggested by the term bureaucracy.   Are
there efficient and more humanly satisfying ways of
organizing people to get the work of society done in
a complex society than by the hierarchy and command
model of large bureaucracies?   3.   Finally, we are confronted with a wide range of ecological problems.   How
can we balance environmental sanity in the use of
resources and controlling pollution with the values of
economic growth?   Must growth finally go, or can we
have a sustainable society with justice and continuing
enlargement of the economic pie?   Neither of these three
is system-specific but must be faced by all economies
in the modern world both capitalist and socialist.

     In addition, there are structural issues within
our capitalist society that must be dealt with.   While
these matters confront us in a particular form given
our own economy, it is not clear that we could avoid
them or their counterparts in some other system.   Here
again let me mention three.   1.   How can we curb inflation under conditions of full employment and steady
growth without going into recession?   2.   How can we
promote greater equality among our citizens without
unduly offending efficiency and a consequent loss of

total economic benefits to be shared? 3. How can we have affirmative action to redress the balance in favor of groups previously systematically disadvantaged without falling into reverse discrimination? There are issues of economic justice here, but they are not limited or merely endemic to capitalist societies.

It is against this background that my initial thesis is to be understood. Let me repeat it and amplify it in this framework. A progressively evolving capitalist economy managed and directed by a properly functioning democracy in a culture dedicated to the increase of human welfare and the fullest extension of freedom and equality is not inimical to justice. To summarize, the achievement of justice in our society depends not only on appropriately modifying a capitalist economy but also on making democracy really work and on the values that dominate the minds and hearts of citizens.

In this context I would urge those who are concerned with justice to abandon any dedication to particular ideologies and systems as such. Instead, let us seek open-ended ideologies based on tough-minded empiricism which looks at particular functioning societies and asks what is happening to people and what modes of economic and political functioning would increase human freedom, maximize social welfare, and extend equality. Let our ideologies and our systems evolve to fit the requirements of a given situation rather than try to defend preconceived "isms" in defiance of facts.

II

Let me turn quickly to a brief analysis of the

present state of capitalist society in the context of
the political and cultural orders. To do that I want
to make use of a paradigm found in George Cabot Lodge's
book THE NEW AMERICAN IDEOLOGY.[5] He suggests that the
"old ideology" that prevailed for the first two hundred
years of American history is breaking down, while a
"new ideology" is being born. Central to the emerging
paradigm is what he calls "communitarianism." This he
contrasts with the "individualism" of the "old ideology." In the older view the individual is the basic
unit. Society is the sum total of individuals and
arises by contract. Fulfillment achieved by individual
effort is a basic dogma. In the "communitarian" model
society is seen as an interdependent whole made up of
groups, sub-groups, and individuals. Fulfillment of
the individual comes by participation in a community to
which one contributes and from which one gains benefits.
Justice will refer to the healthy functioning of this
organic system in which one gives in accordance with
ability and receives in accordance with merit and basic
need.

My thesis is that a "communitarian" model has potential which we should help bring to actualization.
It would have at least four implications for witness
and action:

1. It would stress the virtue and necessity of
cooperation and harmonious interdependence rather than
competition alone.

2. It would stress devotion to the common good
as essential to everybody's good in an interdependent
society rather than simply sanctioning the unlimited
pursuit of private gain.

3. It would stress the importance of restraint
and frugality as a way of curbing the appetite for

unlimited consumption and acquisition. Where necessary
frugality might be enforced, as, for example, by taxing
heavily the purchase of gas-guzzling cars.

4. It would pay particular attention to the poor
and disadvantaged and seek ways to equalize their opportunities and resources.

Let me stress that I am not setting forth cooperation, devotion to the common good, frugality, and
equality as mere ideals. They are that. But I am
also saying that these virtues grow organically out of
the realities of the present and emerging future. They
fit the situation factually and morally. To some extent, they are economic and political necessities and
not just moral options. Unless we seek the common
good with self-restraint, exercise frugality, and show
a concern for the least advantaged, none of us may
have good future prospects. In this sense these ideals
set the moral agenda for religious communities and
their leadership in the coming decades.

This thesis, like the first one, rests on some
basic assumptions which I must now spell out briefly.
In the years since World War II this country has experienced an enormous growth of prosperity. Along with
this in the last half century, far-reaching changes have
taken place in the relationship of government to the
economy and the society generally. While national
government has always had a commitment to meet common
needs that individuals alone could not provide, such as
defense, highways, railroads, etc., recent decades have
witnessed the assumption of three new tasks: 1. Since
the time of the depression of the 1930's, the state
has taken responsibility for normative economic policy.
I mean such tasks as reducing unemployment, stimulating
growth, regulating inflation, redistributing income, etc.

2. In the 1950's the government began to underwrite
science and technology at the research and development
level. 3. In the 1960's there emerged a commitment
to normative social policy. I refer to the civil rights
movement, housing policy, environmental concerns, income support through the welfare system, and protecting
the rights and claims of groups that hitherto had been
left out of the main stream.[6] The government is now
committed "not only to the welfare state, but to redress the impact of all economic and social inequalities as well."[7]

One result of all this is that an increasing number of issues are now settled in the political arena.
Value conflicts are heightened and put in the center of
public attention to be resolved in the halls of government. The strains put upon government could be more
easily resolved in a time of economic expansion. More
particularly, those issues involving government expen-
diture to assist the poor were not as acute and controversial as long as these programs could be as paid for
out of the margin of growth. However, when the economy
is stagnant, productivity is virtually at a standstill,
unemployment rises, and we alternate between inflation
and recession, social strife over welfare programs will
inevitably become more severe. The budget of the federal government has become the central focus of a power
struggle and value conflict, since it is the mechanism
of allocation of resources and alleviation of economic
distress. How much the government will spend and for
whom and for what will be a major issue for the coming
decades.

In this framework certain problems become acute.
We live in a time not only of rising expectations but
rising entitlements. More and more people and groups

demand that the government protect their rights and
further their interests. This is a part of the "new
ideology." But the ability of the government to meet
those demands in so far as they require money is more
limited in a time of economic stagnation. Moreover,
the rights of minorities and previously neglected
groups such as blacks and women threaten the advantages
if not the rights of individuals belonging to the privileged groups. So we fight over the Equal Rights Amend-
ment, busing, and affirmative action versus reverse discrimination. Finally, there are those cultural and
moral issues such as the rights of homosexuals, abortion, pornography, etc. which have moved into the political arena and are profoundly divisive.

Every industrial state has to deal with the tension between accumulation and legitimation. By accumulation I mean resources withheld from immediate consumption and invested to insure growth. By legitimation
I mean the consent to government authority that comes
when people's real needs and demands for economic well-
being and social rights are being met. To put it differently, the tension is between future growth and
immediate consumption. When the economic pie is growing, the tension is not so sharp. There can be increasing rates of consumption and enough left over for
investment to insure future growth. But when economic
growth is slow or stagnant, the issue becomes acute.
The resolution can come only if there is a "consensual
agreement on the normative issues of distributive justice, in the balance to be struck between growth and
consumption."[8] And this consensus is just what we do
not sufficiently have.

Now into this picture comes the debate over how
much and how long can we either sustain growth without

too much social and physical burden on resources or
tolerate growth in the face of pollution. When the
issues of the limits to growth are combined with the
economic problems of maintaining justice while balancing consumption and growth, we have the whole range of
issues that we summarize with the term "eco-justice"
or,as I prefer, "biopolitics."

At this point let me quote from Daniel Bell who
summarizes a lot of this:

> The economic dilemmas confronting Western
> societies derive from the fact that we have
> sought to combine bourgeois appetites which
> resist curbs on acquisitiveness, either
> morally or by taxation, a democratic polity
> which, increasingly and understandably,
> demands more and more services as entitle-
> ments, and an individual ethos which at best
> defends the idea of personal liberty and at
> worst evades the necessary social responsi-
> bilities and social sacrifices which a com-
> munal society demands. In sum, we have no
> normative commitment to a public household
> or a public philosophy that would mediate
> private conflicts.9

Continuing with Daniel Bell, up to this point we have
had in this country three unspoken assumptions:
1. "that the values of the individual were to be maximized, 2. that rising material wealth would dissolve
all strains resulting from inequality, and 3. that
continuity of experience would provide solutions for
all future problems."[10] These assumptions have now
been strained or disrupted.

In such a social context what we badly need for
the immediate and long term future is a conception of
and devotion to the common good which puts an appropriate restraint on individual and group wants, while
retaining a sense of legitimate need. A concept of
the common good, of the public welfare, would provide
a framework in which rights of individuals and groups

can be balanced against the rights of others and restrain the illegitimate escalation of rights and
claims into unjustified wants and selfish aggrandizement. Without such a conception and a devotion to
agreed upon normative rules, the only method of settling
problems is a combination of bargaining and a struggle
for power. In Bell's terms what we have lost and need
desperately is "civitas, that spontaneous willingness
to obey the law, to respect the rights of others, to
forego the temptations of private enrichment at the
expense of the public weal -- in short to honor the
"city" of which one is a member."[11] Now anyone with a
realistic view of human nature may think that the curbing of selfishness is the perennial problem of all societies. Nevertheless, it is the special task of religious institutions to contribute to the building of a
sense of social responsibility which restrains private
greed for the sake of common justice, and to do this
within the social context of the next two decades.

This moral task is made exceedingly difficult by
two converging cultural trends with which we are all
familiar. One is the preoccupation with self and individual advancement, growth, fulfillment, success, and
so on that has been variously characterized as the cult
of the "me generation" (Tom Wolfe), "the new narcis-
sism," (Peter Marin), "the narcissistic society"
(Christopher Lasch), and "the therapeutic mentality"
(Donald Miller).[12] The second both reinforces the preoccupation with self-actualization and constitutes an
independent factor. I refer to the sense of bafflement in the face of the complexity and ambiguity of
social problems which so frustrates people that it
drives them away from social concern to preoccupation
with self and to inward consciousness and individual
happiness.

Nevertheless, despite the difficulties, I want to
urge that a major task of the clergy and the institutions they lead is to develop in persons of every age
and social role a devotion to the common good which can
moderate the quest for special advantage on the part
of individuals and groups. I speak to you as moral
leaders who must address the question of the public
welfare in the midst of the conflict between "the old
ideology" and "the new ideology," in an era increasingly conscious of limits, in a time caught between the
demands of groups for more and more economic gains and
social entitlements, on the one hand, and the realities of economic stagnation and mutually exclusive
claims, on the other hand. In an increasingly interdependent society moral educators need a vision of
society as an organic whole made up of many members
whose fulfillment requires that their individual quest
for fulfillment be integrated with the rights of others
to a similar quest within the context of a common good.

This brings us back to the intuition of a new
paradigm which lies before us luring us towards its
actualization in the common life. The individualism of
"the old ideology" needs to be moderated by the communal
focus of "the new ideology." Private gain and the public interest need to be correlated in a vision of a
social order in which individual freedom and social
justice are balanced. This is a perennial problem, but
it has a peculiar focus in our present time. More
specifically the question before us in the next two decades is whether we can learn to live sanely, satis-
factorily, and responsibly in an increasingly complicated world full of limits and in which solutions to
problems are fraught with much ambiguity, compromise,
and trade-offs. We are facing the growth of many limits

in an increasingly interdependent world. We approach
the biological limits of the world in terms of pollution, and resources. We face limits to economic
growth and tough structural limits which generate inflation, unemployment, and recession. There are limits
to the rise in affluence. We face limits to which
problems have solutions without undesirable side effects. Many involve conflict between right and right,
not between right and wrong. We see a conflict between rising entitlements and the limits to providing
them. With pluralism and diversity, there are many
competing groups with different agendas among white
males, women, blacks, and other minorities. We confront a limit to our power in the world to work our
way. To live successfully, religious maturity in this
situation requires a high tolerance for complexity and
ambiguity. We need a theology of limits and a doctrine
of grace which can save us from our bafflement and
frustration in dealing with issues as well as from sin
and doubt. We have to learn to live with trade-offs
and compromise and limited gains in trying to balance
competing good things. No group can expect to get all
it wants. It is within this context that we need a
new vision of the common good which can help us mediate
the conflicts between individuals and groups.

In this situation several possibilities arise for
religious institutions. 1. We can retreat into individual and other-worldly piety and let the world go.
2. We can confront the world with a reactionary theology and politics which seek to impose a set of cultural
and economic values from the past onto the present.
These two are the temptations of conservative groups.
We have seen an illustration of the second in the new
right-wing politics of some branches of fundamentalist

Christianity. 3. We can retreat into a concern with
self-development, personal growth, and the cultivation
of the inner spiritual life of individuals and congre-
gations. This has been the temptation of many main line
and liberal groups in the 70's, and it will continue to
have a seductive appeal. 4. Or we can develop a soph-
isticated social concern and a program of action based
on a refined ethics of ambiguity and a theology of
limits which generates a tolerance for complexity and
trade-offs along with a quest for a harmonious, just
and fulfilling society in a world of peace. It will
not surprise you to hear that I contend for this fourth
option as the way of responsible morality which religious leaders should promote.

        To conclude, let me summarize briefly what I have
said. 1. First, a democratic capitalist society is
potentially just. 2. Second, we need a model of a
"communitarian" society as a guide for the reformation
of our existing capitalist order for the sake of justice. This means that cooperation, mutual interdependence, restraint, and devotion to the common good will
transform or at least modify the dominant ethos of
competition, independence, unrestrained acquisitive-
ness, and selfish individualism. This is no small
challenge, but I think it marks out the path to economic justice in a capitalist society.

NOTES

PREFACE

1. James Gustafson, ETHICS FROM A THEOCENTRIC PER-
    PECTIVE: THEOLOGY AND ETHICS (Chicago: The
    University of Chicago Press, 1981), p. 59.

INTRODUCTION

1. John Cobb, A CHRISTIAN NATURAL THEOLOGY (Philadelphia:
    The Westminster Press, 1965); David Griffin, GOD,
    POWER AND EVIL (Philadelphia: The Westminster
    Press, 1976).

CHAPTER I

1. See John Cobb, A CHRISTIAN NATURAL THEOLOGY
    (Philadelphia: Westminster Press, 1965). I
    freely acknowledge the ambiguity of speaking of
    a Christian natural theology. Despite the
    objections of David Tracy and Schubert Ogden,
    the designation still seems apt. One might
    ask, "What's in a name? A theology by any
    other name would come out the same." Cobb's
    defense of the title is refreshing by virtue
    of its honesty in acknowledging that his
    philosophical views, like all others, are
    historically conditioned. In his case Cobb
    is simply confessing that his Christian background
    influences him in the choice of a particular
    philosophy. Tracy and Ogden, on the other hand,
    seem to make rather less of historical relativity
    than the facts warrant, while accusing Cobb
    of just the opposite fault. They seem to harbor
    the view that some philosophies, notably White-
    head's in this case, can be known to be true or
    more true than alternatives rather than simply
    believed to be so by their adherents. My view
    is that the efforts to prove the validity of
    a particular philosophy assume its truth as the
    basis of the proof rather than establish its
    veracity on universally convincing grounds.
    Validation is a circular procedure although
    not hopelessly nor absolutely so. The history
    of philosophy may well represent some degree
    of progress in eliminating error and clarifying
    thought. But whatever transcendence there may be
    of the circularity of verfication does not take away

the fundamental relativity which characterizes
all world views. Nor does it make possible the
non-adjectival natural theology to which Ogden
and Tracy still in some measure apparently
aspire. See the article by David Tracy in
JOHN COBB'S THEOLOGY IN PROCESS, ed. by David
Griffin and Thomas Altizer (Philadelphia:
Westminster Press, 1977) , pp. 25-38, and
Cobb's response, pp. 150-154. For Ogden's
objections see Brown, et. al., PROCESS PHILOSOPHY
AND CHRISTIAN THOUGHT (Indianapolis: Bobbs-
Merril Co., Inc., 1971), pp. 111-115. In an
important review Langdon Gilkey makes an opposite
charge. He doubts whether, in some fundamental
respects, Cobb's Christian natural theology is
really Christian. Cobb's reply is that he was
in that book doing natural theology and not the
specific work of Christian theology based on
Scriptural sources and norms. While pertinent,
Cobb is not fully convincing. His Christian
views do not seem to differ much from his
Whiteheadian views, at least when speaking of God.
Whether his Whiteheadian views are compatible with
Christian doctrine is a substantive and not
simply a methodological question. See Langdon
Gilkey, "Review of A CHRISTIAN NATURAL THEOLOGY,"
THEOLOGY TODAY (January, 1966), pp. 530-545.
Cobb's reply is found in THEOLOGY TODAY (April,
1966), pp. 140-142, under the title, "Can Natural
Theology be Christian?"

2.   H. Richard Niebuhr, CHRIST AND CULTURE (New York:
     Harper & Row, 1951).

3.   Paul Lehmann, ETHICS IN A CHRISTIAN CONTEXT (New
     York: Harper & Row, 1963), pp. 251-284.

4.   Paul Tillich, SYSTEMATIC THEOLOGY, (Chicago:
     University of Chicago Press, 1951), Vol. I, pp.
     23-24.

5.   This way of putting it may overstate the element
     of rational clarity that is actually available.
     Real life is too dense, thick, complex, ambiguous,
     and paradoxical for any interpretive pattern to
     clarify absolutely and perfectly. Streams of
     intellectual light only partially dispel the
     mystery of existence, although there are moments
     of special illumination when all seems clear and
     plain.

6.   John Cobb, LIVING OPTIONS IN PROTESTANT THEOLOGY
     (Philadelphia: Westminster Press, 1962), p. 313.

7.   Alfred North Whitehead, SCIENCE AND THE MODERN
     WORLD (New York: The Macmillan Co., 1925).

8.   SYSTEMATIC THEOLOGY, Vol. I, p. 27.

9.   Carl Becker, THE HEAVENLY CITY OF THE 18th CENTURY
     PHILOSOPHERS (New Haven: Yale University Press,
     1932).

10. Karl Barth, CHURCH DOGMATICS (Edinburgh: T & T
     Clark, 1956), Vol. I, part 2, p. 729.

11. Ibid., p. 733.

12. Barth, CHURCH DOGMATICS, Vol. I, part 2, p. 537.

13. Ibid., pp. 457-585.

14. Henry Nelson Wieman, THE SOURCE OF HUMAN GOOD
     (Carbondale: Southern Illinois University Press,
     1946), p. 268.

15. JOHN COBB'S THEOLOGY IN PROCESS, pp. 22-23. While
     there are problems enough with the effort to
     find a universal essence of Christianity, David
     Griffin shows that there are equally formidable
     difficulties with the alternative Cobb proposes.
     Cobb wishes to preserve Christian identity by
     tracing through history the operation of the
     principle of creative transformation, which he
     identifies with Christ or Logos. But if one
     is to judge which transformations are "creative,"
     then some criterion of judgment must be presup-
     posed. This takes us right back to the question
     of Christian essentials or to an essence or norm
     which enables us to distinguish creative from
     destructive transformations in the history of
     the church.

16. Harold DeWolf, A THEOLOGY OF THE LIVING CHURCH
     (New York: Harper and Brothers, 1953), pp. 33-
     36.

17. For a more detailed discussion of these methodol-
     ogical issues, see Kenneth Cauthen, SCIENCE,
     SECULARIZATION AND GOD (Nashville: Abingdon
     Press, 1969), pp. 61-89, 196-210.

18.   Cf. David Tracy, A BLESSED RAGE FOR ORDER (New
      York: Seabury Press, 1975).

                        CHAPTER II

1.   For a brief but excellent discussion of these dis-
      tinctions see William K. Frankena, ETHICS
      (Englewood Cliffs: Prentice-Hall, Inc., 1973),
      Second edition, pp. 12-60. For more extended
      discussions of the standard problems in philos-
      ophical ethics, see Richard T. Garner and
      Bernard Rosen, MORAL PHILOSOPHY (New York: The
      Macmillan Co., 1967). A standard treatment of
      issues in contemporary moral philosophy is found
      in Richard Brandt, ETHICAL THEORY (Englewood
      Cliffs: Prentice-Hall, Inc., 1959). A history
      of developments in ethics during the twentieth
      century, largely British, can be found in Roger
      N. Hancock, TWENTIETH CENTURY ETHICS (New York:
      Columbia University Press, 1974).

2.   It may appear that I am in a subtle way using
      teleological reasoning at the point of making
      comparisions between greater and lesser offenses
      against or enhancement of intrinsic human worth.
      Telling a small "white lie" to a spouse to avoid
      hurting his/her feeling is more acceptable than
      secretly committing adultery. However, this
      measurement is made in terms of what honors or
      offends human worth as a present fact, not in
      terms of future consequences for good or ill,
      as in the case of teleological procedures. Surely
      some rationale distinguishing between prima facie
      and actual duty is needed that is not purely
      arbitrary. And must not this rationale finally
      be based on some order of being and value
      that is objective and real and in terms of which
      comparative judgments can be made but related
      to present structure and fact not in accordance
      with future outcomes and potential alone?

3.   W. D. Ross, THE RIGHT AND THE GOOD (New York:
      Oxford University, 1930), and THE FOUNDATIONS
      OF ETHICS (New York: Oxford University Press,
      1939), pp. 83-95.

4.   This case is taken from J.J.C. Smart and Bernard
      Williams, UTILITARIANISM (New York:Cambridge
      University Press, 1973), pp. 69ff.

5. J.J.C. Smart defends himself against H.J. McCloskey,
    who suggests that he is happy with this consequence
    of utilitarianism. He responds that he is not happy
    but admits that it is theoretically possible that
    utilitarianism might sometimes require one to do
    something unjust for the sake of the good. UTILI-
    TARIANISM, pp. 70-71.

6. This is the charge made by D.H. Hodgson, CONSEQUENCES
    OF UTILITARIANISM (New York: Oxford University Press,
    1967).

7. Brand Blanshard, REASON AND GOODNESS (New York: The
    Macmillan Co., 1961), pp. 139-160, 324-329.

8. On this point see Frankena, ETHICS, pp. 34-43, and
    Nicolas Rescher, DISTRIBUTIVE JUSTICE (Indianapolis:
    The Bobbs-Merrill Co., Inc., 1966), pp. 25-69.

9. For example, one has to look into the difference
    between asking about the consequences for good
    and ill if I do act A in circumstance B and asking
    what if everybody did act A in circumstance B. The
    act utilitarian might argue that most people probably
    will not do act A in this circumstance so that I
    only have to ask what is the probable influence of
    my doing act A in circumstance B on others to do
    act A in circumstance B. Let us suppose that act A
    is cutting across the grass to get to a class that
    a student is about to be late for. The general
    utilitarian might respond that one must universalize
    one's own actions in order to determine rightness
    and that making exceptions for oneself is not
    legitimate. My conclusion is that this is a stand-
    off with the act and general utilitarian having
    about as much claim to being correct as the other.
    Likewise, the rule utilitarian who makes no excep-
    tions to rules is not as likely to maximize good
    as the one who make rare and judicious exceptions.
    But to begin to make exceptions opens up the pos-
    sibility of losing the distinctiveness of the rule
    position and to fall into some form or modified
    act or summary rule theory. See Frankena, ETHICS,
    pp. 34-43, for a brief but perceptive account of
    some of the arguments. M.G. Singer is well known
    for his development of the generalization theme.
    See his GENERALIZATION IN ETHICS (New York: Random
    House, 1961). Singer's views are discussed in
    Hancock, TWENTIETH CENTURY ETHICS, pp. 164-181.

10. J.J.C. Smart and Bernard Williams, UTILITARIANISM, pp. 69ff.

11. John Rawls, A THEORY OF JUSTICE (Cambridge: Harvard University Press, 1971), p. 30.

12. While utilitarianism appears to provide the most immediate and clear way of justifying the right of <u>eminent</u> <u>domain</u>, equally persuasive warrants can be derived on deontological grounds. Nevertheless, utilitarianism does not take seriously enough the distinction among persons (Rawls), and it does seem to me an offense against the dignity and worth of these Polish citizens in Detroit to take their homes for the sake of building an automobile factory. Utilitarianism would merely subtract the disadvantage to the Poles from the sum total of benefit to be derived for the entire city of Detroit to arrive at a net sum of good over bad, without allowance being made for the rights of persons as persons.

13. Perhaps it would be more accurate to say that a person has the privilege of respecting his/her own rights and the obligation to respect the rights of another.

14. I shall discuss later in Chapter VI the implications for moral theory of the fact that persons as persons are equal and yet have different potential in specific respects.

15. An impasse with no resolution? A lottery would be permissible but not mandatory. Only those who wished to participate should. No one should be forced, but anyone who did not choose to be involved in the lottery should not feast on the results. Of course, once the lottery became voluntary, the numbers involved might not be sufficient to gain the desired ends.

16. These formulations, of course, have been strongly influenced by the process philosophy of Alfred North Whitehead. In particular, see PROCESS AND REALITY (New York: The Macmillan Co. 1929), and MODES OF THOUGHT (New York: The Macmillan Co., 1938). See also my SCIENCE SECULARIZATION AND GOD (Nashville: Abingdon Press, 1979), pp. 90-130.

17. Whiteheadians will doubtless be dismayed at what
    appears to be either my ignorance or my ignoring
    of the specifics of the theory of actual occasions
    in relation to societies, while generally praising
    the master himself and hooking on to some of his
    views. In describing organisms or life processes,
    I am centering phenomenologically on their macro-
    manifestations in animals (and maybe plants too),
    which are of more ethical relevance. I believe
    that at this level my generalizations will hold.
    It may be true that a consistent and complete
    accounting of these processes cannot finally be
    given without adopting the Whiteheadian theories
    in detail. I am aware that a person or an animal
    is, in Whiteheadian terms, a complex society,
    while I seem to be treating them as individuals
    with a history. Upon reviewing at this moment
    the lines in the text that were written some time
    ago, I am acutely conscious of a tension between
    the virtues of the microanalysis of Whitehead in
    explaining macrochange and the problems raised
    with respect to the identity and historical
    continuity of the self. I feel the need to de-
    scribe an animal or a person as a real individual.
    Many critics have doubted whether Whitehead can
    properly account for self-identity in persons in
    a way which grounds moral agency. Doubtless it
    is true that I am not in possession in my own mind,
    much less in the text, of a completely coherent,
    adequate, and applicable theory of selfhood, of
    individuality, identity, and in general of the
    relationship between discrete individual occasions
    and societies. But it is not beyond doubt that
    Whitehead was either. So for this purpose I
    persist in my own way of stating what an individual
    organism is, a view which seems to fit at the
    macrolevel of animals and persons, leaving open the
    final resolution of the technical metaphysical ques-
    tions.

                         CHAPTER III

1. Richart T. Garner and Bernard Rosen, MORAL PHILOS-
    OPHY (New York: The Macmillan Co., 1967), p. 220.
    See also, William K. Frankena, ETHICS (Englewood
    Cliffs: Prentice-Hall, Second edition, Inc., 1973),
    pp. 95-116.

2. Garner and Rosen, MORAL PHILOSOPHY, p. 220.

3. Ibid., pp. 273-274.

4. John R. Searle, "How to Derive 'Ought' from 'Is,'"
    READINGS IN CONTEMPORARY ETHICAL THEORY, ed. by
    Kenneth Pahel and Marvin Schiller (Englewood
    Cliffs: Prentice-Hall, Inc., 1970), pp. 156-168.

5. William K. Frankena, PERSPECTIVES ON MORALITY
    (South Bend: University of Notre Dame Press,
    1976), p. 142.

6. Ibid., p. 141.

7. Ibid., p. 213.

8. W. David Ross, FOUNDATIONS OF ETHICS (New York:
    Oxford University Press, 1939), pp. 27-28.

9. Ibid., pp. 83-85. See also, Ross, THE RIGHT AND
    THE GOOD (New York: Oxford University Press,
    1930).

10. See my SCIENCE, SECULARIZATION AND GOD (Nashville:
    Abingdon Press, 1969), p. 156.

11. Frankena, PERSPECTIVES ON MORALITY, p. 139.

12. Kenneth Cauthen, SCIENCE, SECULARIZATION AND GOD.

13. Frankena, PERSPECTIVES ON MORALITY, pp. 6-9.

14. Ibid., p. 9.

15. Cf. H. Richard Niebuhr, THE RESPONSIBLE SELF (New
    York: Harper & Row, 1963). While I agree with
    theological definists who say that right means
    commanded by God, I presumably differ from them
    in saying that it is equally true that God
    commands the right because it is right. Can this
    seeming double talk be clarified? God wills the
    right and the good because it is right and good.
    But right and good are not alien or extraneous
    to God but define the structure and aim of the
    divine nature and character. Hence, right and
    good are intrinsic to or immanent in the divine
    being and not foreign or external constraints to
    which God must conform. In short, God's com-
    mand is a free expression of the divine character,
    while at the same time the divine char-

acter provides the determinative context with
which freedom is exercised. See my SCIENCE,
SECULARIZATION AND GOD, pp. 191-192. Paul Tillich's
way of putting this would be to say that in God
freedom and destiny are identical. See his
SYSTEMATIC THEOLOGY (Chicago: University of
Chicago Press, 1951), Vol. I, pp. 182-186, 248-249.

16. H. Richard Niebuhr, THE RESPONSIBLE SELF (New York:
Harper & Row, 1963).

17. Hence, in this respect I join with those "revisionist"
theologians who argue that an adequate analysis of
human existence points to a dimension of transcendence
and shows the insufficiency of a purely secular philosophy of life. See David Tracy, A BLESSED RAGE FOR
ORDER (New York: Seabury Press, 1975). However,
I also believe that an adequate analysis of nature,
especially the evolutionary process, also points to
the reality of a Transcendent Purpose. See my SCI-
ENCE, SECULARIZATION AND GOD.

18. I am well aware that the ambiguous and tragic dimensions of life as aspects of "the problem of evil"
constitute a formidable barrier to belief in divine
goodness. To meet this objection, I believe that it
is necessary to speak of metaphysical limitations on
the power of God. A good case can be made, I think,
for the reality of a Cosmic Purpose which works within the limits of the finitude of being and the freedom of persons (and other subhuman creatures) to
actualize to the fullest emergent and emerging possibilities of enjoyment (goodness). See my SCIENCE,
SECULARIZATION AND GOD.

19. Paul Lehmann, ETHICS IN A CHRISTIAN CONTEXT (New
York: Harper & Row, 1963), pp. 251-284.

20. Paul Tillich, SYSTEMATIC THEOLOGY, VOL. I, pp. 59-66.

CHAPTER IV

1. H. Richard Niebuhr, THE RESPONSIBLE SELF (New York:
Harper & Row, 1963).

2. Kenneth Cauthen, THE ETHICS OF ENJOYMENT (Atlanta:
John Knox Press, 1975).

3. C. H. Dodd, GOSPEL AND LAW (New York: Cambridge
University Press, 1951), pp. 64-83.

4. Gene Outka, AGAPE: AN ETHICAL ANALYSIS (New Haven:
    Yale University Press, 1972),   pp. 9-13.

5. Reinhold Niebuhr, AN INTERPRETATION OF CHRISTIAN
    ETHICS (New York: Scribners, 1935). Paul Ramsey,
    DEEDS AND RULES IN CHRISTIAN ETHICS (Oliver and
    Boyd, 1965).

6. William Frankena, ETHICS (Englewood Cliffs: Prentice-
    Hall, Inc., 1973), and William Frankena, "Love and
    Principle in Christian Ethics," FAITH AND PHILOSOPHY,
    ed. by Alvin Plantinga (Grand Rapids: Wm. B. Eerdmans,
    Co., 1964), pp. 203-225.

7. W. D. Ross, THE RIGHT AND THE GOOD (New York: Oxford
    University Press, 1939), p. 21.

8. Anders Nygren, AGAPE AND EROS (London: S-P-C-K, 1957).

9. Ibid., pp. 75-79.

10. Reinhold Niebuhr, THE NATURE AND DESTINY OF MAN (New
    York: Charles Scribner's Sons, 1949), Vol. II, pp. 68-
    97, 244-286; FAITH AND HISTORY (New York: Charles
    Scribner's Sons, 1949), pp. 171-195. See also, Outka,
    AGAPE, pp. 24-25, and Paul Ramsey, NINE MODERN
    MORALISTS (Englewood Cliffs: Prentice-Hall, Inc.,
    1962), pp. 111-147.

11. Reinhold Niebuhr, AN INTERPRETATION OF CHRISTIAN
    ETHICS, pp. 103-135.

12. Outka, AGAPE, pp. 68-70.

13. Paul Ramsey, BASIC CHRISTIAN ETHICS (New York:
    Scribner's, 1951), pp. 153-166.

14. W. D. Ross, FOUNDATIONS OF ETHICS (New York:
    Oxford University Press, 1939), p. 277. See also
    pp. 72-75, 272-278.

15. Cf. Ramsey, BASIC CHRISTIAN ETHICS, pp. 24-45.

16. Gordon Harland, THE THOUGHT OF REINHOLD NIEBUHR
    (New York: Oxford University Press, 1960); Niebuhr,
    THE NATURE AND DESTINY OF MAN, Vol. II, pp. 244-
    286. Cf. Ramsey, NINE MODERN MORALISTS, pp. 111-
    131.

17. Niebuhr, THE NATURE AND DESTINY OF MAN, Vol. II, p. 88. Outka, AGAPE, pp. 274-279.

18. Paul Tillich, SYSTEMATIC THEOLOGY (Chicago: University of Chicago Press, 1951), Vol. I, pp. 174-178.

19. Daniel Day Williams, THE SPIRIT AND THE FORMS OF LOVE (New York: Harper & Row, 1968), pp. 192-213.

20. Paul Lehmann, ETHICS IN A CHRISTIAN CONTEXT (New York: Harper & Row, 1963), pp. 16-17, 53-56, 219-223, 282-283.

21. Alfred North Whitehead, THE FUNCTION OF REASON (Boston: Beacon Press, 1958), p. 8.

22. Kenneth Cauthen, SCIENCE, SECULARIZATION AND GOD (Nashville: Abingdon Press, 1969), pp. 90-130.

23. In this respect my usage of eros is more akin to that of Aristotle than of Plato. Cf. Nygren, AGAPE AND EROS, pp. 160-186.

24. See my SCIENCE, SECULARIZATION AND GOD, pp. 188-194.

25. For a more detailed discussion of the nature of God, see SCIENCE, SECULARIZATION AND GOD, pp. 131-194.

26. Paul Tillich, BIBLICAL RELIGION AND THE SEARCH FOR ULTIMATE REALITY (Chicago: University of Chicago Press, 1955).

27. Cf. John Knox, THE CHURCH AND THE REALITY OF CHRIST (New York: Harper & Row, 1962), pp. 37-59.

CHAPTER V

1. Emil Brunner, THE DIVINE IMPERATIVE (Philadelphia: Westminster Press, 1947), p. 221.

2. Emil Brunner, JUSTICE AND THE SOCIAL ORDER (New York: Harper & Brothers, 1945), pp. 128-129.

3. Brunner, THE DIVINE IMPERATIVE, pp. 227.

4. Gene Outka, AGAPE: AN ETHICAL ANALYSIS (New Haven: Yale University Press, 1972), pp. 210-212.

5. Paul Ramsey, BASIC CHRISTIAN ETHICS (New York:
    Charles Scribner's Sons, 1951), pp. 2-24.

6. Roderick Firth, "Ethical Absolutism and the Ideal
    Observer," PHILOSOPHY AND PHENOMENOLOGICAL RE-
    SEARCH, Vol. 12, 1952. For a brief discussion and
    other references, see John Rawls, A THEORY OF
    JUSTICE (Cambridge: Harvard University Press, 1971),
    pp. 184-195. See also Vernon J. Bourke, "The Ethical
    Role of the Impartial Observer," THE JOURNAL OF
    RELIGIOUS ETHICS (Fall, 1978), pp. 272-292.

7. John Rawls, A THEORY OF JUSTICE, pp. 11-22, 118-
    192.

8. Ibid., pp. 60-61, 302-303.

9. J. R. Lucas, ON JUSTICE (Oxford: Clarendon Press,
    1980), p. 186.

10. Robert Nozick, ANARCHY, STATE AND UTOPIA (New York:
    Basic Books, Inc., 1974), p. 202.

11. Richard B. Brandt, A THEORY OF THE GOOD AND THE
    RIGHT (New York: Oxford University Press, 1979),
    p. 238.

12. Cf. Derek L. Phillips, EQUALITY, JUSTICE AND
    RECTIFICATION   (New York: Academic Press, 1979),
    p. 30-36.

13. Rawls, A THEORY OF JUSTICE, pp. 34-40, 60-65,
    150-160, 541-548.

14. Ibid., p. 542.

15. Ibid., pp. 121-125, 161-175, 315-325.

16. William Frankena, ETHICS (Englewood Cliffs:
    Prentice-Hall, Inc., 1973), Second ed., p. 53.

CHAPTER VI

1. Quoted by Paul Ramsey, BASIC CHRISTIAN ETHICS
    (New York: Charles Scribner's Sons, 1950), p. 156.

2. Alfred North Whitehead, PROCESS AND REALITY, 1929
    (New York: Harper Torchbook, 1960), p. 41.

3. Emil Brunner, THE DIVINE IMPERATIVE (Philadelphia:
    The Westminster Press, 1947), p. 230.

4. Kenneth Boulding, THE ORGANIZATIONAL REVOLUTION
    (New York: Harper & Brothers, 1953), pp. xvi-
    xxxiv, 66-68.

5. Alfred North Whitehead, ADVENTURES OF IDEAS, 1933
    (New York: Mentor Books, 1955), p. 24.

6. Ibid., p. 25.

7. Cf. Henry Nelson Wieman, THE SOURCE OF HUMAN GOOD
    (Chicago: The University of Chicago Press, 1946).

8. Whitehead, PROCESS AND REALITY, p. 23; ADVENTURES
    OF IDEAS, 251-264.

9. Whitehead, PROCESS AND REALITY, p. 41.

10. Whitehead, ADVENTURES OF IDEAS, pp. 290-291.

11. Whitehead, PROCESS AND REALITY, pp. 512-513;
    ADVENTURES OF IDEAS, pp. 290-291; MODES OF THOUGHT,
    1938 (New York: Free Press Paperback, 1968), pp. 13-
    14.

12. Robert L. Heilbroner and Lester C. Thurow, FIVE
    ECONOMIC CHALLENGES (Englewood Cliffs: Prentice-
    Hall, Inc., 1981), pp. 3-51.

13. An earlier version of this section of the chapter
    appeared in THE CHRISTIAN CENTURY under the title
    "The Legitimacy and Limits of Freedom of Choice,"
    (July 1-8, 1981), pp. 702-704. Copyright by The
    Christian Century Foundation, 1981. Used by per-
    mission.

14. Cf. Nicholas Rescher, DISTRIBUTIVE JUSTICE
    (Indianapolis: Bobs-Merrill Co., Inc., 1966),
    pp. 28-41. See also Arthur Okun, EQUALITY AND
    EFFICIENCY (Washington: The Brookings Institution,
    1975), pp. 88-120. Okun points out that economists
    and laymen alike point to one-half the average in-
    come as the point of deprivation from a subjective
    point of view.

15. John Rawls, A THEORY OF JUSTICE (Cambridge: Harvard
    University Press, 1971), pp. 284-293.

16.   See Daniel Bell, THE COMING OF POST-INDUSTRIAL
       SOCIETY (New York: Basic Books, 1973), pp. 450-
       451.

17.   On this point I side with Nozick against Rawls.
       See Robert Nozick, ANARCHY, STATE AND UTOPIA
       (New York: Basic Books, 1974), pp. 213-231, and
       Rawls, A THEORY OF JUSTICE, pp. 101-102.

18.   See Philip Wogaman, THE GREAT ECONOMIC DEBATE
       (Philadelphia: Westminster Press, 1977), pp. 93-
       97, 132-133. Wogaman takes this statistic from
       A. B. Atkinson, THE ECONOMICS OF EQUALITY (Oxford:
       The Clarendon Press, 1975). See also, Michael
       Harrington DECADE OF DECISION (New York: Simon
       and Schuster, 1980), pp. 148-177.

19.   For two differing discussions, see Nozick,
       ANARCHY, STATE AND UTOPIA, pp. 232-275, and
       Sanford A. Lakey, EQUALITY IN POLITICAL PHILOSOPHY
       (Harvard University Press, 1964), pp. 156-193.

20.   Bell, THE COMING OF POST-INDUSTRIAL SOCIETY,
       pp. 408-451. See also, Christopher Jencks,
       et. al., INEQUALITY (New York: Basic Books, 1972),
       and Michael Lewis, THE CULTURE OF INEQUALITY
       (Amherst: U. of Massachusetts Press, 1978).

21.   Information taken from an article by William F.
       Buckley, Jr., in the Editorial section of the
       LOS ANGELES TIMES, November 12, 1978.

22.   Nozick, ANARCHY, STATE AND UTOPIA, pp. 149-231.

23.   Ibid., p. 163.

24.   Derek Phillips, EQUALITY, JUSTICE AND RECTIFICATION
       (New York: Academic Press, 1979), pp. 106-108.

25.   George Cabot Lodge, THE NEW AMERICAN IDEOLOGY
       (New York: Alfred Knopf, 1975).

26.   Bell, THE COMING OF POST-INDUSTRIAL SOCIETY,
       pp. 425-465.

APPENDIX

1.   I am following Daniel Bell, THE CULTURAL CON-
      TRADICTIONS OF CAPITALISM (New York: Basic Books,
      1976), pp. xi-xii, 3-30.

2.   No one has analyzed the complexities, ambiguities,
     and contradictions in contemporary American life
     more perceptively than Daniel Bell in the book
     referred to in note 1, on which I am heavily
     dependent throughout this paper.

3.   In this sketchy account I have taken capitalism
     and socialism as more or less "ideal types."
     In their actual embodiments in particular
     societies and in their various combinations in
     the 20th century, the truth gets much more com-
     plicated, partly because economic systems always
     exist in the context of political orders and
     cultural contexts (the realms of values, meanings)
     which have their own distinctiveness.

4.   Along with many Christian intellectuals I have
     been attracted by what I would call the "socialist
     myth," which even a critic like Michael Novak
     admits has potent moral power. However, I think
     it is frequently the case than an idealized
     socialism is contrasted with an actually function-
     ing capitalist society to the comparative dis-
     advantage of the latter. Moreover, whatever else
     may be said about socialism as an ideal, history
     seems to teach us that it does not fit the dominant
     ethos of America for many reasons -- open frontier
     with vast opportunities for individual enterprise,
     immigrants fleeing from oppressive societies and
     bringing with them a deep dedication to individual
     freedom, etc. Hence, let us work with the society
     in which we actually find ourselves and engage in
     the reform of capitalism rather than indulge in a
     futile quest of an idealized socialism. However,
     as critics and as representatives of a transcendent
     moral norm, it is fitting for clergy "to press the
     socialist questions" (John Bennett) while being
     critical of prepackaged socialist answers in
     doctrinaire dress. See John Bennett, THE RADICAL
     IMPERATIVE (Philadelphia: The Westminster Press,
     1975), pp. 142-164; Michael Harrington, DECADE OF
     DECISION (New York: Simon and Schuster, 1980);
     Philip Wogaman, THE GREAT ECONOMIC DEBATE
     (Philadelphia: Westminster Press, 1977); Robert
     Benne, THE ETHICS OF DEMOCRATIC CAPITALISM
     (Philadelphia: Fortress Press, 1981), pp. 1-19;
     Michael Novak, THE AMERICAN VISION (Washington:
     American Enterprise Institute, 1979), pp. 7-17.

5.   George Cabot Lodge, THE NEW AMERICAN IDEOLOGY
      (New York: Knopf, 1975).

6.   Bell,THE CULTURAL CONTRADICTIONS OF CAPITALISM,
      pp. 224-227.

7.   Ibid., p. 226.

8.   Ibid., p. 237.

9.   Ibid., pp. 248-249.

10.   Ibid., p. 251.

11.   Ibid., p. 245.

12.   Donald E. Miller, THE CASE FOR LIBERAL CHRISTIANITY
      (New York: Harper & Row Inc., 1981), pp. 114-126.

INDEX OF NAMES

INDEX OF SUBJECTS

TORONTO STUDIES IN THEOLOGY